Dear Ambassador Herbst,

As a token of my gratitude for the opportunity you and S/CRS have given me to apply in the government some of the theories Political Science academics have developed — for good or ill — I present you with my own theoretical musings of the course of European integration.

It has been my sincere pleasure to learn at your side about how U.S. foreign policy is conducted, and I have enjoyed our discussions over time — particularly overseas.

My very best to you in your next post at CCO. I am now confident all our problems over there will now be solved —

Jeff Stacy

Integrating Europe

Informal Politics and Institutional Change

Jeffrey Stacey

OXFORD
UNIVERSITY PRESS

Great Clarendon Street, Oxford OX2 6DP

Oxford University Press is a department of the University of Oxford.
It furthers the University's objective of excellence in research, scholarship,
and education by publishing worldwide in

Oxford New York

Auckland Cape Town Dar es Salaam Hong Kong Karachi
Kuala Lumpur Madrid Melbourne Mexico City Nairobi
New Delhi Shanghai Taipei Toronto

With offices in

Argentina Austria Brazil Chile Czech Republic France Greece
Guatemala Hungary Italy Japan Poland Portugal Singapore
South Korea Switzerland Thailand Turkey Ukraine Vietnam

Oxford is a registered trade mark of Oxford University Press
in the UK and in certain other countries

Published in the United States
by Oxford University Press Inc., New York

© Jeffrey Stacey 2010

The moral rights of the author have been asserted
Database right Oxford University Press (maker)

First published 2010

British Library Cataloguing in Publication Data
Data available

Library of Congress Cataloging in Publication Data
Data available

Typeset by SPI Publisher Services, Pondicherry, India
Printed in Great Britain
on acid-free paper by the
MPG Books Group, Bodmin and King's Lynn

ISBN 978–0–19–958476–5

Contents

Acknowledgments

I would like to thank many instrumental individuals, firstly the EU officials who kindly allowed me to interview them for this study: Takis Anastopoulos, Maria Arpio, Jill Assant, Auke Bass, Martin Bauer, Sally Bliss, Antonio Broggi, Gianluca Brunetti, Emilio de Capitani, George Caravelis, Joseph Coolegham, Cesar Cortez, Christopher Docksey, Piedro Ducci, Jean Claude Eckout, David Elliot, Alfredo de Feo, Csilla Fikele, John Forman, David Galloway, F. Gennison, Ricardo Gonsalbo-Bono, Mario Gonsalez-Sanchez, Silvio Ganzato, Norbert Gresch, Jurgen Grunwald, Otto Harnier, Jean Paul Jacquez, Wolfgang Leonhardt, Joost Korte, Rainer Lau, Giorgio Maganza, Gary Miller, Lars Mitek Peterson, Lars Moller, Michael Moore, Karl Heinz Neunreither, Una O'Dwyer, Hartmut Offele, Paolo Panzano, Jose-Luis, Etzo Perillo, Andrea Pierucci, Carmen Preising, Anne Pringle, Charles Reich, Rufus-Quintana, Hans-Peter Schiffauer, Denise Sorasio, Olivier E. Souza, James Spence, Palolo Stancanelli, Neil Turns, Roger Van Haeren, Peter Van Nuffel, Alain Van Solinge, Jerome Vignon, Yohannes Vos, Evelyn Waldherr, Frank Wall, Klaus Welle, and Clare Wells.

Special thanks to those officials who not only granted me multiple interviews but also provided me with feedback: Kieran Bradley, Richard Corbett, Youri Devuyst, John Fitzmaurice, Wilhelm Lehman, Wolfgang Leohhardt, Dietmar Nickel, Miguel Sagredo, Martin Westlake, and in particular Francis Jacobs and Michael Shackleton.

I gratefully acknowledge the financial assistance of St Antony's College (Oxford), the Council for European Studies (in New York), the Institute for the Study of World Politics, the Columbia University Graduate School of Arts and Sciences, and the Center for European and Mediterranean Studies (NYU).

I would especially like to thank David Andrews, Joseph Bafumi, George Bermann, Matthew Bothner, Tim Buthe, James Caporaso, Phil Cerny, William Clark, Joseph Foudi, Erik Gartzke, Adrienne Heritier, Simon Hix, Liesbet Hooghe, Christopher Jackson, Annie Kreppel, Paulette Kurzer, Patrick Leblond, Quan Li, Gary Marks, Kathleen McNamara, Anand Menon,

Jeannette Money, Andrew Moravcsik, B. Guy Peters, Jeremy Richardson, Berthold Rittberger, Ben Rosamond, Glenda Rosenthal, Shanker Satyanath, Martin Schain, Holger Schmidt, Ioannis Sinanoglou, Julie Smith, Jack Snyder, Nicholas Toloudas, and Helen Wallace, as well as my stand-in defense committee (Jack Snyder, Erik Gartzke, John Huber, Glenda Rosenthal, and Volker Berghahn), and most particularly my advisors David A. Baldwin, Walter Mattli, Helen V. Milner, Lord Wallace of Saltaire, and the late Vincent Wright for their superb feedback and guidance. My deepest gratitude goes to the late Sir Edward Heath KG MBE for the opportunity of a lifetime—in particular, for being able to observe and participate in European politics and learn at the feet of a master. Any and all errors are my own.

List of Figures

List of Tables

List of Abbreviations

BIS	Bank of International Settlements
CAP	Common Agricultural Policy
CFSP	Common Foreign and Security Policy
DG	Directorate General
DV	Dependent Variable
EC	European Community
ECU	European Currency Unit
EEA	European Economic Area
EEC	European Economic Community
ECJ	European Court of Justice
EMU	Economic and Monetary Union
EPP	European People's Party
EU	European Union
FSAP	Financial Services Action Plan
GNP	Gross National Product
HI	Historical Institutionalism
IAIS	International Association of Insurance Supervisors
ICC	International Criminal Court
ICTY	International Criminal Tribunal of the former Yugoslavia
IEC	International Electrotechnical Commission
IGC	Intergovernmental Conference
IIAs	Interinstitutional Agreements
IOSCO	International Organization of Security Commissions
ISO	International Organization for Standardization
IVs	Independent Variables
LI	Liberal Intergovernmentalism

MCAs	Monetary Compensatory Amounts
MEPs	Members of the European Parliament
MLG	Multilevel Governance
NGOs	Nongovernmental Organizations
NIE	New Institutional Economics
OJ	*Official Journal*
P/A	Principal–Agent
QMV	Qualified Majority Vote
RCI	Rational Choice Institutionalism
SEA	Single European Act
SI	Sociological Institutionalism
SIE	Structure Induced Equilibrium

1

Introduction

Politics and institutions

When it comes to politics, is it important to play by the rules? When we think of politics, we tend to conjure up images of "office politics" or a pair of politicians squaring off in a media interview or on the floor of Congress. Politics as a social phenomenon is not confined to the hallowed halls of government. In fact, wherever there are disagreements among individuals or groups we have politics on our hands, contests among individuals or groups of some kind to get what they want. From children arguing on the playground all the way to US senators fighting it out over national budget resources, politics appear to be everywhere in social life. Often it seems that whoever is stronger or smarter tends to win the contest, sometimes in a no-holds-barred sort of way.

But take a closer look and you will find that just like maneuvering the checkout lines at a busy supermarket or playing a pickup game of basketball, in every sort of contest imaginable the actors are competing according to some set of rules. These can be either implicit and generally understood by those interacting, or more explicit with a written down set of rules that competitors can appeal to, if necessary. In the study of politics rules are referred to as institutions, and if politics is about playing some sort of game, then institutions constitute the rules of the game. But it goes beyond that, for virtually all aspects of social life have institutional elements that govern human behavior. For even social interactions devoid of disagreement and overt politics are governed by rules; moreover, institutions structure the behavior of actors in normal everyday situations, such as an understood rule in Japan that no employees can leave for the day until the boss goes home first.

Institutions clearly constitute the sinews of politics, the stuff that defines a given political arena and sets out the rules for competition. While it is important how powerful or skilled political actors are, institutions are often just as important in explaining the outcome of the competition. Change the rules, and more than likely you change the outcome. Just like standard actors like politicians or nation-states rarely play only one round of the games they participate in, the rules of the game normally do not remain static. If institutions matter to our understanding of why different actors in society behave the way they do, then institutional change may matter even more. But understanding why the rules of political contests may all of a sudden change, after having been in place and adhered to possibly for long periods of time, constitutes a puzzle.

Take the European Union (EU), for instance. The conventional wisdom that European integration is explained largely by negotiations of treaties by its Member States is something of a myth, albeit a powerful one in light of today's reigning scholarship. It seems scholars and journalists alike have trouble ascertaining what EU insiders encounter in Brussels on a daily basis. In essence, the intermittent treaties that formally transfer sovereignty from Member States to the EU's supranational level tell only part of the story.

Instead of being the sole origin for such transfers, formal treaties often function as repositories of previously arranged sovereignty transfers that have already taken place, in the EU's informal sphere. These earlier outcomes stem from efforts of the EU's three principal policy-making actors—the Council of Ministers, the European Commission, and the European Parliament, also known as the Three—to broker informal agreements between them, which systematically serve to alter policy-making rules. What is more, the new informal rules occasionally serve to alter the balance of power among these actors, all of which occurs outside of the EU's cumulative Treaty. As such the amending treaties not only create new formal rules, but they also serve to gather together extant informal rules and infuse them with a legal component they lack—in a word, they *formalize* them. Even prior to this step, however, to the extent that informal rules have already transferred power from the Council's Member States to the Parliament, Europe has previously become more integrated.

This is the untold story of European integration. While these mundane matters for EU policy-makers remain fairly obscure to the scholarly ranks, national politicians have in recent years begun to take notice, particularly in the Danish and British parliaments. What they have grown concerned about is the mushrooming phenomenon of informal horse-trading in Brussels, for in the eyes of critics what began as a way of making formal legislation work in practice has become a threat to democracy. Take the EU's most recent informal agreement, for example. Bilateral in nature, it was negotiated between the Council and Parliament as a result of the Parliament's long-standing desire to augment its feeble authority over policy implementation—known in EU circles as comitology. In traditional democracies, legislatures have a system of holding the executive branch accountable for the ways in which it implements legislation, but in the EU the Parliament has for much of its existence lacked such a system to hold the Commission to task for its implementing decisions.

As of 2006, the Parliament has made major inroads into the Council's sturdy redoubt, whose committees of national civil servants have long held singular sway over their Commission counterparts when it comes to comitology. But pressure from the Parliament boiled over after the Member States failed to ratify the recently proposed Constitutional treaty due to French and Dutch vetoes the year before. Informal bargaining went on for months before the Council capitulated, and in an informal agreement granted the Parliament a newfound veto power (over Commission implementation decisions for all legislation created under the EU's codecision policy-making procedure, that is, the vast majority of EU legislation).[1] This is not a formal institutional change; instead it constitutes an informal change in the rules, and one that is not prescribed by the Treaty and therefore technically not even legal.

Informality is important not only because informal rules are ubiquitous, but also because they frequently serve as the direct forerunner to formal institutional change. In other words, as evidenced repeatedly in the EU, formal laws are frequently tried out first as informal rules; as such, the political contest to create them occurs much earlier than most observers realize. The study of informal rules is surprisingly rare given that they are fought over just as fiercely as formal rules are; EU actors engage in contentious bargaining sessions, not only over treaties but informal agreements as well. The informal rules comprising them are neglected largely due to scholars' erroneous assumption that political actors will refuse being bound by them in light of their nonlegal status; in fact, actors pay a price for violating them. In the EU, weaker actors in fact will cease cooperation across the board if stronger actors do this.[2] Informal rules are nonetheless frequently created either because they constitute a tryout for formal

---

[1] EU official, interview by the author, European Commission, Brussels, July 4, 2007.
[2] EU official, interview by the author, European Parliament, Brussels, July 6, 2007.

institutional change or because the formidable creation of laws proves too prohibitive.[3]

The new rules bundled together play a critical role in shaping the strategic interaction among the Three. In the context of an institutional framework of rules that structure their interaction, the Three bargain competitively not only over policy outcomes, but also over the rules that allocate the very powers they use to make policy. In the course of this incessant strategic interaction, whenever such a power game outcome cannot be fed into an amending treaty in the making, they take the form of new informal agreements. The intermittent result of a single round of this competition is a bundle of new rules, that is, informal institutions—which then recursively feed back to and become a part of the institutional framework that structures the next round; actors thus comply with an altered set of rules in making their subsequent strategic choices.

This book makes two major inquiries. On one level it examines the widely regarded but vaguely understood phenomenon of institutional change, seeking to map uncharted territory with application across various social and political arenas. This book maintains that informality, understood as the dynamics surrounding nonlegal rule creation, offers an insight into how institutions change. More fundamentally, it employs a rationalist theory of institutional change in which institutions are not taken as given, or exogenous. Instead, the rules of the game so to speak are supplied by the players themselves, or endogenous. An institution comprises shared expectations among actors to interact with one another in accordance with a particular pattern. This equilibrium persists until actors alter them, either at the behest of a power play by a strong actor—perhaps a coalition of actors—or as a result of bargaining among actors of various strength.

This theoretical approach differs from others in which institutions are assumed to be "thick" and thus difficult to change, even by powerful actors; such theories view institutions as accretions that either congeal or become malleable only gradually over time almost in the absence of actors' behavior, that is, agency. Rather, it assumes that institutions are often "thin" and thus more amenable to being changed, depending on a given arena's configuration of actors (i.e., their preferences, their power, and the nature of their strategic interaction). In deploying this variant of rational institutionalist theory, this book further seeks to compensate for the irony of how numerous rationalist scholars tend to apply the theory most ideally suited

---

[3] EU official, interview by the author, European Commission, Brussels, July 4, 2007.

4

for explaining the phenomenon of change to arenas of institutional stasis, namely the structure-induced equilibrium approach.[4]

On a second level, the book illuminates institutional change in the EU, revealing a causal component of European integration not incorporated in conventional accounts of how nation-states relinquish their sovereignty. Reigning theoretical accounts in the Regional Integration field posit that integration stems from formal intergovernmental treaties between governments, such as EU Member States. Andrew Moravcsik's *tour de force* is a case in point, falsely attributing the source of a trove of primary EU laws to the preferences of the EU's most powerful Member State governments.[5] Moravcsik is hardly alone in this insistence; he is merely the most insistent and therefore the most open to criticism. While this book, like his, makes use of the theoretical concept of incomplete contracting, its findings about the importance of the EU's informal sphere place it along with Craig Parson's more ideas-based approach as one of the more "anti-Intergovernmentalist" works in the field.[6]

Instead, what if a broad swathe of the laws in EU treaties were not created by the Member States, let alone the most powerful ones? What if supranational actors like the European Parliament were instrumental in their creation? And what if the laws in question not only were originally conceived as informal institutions without legal force, but furthermore that whenever one of these clashes with a formal law EU actors actually were to abide by the former? Finally, what if all these things served to decrease the so-called democratic deficit of the EU, albeit in a manner woefully lacking in legitimacy? Whatever accounts for these outcomes amounts to an enormous puzzle, and this book seeks to explain them.

Theories of European integration

As Mattli and Slaughter and others have called for a transcendence of the conventional debate over legal integration in the EU, so too there needs to be a transcendence of the conventional debate over the EU's political

---

[4] For exemplars of the structure-induced equilibrium approach that treats institutions as exogenous, see Shepsle (1979) and North (1990); for exemplars of the rationalist approach that threats them as endogenous, see Schotter (1981) and Calvert (1995).

[5] See Moravcsik (1998). Note that the reference is to primary law and the sources of EU treaties, as opposed to secondary legislation and the policy sphere in which the Commission and Parliament are formally involved (for all policies made according to the EU's codecision procedure, the Parliament and Council are coequals).

[6] See Parsons (2003).

integration.[7] Whether transcendence can achieve synthesis some four decades on from the inception of this debate, however, is open to doubt. As long as work on European and regional integration meets rigorous methodological standards, endeavoring to explain outcomes either within or across discrete spheres of the colossal EU political system will represent a sound theoretical enterprise.

The main theoretical contenders in the ongoing effort to account for the impetus, pace, and variance of European integration amount to the Neofunctionalist, Intergovernmentalist, and Governance approaches, as well as more recent arrivals on the scene: the ideational approach, the formal modeling approach, and the "new institutionalism" approach.[8] Although not altogether different, these and other late contenders cannot, as some have suggested, be equated with Neofunctionalist theory—the thoroughbred first out of the gates and the only full-fledged theory "born and raised in EU territory."[9]

Neofunctionalist theory nonetheless has proved to be considerably deficient.[10] While often astute with regard to process, it has fared poorly with regard to predicted outcomes. In essence, various empirical developments exposed the inadequacies of focusing too intently on interest groups and functional linkages, while not enough on the capacity of governments to withstand the allegedly inherent momentum of integration. Despite the resurgence of formal integration in the forms of the Single European Act (SEA), the Maastricht Treaty, the Amsterdam Treaty, and most recently the Nice Treaty, Neofunctionalism remains in ill theoretical repute.

An important exception to this trend has been something of a renaissance for the theory with regard to the legal sphere of European integration, in which Mattli and Slaughter have a cogent series of arguments for

[7] Mattli and Slaughter (1998: 177–209). See also Hix (1994), Dowding (2000), Schneider (2000), and Rosamond (2000, 2006).

[8] Whereas the Political Science literature is all but silent about the role of informal accords in European integration, the Legal literature has recently produced a small spate of interesting work that does take the EU's informal sphere seriously; however, their being exercises in classification and significance highlighting, these studies do not feature causal explanations that meet customary social science standards. See Monar (1994), Driessen (2007, 2008), Eiselt et al. (2007), Hummer (2007), Keitz and Maurer (2007), and Puntscher Riekmann (2007).

[9] Despite something of a resurgence, in recent years practically any argument challenging Intergovernmentalism has had the "Neofunctionalist" label applied to it, often neglecting the actual propositions of Neofunctionalism. Leon Lindberg *inter alia* has cautioned scholars of European integration to avoid this blurring of theoretical clarity: Acceptance speech, European University Studies Association, seventh biennial conference, Madison, Wisconsin, June 1, 2001.

[10] The literature on Neofunctionalist theory is vast; hence, only the seminal works of the two pioneers of the theory will be referenced: Haas (1958) and Lindberg (1963).

Neofunctionalism's ability to account for the ways in which the European Court of Justice (ECJ), in conjunction with national courts, has furthered the course of integration.[11] Nonetheless, it would appear that any residual explanatory power of the theory is confined to the legal sphere, with the possible exceptions of several theories to be discussed below that one might construe as Neofunctionalist offshoots.

The breakdown of Neofunctionalism in the 1950s to 1970s was evident in several ways: the expanded role of the Commission did not occur; functional linkages between different economic sectors were not as extensive as predicted; the expected transfer of elites' political loyalties to a new core of officials in Brussels did not transpire; a massive blurring of what was perceived to be technical and political took place; and the economic–political continuum did not prove to be wholly linear, that is, functional spillover did not occur to the extent envisaged.

As such, Neofunctionalism's pluralistic conception of creative transnational interchange in the construction of functional coalitions did not materialize, and the few functional cross-sectoral linkages that did develop proved unable to act as an impetus for widening the scope of EU lawmaking. Contrary to the expectations of Neofunctionalists, economic integration did not prove to be a gradual, stage-by-stage process leading to further and further integration, nor did the creation of the European Economic Community (EEC) customs union, among other things, lead inexorably to greater political integration.[12]

Over the course of the fifty-year history of the EU, the theory of Intergovernmentalism has fared somewhat better. According to Intergovernmentalism, EU Member States generally not only prefer to retain their sovereignty, but they also possess the ability to prevent the transfer of sovereignty to supranational organizational actors whenever they wish to exercise it. Member States desire collective, or supranational, action only when the benefits are obtainable without having their sovereignty unnecessarily impinged upon. Only on rare occasion do they intend to transfer limited amounts of their sovereignty, but they always maintain the ability to oversee it—and even to recapture it if circumstances necessitate.

In other words, as principals Member States delegate specific responsibilities to organizational agents in the EU, oversee them vigilantly, and rein them in whenever they seek to exercise their delegated authority beyond the intended scope. In addition, the important bargains exist only in the

---

[11] Mattli and Slaughter (1993, 1995, 1998).

[12] The EEC was formed in 1957 and formally became the European Community (EC) in 1972.

formal sphere of the EU and occur only between Member States in the form of treaties. The EU's *acquis communautaire* exists insofar as the treaties prescribe specific institutional designs and the procedures to which organizational actors must adhere.[13] Informal agreements are insignificant in the Intergovernmentalist perspective; indeed, they go thoroughly unconsidered.

Although Intergovernmentalism fared better regarding the so-called Eurosclerosis of the 1970s than Neofunctionalism, subsequent to the "relaunch" of European integration in the mid-1980s it has struggled somewhat to retain its beacon status. As the principal proponent of Intergovernmentalist theory, Andrew Moravcsik has attained the status of the Kenneth Waltz of European integration. His work is, if not necessarily the omega, certainly the alpha of the European integration literature: practically all serious theoretical contenders begin with Moravcsik's Liberal Intergovernmentalism (LI) variant as their starting point—drawn from both neorealism and neoliberal institutionalism—and necessarily so.[14]

With its rationalist, state-centric, and government-motivational assumptions, LI purports to explain the enduring integration puzzle by claiming

> that the broad lines of European integration since 1955 reflect three factors: patterns of commercial exchange, the relative bargaining power of important governments, and the incentives to enhance the credibility of interstate commitments. The most fundamental of these was commercial interest.... At its core, I argue, European integration has been dictated by the need to adapt through policy coordination to these trends in technology and in economic policy.... Where such interests converged, integration advanced.[15]

Moravcsik's important contribution has made the case for Intergovernmentalism as no one has before.

LI indeed has seemed capable of explaining a substantial amount of amending treaty outcomes. As much of an achievement as this purports to be in theoretical terms, it nonetheless fails to explain all the variance of the integration outcome. The standard and fairly sustainable critiques of LI comprise tautological problems, disagreements about the state and what constitutes it, and what has been described as the problem of sovereignty

---

[13] The *acquis communautaire* is the EU term for all the formal rules of the EU, comprising everything from the primary law of treaty provisions to the secondary law of policy-making results and the rulings of the ECJ. Informal accords and their rules are not considered a part of the *acquis*.

[14] For his most prolific LI exposition, see Moravcsik (1998).

[15] Moravcsik (1998: 3).

discourse, that is, how Intergovernmentalist images of European integration are privileged ontologically.[16]

From an informal institutionalist perspective, the primary problem with LI is its propositional insistence that Member State preference formation is confined entirely to the domestic level of analysis, that is, domestic politics. Based on evidence of the impact on integration from the EU's informal sphere, LI's principal deficiency is two-part. First, it fails to allow for the fact that certain Member State preferences for Intergovernmental Conference (IGC) outcomes stem not from domestic political actors—or any global economic interests that may filter through to the domestic level—but from supranational political actors; not all, but a substantial amount.[17] LI allows for national governments to transfer sovereignty *to* supranational organizations, but, crucially, it abjures their incorporating any constitutional content *from* them.

At issue here is a crucial difference between ultimate and proximate preferences. In the context of the EU, the former constitute formal bargain preferences that have Member State governments as their sole origin, that is, preferences formed prior to any interactions with other governments or supranational organizations. These preferences are formed solely with a given state's national interests in mind, as governments interact with citizens, interests groups, and the press and weigh their needs and the strategies to meet them in the context of IGCs. Whereas proximate preferences involve shifts from certain ultimate preferences to updated preferences incorporating the results of interactions with other Member States and supranational organizations, that is, discussions with them, early negotiations with them, pressure from them, trade-offs with them, etc. The EU's supranational organizations influence formal constitutional content through Member States' proximate preference formation, more often than not through a majority of Member States determining that a certain informal accord has worked well enough in practice that it makes sense to them to formally incorporate its rules in treaty form.

The closest LI comes to allowing for supranational influence on Member State preference formation is Moravcsik's openness to issue linkage in his theoretical framework. The problem is that LI forecloses the influence of supranational organizations because the only actors that national governments are allowed to link issues with are other national governments,

---

[16] For a good review of these critiques, see Rosamond (2000).

[17] IGCs comprise the Member States' traditional formal treaty negotiating sessions (now supplemented by the European Convention).

just as coalitions in his model can only comprise constellations of Member States. In fact, Member States bargain with the Parliament and the Commission through the Council on a regular basis in the informal sphere. As a result, either to exchange something with them or appease them, in certain instances this bargaining results in the incorporation of supranational preferences in formal treaty bargains. The proximate preferences of Member States act as the conduit in such cases, in ways for which LI cannot account—indeed, ways inconsistent with the LI model's assumptions and predictions.

As the evidence presented in later chapters will support, national governments in specific instances adjust their formal bargain preferences via either bargaining indirectly with supranational organizations (e.g., trading off Parliament's preference for a specific codecision treaty provision for a Council preference for a reduction in the Parliament's procedural delaying tactics) or simply being persuaded by the efficacy of the rules of a given informal accord (e.g., recognizing the utility of having the Parliament officially "invest" a new college of Commissioners and formalizing this informal accord via including a provision for such in the Treaty). Hence, the empirical record will show that a fair number of Member State preferences stem not from the preference formation process predicted by LI, but rather proximate preferences that have supranational actors as their source. To the extent that the Council formally incorporates preferences of supranational origin in treaty form, a key LI hypothesis is falsified: national governments do not control all aspects of the grand bargains that generate amending treaties; what Moravcsik terms "the process-level intervention of institutional entrepreneurs" do, to a lesser but significant extent.

Second, LI cannot sustain empirical evidence not only that the integration process is furthered *in-between* the occasional amending treaties, but also that the primary source of this type of integration is not the Member States, but rather the Council's supranational competitors (particularly the Parliament). Temporally speaking, such can be conceived of as *interregnum integration*—informal accords interpolated in-between treaties during normal periods of EU activity—as opposed to *history-making integration*—that which is part and parcel of formal treaty-amending accords that radically reconfigure the EU's constitutional landscape.[18] In terms of the source of integration, Member States may dominate history-making integration—despite a certain portion of their treaty preferences being derived from

---

[18] See Stacey and Rittberger (2003).

10

nonnational and noneconomic origins—but supranational political actors are a force in interregnum integration: formally in terms of the ECJ's jurisprudence but informally in terms of the Commission and Parliament.

It is in the course of day-to-day EU policy-making, or governance, that informal institution-building dynamics can and does engender interregnum integration. As this book will lay out below, this type of integration occurs more on the margins of normal governance, as opposed to the highly salient, headline-grabbing IGCs that formally amend the Treaty every so often. More obscure but no less important, activities in the informal sphere of the EU have tended to be either unknown or taken for granted. LI cannot account for the vicissitudes of informal accord haggling, despite Moravcsik's contention that although his emphasis lies elsewhere LI is applicable to everyday EU decision-making.[19] Thus, on both the demand side and the supply side of integration LI is unable to take informal interorganizational dynamics into account: the preferences of EU organizational actors on the demand side, and informal agreements on the supply side.

Another contender involves Multilevel Governance (MLG) and other contributions to the Governance approach. MLG is best depicted as a valuable attempt to describe the EU accurately as the proto-political polity that it is. Less a theory and more a complex metaphor, its principal proponents Gary Marks and Liesbet Hooghe have spearheaded what has been termed the "governance turn" in European integration literature.[20] MLG and its successors have expanded our understanding of the EU with such important insights as the existence of overlapping competencies among multiple levels of governments and interaction of political actors across those levels.

Nonetheless, MLG overstates the degree to which the EU has become a political system not unlike traditional nation-states. Moreover, three other deficiencies mark the approach: not a full-fledged theory, it neither generates tight, testable hypotheses nor offers propositions that account for why and how sovereignty is transferred; moreover, while it casts the EU as a recently developed pattern of politics, it suffers from the fact that a great many Member State decisions are responsible for this; and most pertinent to informal interorganizational dynamics, it does not depict this putative polity as one governed by constitutional rules dictating the allotment and use of specific powers.

---

[19] Moravcsik (1998: 613).
[20] See Kohler-Koch and Rittberger (2006), Hooghe and Marks (2001), Hix (1998), Jachtenfuchs (1995), Marks et al. (1996).

Governance more generally involves a sprawling theoretical approach. It broadly depicts policy-making arenas as those in which public and private actors engage in intentional regulation of societal relationships and non-hierarchical decision-making. Some theoretical projects under this rubric are state-centered, with the state driving the policy-making process albeit in a network of nonstate actors; whereas others are society-centered, with nonstate actors driving the process in a network that includes the state as an actor. However, useful though this approach is in conceptual and mapping terms, its potential for explaining political outcomes is rarely attained by its proponents. More often than not, applications of the Governance approach are description dominant, even moving beyond the analytical realm into all things normative such as the pursuit of the "public good." At times, it takes the EU political system as a given and examines its impact on national political systems; at others, it argues that the EU has become a "regulatory state" akin to national governments, with certain appeals to legitimation questions.[21]

Supranational Governance theory amounts to a more sophisticated enterprise. Wayne Sandholtz, Neil Fligstein, and Alec Stone Sweet have served up the second installment of the project that first gave birth to the 1998 Sandholtz and Stone Sweet volume, comprising one of the more compelling reformulations of Neofunctionalist theorizing to date.[22] In essence, their theory comprises five successive causal steps: Increased transnational exchange begets pressure on EU Member States to create supranational organizations, which in turn begets new rule creation by these actors, which in turn begets political spillover, which in turn begets integration.

Despite how the 2001 volume's contributors both map new empirical ground and challenge conventional perspectives, strengths notwithstanding they suffer from deficiencies that are primarily set in motion by the authors' framing chapter and echoed in the conclusion. First, despite a format apparently designed for empirical chapters to test hypotheses generated by the theory chapter, Sandholtz et al. tend to downgrade the theoretical element of their enterprise. Unlike their previous volume, which proffers a fairly rigorous causal argument with testable hypotheses, its successor does not measure up.

Even though the theoretical approach of the second volume comes right out of the first, the authors do not so much as explain the "institutionalization" process as describe it, albeit in a compelling manner. Whereas the first

---

[21] See Majone (1996) and Jachtenfuchs (2001).

[22] Sandholtz and Stone Sweet (1998) and Stone Sweet et al. (2001).

line of argument in the previous volume sets out a plausible theory of the demand for supranational rules—although the authors apparently have yet to acknowledge their intellectual debt to Walter Mattli's work as they now have with Ernst Haas's—they import the more dubious second line of argument to act as the theoretical crux for the follow-up volume. In doing so, however, the authors recoil from sound theorizing, preferring instead to "focus on" institutionalization—the creation of behavior constraining rules—rather than explain it. As such, their vaunted argument has to be ferreted out of a dense thicket of institutionalist discussion.

Moreover, without some sort of theoretical test, the claims cannot be evaluated. In order to distinguish their argument from the LI arguments they enthusiastically reject in the conclusion, the authors need to furnish something that demonstrates that the outcomes they observe cannot be explained by their nemesis. In particular, by not paying close attention to the actor sources of many of the new rules, this volume fails to recognize that amending treaties, Council common positions, and comitology committee decisions are often the sources of new rules. As such, a rigorous test should comprise two basic hurdles: Do the new rules have sources other than the Council and the Member States, and does the content of the new rules do anything other than reinforce the status quo? By contrast my own book employs a test of this type, seeking to ascertain when and whether new rules are integrative.

The Achilles heel of this work involves the argument itself. To begin with, the proposition that existing rules motivate supranational actors not only to exploit them but also to create new rules of their own accord—and expand their organizational capacity in the process—amounts to a tautology: institutions $\Rightarrow$ institutions. While it is accurate that organizational actors other than the Council do indeed exploit the opportunities of status quo constellations of rules, they do not do so in a vacuum; instead, they compete and bargain with a Council that vigorously defends its prerogatives. The primary problem with this Neofunctionalist argument is that it fails to theorize the quotidian strategic interaction of the primary EU actors and demonstrate how the Commission and particularly the Parliament are occasionally able to pressure the Council to accede to their preferences. In sum, while Sandholtz et al. commendably theorize the demand for new institutions, they largely fail to explain why and when those institutions will be successfully supplied.

Mark Pollack has written the standard-setting principal–agent (P/A) theoretical contribution to EU studies, which along with his rational institutionalist followers together comprise something of the new institutionalist state of the art in this field.[23] Pollack argues that the autonomy of the Commission varies across EU policy areas as a function of Member States control mechanisms' efficacy and their need for expert information and credible commitments (I review his book more thoroughly in Chapter 2).

Joseph Jupille's account of EU policy-making continues the rationalist surge in EU studies.[24] His original examination of what he terms "procedural politics" on the part of the Three is compelling. Jupille analyzes strategic interaction in EU policy-making from an interesting angle, namely that of competition among the Three under conditions of policy issue jurisdictional ambiguity. Under such conditions—when a policy proposal coming down the pipeline does not fit unambiguously with a particular Treaty-based policy-making procedure—any of the Three can maximize their policy impact by hunting for opportunities to frame the proposal in such a way that it will get designated to adhere to a procedure that most advantages that actor. Jupille's book unlike this book is not a study of the politics of institutional change, at least as this term is traditionally understood; instead, he focuses on a designating or framing competition among the Three in an exogenous context of prevailing rules.

Jupille's account is methodologically sophisticated, incorporating both qualitative and quantitative methods and thus augmenting the convincing nature of his argument. However, his analysis necessarily leaves out a sizable swath of policy-making instances in the EU: He only examines instances of ambiguity over policy definitions that are indicated by legal disputes in the ECJ among the Three over the appropriate policy-making procedure to be designated for a given policy proposal. Moreover, Jupille's own statistical analysis results are weak for his hypothesis that "procedural politics" affects institutional change. Nonetheless, he provides a convincing account of a salient slice of EU policy-making outcomes.

Jonas Tallberg carries the rational institutionalist torch farther in his important study of the critical role played by the holder of the rotating EU Presidency in policy outcomes.[25] He argues that the Member State in the Council's driver seat possesses critical informational and procedural advantages in their interaction with other Member States, thereby allowing them to achieve more of their own policy preferences than their counterparts'. With these power resources in hand, the Presidency occupant is able to overcome the Council's internal collective action problems and other

---

[23] Pollack (1997, 2003).
[24] Jupille (2004).
[25] Tallberg (2006).

bargaining impediments so as to significantly impact the outcome of EU policy negotiations. At first glance, it would appear this work lends support to Intergovernmentalist claims.

But what about others among the Three? While in his case studies Tallberg acknowledges the existence of the obvious roles played by the Parliament and Commission in EU policy-making outcomes, his analysis of the cases diminishes the overall importance of the roles the Council's counterparts play in these very outcomes. Tallberg can thus be accused of subordinating the inter-actor game at the next political level up to his privileged intra-actor game that exclusively involves the Council. This exclusive emphasis on a particular unit of analysis amounts to a fundamental deficiency in the explanation namely failing to examine the game in which the intra-Council game is nested and thereby leading to a major lacuna in his findings. Without examining the Council's strategic interaction with the Parliament and Commission, a comprehensive explanation of policy outcomes is lacking.

Fabio Franchino's tour de force involves a rational institutionalist account of delegation in the EU sphere not of policy-making but instead of policy implementation.[26] Franchino asserts not only that comitology outcomes can be systematically explained, but furthermore that comitology committee selection has an impact on subsequent policy outcomes. He specifically argues that different aspects of the executive authority regularly delegated to the Commission are explained by political and institutional factors including the degree of conflict among Member States, voting rules in the Council, the degree of conflict between the Council and the Commission, complexity of the policy area, and the occasional role played by the Parliament.

Franchino relies on the principal–agent theory P/A model to demonstrate that these causal factors account for decisions to delegate implementing powers to the Commission as well as the choice of comitology procedure, motivated chiefly by the Council's preference for credible commitment devices and policy-making efficiency. Combining qualitative and quantitative methods involving data spanning five decades, Franchino successfully builds on a trove of recent comitology studies—including his own—to demonstrate that while most EU policies are implemented by national administrations, the exceptions to this rule are explained largely by vicissitudes in

---

[26] Franchino (2007). See *inter alia* Joerges and Neyer (1997), Heritier (1999), Hix (2000), Meunier (2000), Kelemen (2002), Ballmann et al. (2002), Franchino (2002, 2004), Hug (2003), and Jun (2003).

Council dynamics. However, the Parliament has continued to make inroads in the comitology sphere, as it won a significant new power from the Council in the form of an informal accord as Franchino's book was going to press.

Rational choice institutionalist studies of the EU have proliferated in recent years, a welcome development in the literature as indicated by this series of book-length studies. Formal modeling approaches in the rationalist vein have also come late to EU and regionalism studies, but a more robust series of debates have grown up around them. In terms of the EU, most of this work centers either on modeling the power relationships among the EU's organizational actors—the power index approach—or modeling the agenda-setting powers of the Council, the Commission, and the Parliament.

Based on cooperative game theory, power index models not only model the voting power of actors, but also actors' ability to achieve their aims. In EU studies, they have been used to model the power of the different Member States within the Council or different political groups, that is, parties within the Parliament.[27] However, this approach has proved deficient due to score normalization and misspecification problems, failure to incorporate nested games at other political levels, and a lack of dynamism in the explanatory models rendering them exercises in description rather than explanation.

Spatial modeling based on noncooperative game theory is superior to the power index approach, largely because the strategic nature of competition is modeled both within and between EU organizational actors. Yet, it is nonetheless problematic when special care is not taken with regard to microfoundations, assumptions, specifications, etc. Garrett and Tsebelis have been prolific with their attempts at modeling the agenda-setting of EU organization actors.[28] However, despite numerous publications and updated models, their efforts have largely proved somewhat deficient.[29]

Primarily due to overly literal interpretations of the EU's formal rules, Garrett and Tsebelis have doggedly stuck to their well-known argument, namely that outcomes under the codecision procedure are less integrationist than those under the cooperation procedure (now defunct). Not only does this model-based argument fly in the face of mountains of empirical evidence—the Parliament is near indisputably better off under

---

[27] See *inter alia* Herne and Nurmi (1993); Johnson (1995); Lane and Maeland (1995), Hosli (1996, 1997), Lane and Berg (1999), Nurmi and Maskanen (1999), and Dowding (2000).

[28] Tsebelis (1994, 1995, 1996), Garrett (1995), and Garrett and Tsebelis (1996, 1997, 2001).

[29] Crombez (1996, 2000), Moser (1996*a*, 1996*b*, 1997), Scully (1997*a*, 1997*b*), Hix (1999, 2000), and Corbett (2000).

codecision—but it further suffers from misspecification not only of informal rules that bind the organizational actors, but also the formal rules themselves. The authors have failed to account for the fact that agenda-setting power does not shift to the Council during the final conciliation stage of the procedure. Moreover, they have underestimated the degree to which the Parliament prefers improved policy-making powers over specific policy outcomes, that is, they have misspecified the Parliament's choice function.

Despite Garrett and Tsebelis's sustained attempt to eke out a degree of traction for their original argument (2001), the evidence still demonstrates that even under the rather rare set of circumstances in which the Council is capable of putting the Parliament in a "take it or leave it position," invariably the Council exhibits some degree of movement toward the Parliament's ideal point—namely because the Parliament consistently links issues across individual policy or power games, resorting to political sanctions whenever the Council seeks to deviate from established equilibria (see Chapter 3). Garrett and Tsebelis would be on safer ground, if they were to relax their single round of play assumption and specify their model in accordance with the gains achieved by the Parliament in the sphere of informal bargaining beyond the scope of the formal treaty.

Challenging these formal and rational institutionalist accounts, a menagerie of ideational and constructivist accounts have abounded in the field. While a considerable swathe of constructivist studies share the chief deficiency of network analysis studies—being exercises more in description than explanation—some recent ideational arguments stand out.[30] Craig Parsons offers up a compelling carefully researched account primarily of the early phases of European integration that centers largely on domestic debates among French elites and nonetheless exercises a significant impact on EEC and European Community (EC) outcomes.[31] Working with a trio of ideational causal models, Parsons is able to account for both the success and failure of a series of highly salient outcomes all the way up to the Maastricht Treaty. Moreover, he is particularly skilled at demonstrating how ideas get engaged in battles among the Three, leading them to redefine their interests. The only limitations relate to some minor ill-fitting empirics, absence

---

[30] Nonetheless, an array of constructivist accounts are noteworthy: DiMaggio and Powell (1991), Jachtenfuchs et al. (1998), Caporaso (1996), Checkel (1999, 2001), Diez (1999), Christiansen et al. (2001), Jupille et al. (2003), Risse (2004), and Diez Medrano (2006).

[31] Parsons (2003).

of any account of how other government elites interacted with their French counterparts, and questions about the generalizability of the argument.

Historically speaking, Nicolas Jabko's work in the ideational vein practically picks up where Parsons's left off and bears a strong resemblance to Kate McNamara's important work.[32] Jabko aims to explain the relaunch of European integration in the late 1980s, depicting the Commission as a catalytic agent of change that procured the support of Member States for its single market goal by framing it in politically strategic ways. Jabko underpins his argument with constructivist theory, that is, "strategic contructivism" in which ideas are used instrumentally. In his view, the content of certain ideas matters less than the degree to which they are rationally exploited to accomplish an actor's specific aims, thereby making it a more rationalist, utilitarian account than he is willing to venture.

Once Jabko extracts the causal force from the market idea—and it becomes a mere rhetorical vessel that is varied as dictated by an intentionally purposive actor relying on a shrewd, overtly political strategy—then his theoretical project ventures outside the constructivist realm. According to Jabko's evidence, the identity and values of business and government leaders are not altered; rather, they are effectively duped by being persuaded that these unchanged interests will be served by offering their support for the Commission's suggested course of action. This strategic, goal-oriented action by Jaque Delors et al. is more redolent of rational institutionalism than the sociological institutionalism connoted by constructivism. Moreover, the timing of this absorbing and compelling account is ironic.

Perhaps Jabko's approach could be applied to how Member States attempted to play the role of catalytic actors, exploiting political language and duping their publics to believe that the seemingly doomed Lisbon Treaty was changed not just symbolically but also substantively.

Institutional change in the EU

Explanations of institutional change in Europe, including the phenomenon of European integration itself, tend to skim the surface of EU activities. Confined largely to national–supranational conflict and the ins and outs of individual policy areas, as indicated above scholarly studies generally fail to

---

[32] Jabko's work (2006) strongly echoes that of Kathleen McNamara, who demonstrates that the neoliberal idea strongly influenced the early 1970s phase of Economic and Monetary Union (EMU) (1998).

uproot an important if somewhat obscured level of political activity in the EU.[33] While most studies focus principally on the formal sphere of European integration, they pay scant attention to the informal sphere: the activities of policy-making actors that are not subject to ECJ oversight and occur on a level parallel to but separate from the EU's formal Treaty-based level (including the customs, routines, and various ad hoc procedural rules that often complement, and occasionally contradict, but never officially constitute the formal sphere).[34]

This book focuses on a prominent instance of what happens when political systems lack constitutional settlements. Unlike the US Congress, where the incidence of institutional change of even an informal sort is somewhat rare, informal dynamics in the EU are rampant despite long-standing constitutional settlements in virtually all of its Member States. The considerable array of formal and informal rules in the EU can be nothing short of dizzying, thereby making this political arena an apt area for institutionalists to ply their trade. Precisely because the EU lacks a constitutional settlement, actors are motivated to press for advantage not only to achieve their policy aims but also to reallocate political power.[35] The phenomenon institutional change is thus prevalent in the EU, an ideal laboratory for inquiring into the conditions under which we can expect both institutional change.

While the book aims to explain the causes of rule-creating activity in the EU's informal sphere, it further seeks to determine whether or not this activity gives rise to any additional integration of the EU's Member States. That it may well lead to such an outcome lends credence to the importance of such an inquiry. Nonetheless, it is necessary to map some important segments of the EU terrain which hitherto have been hidden from view. The informal activity of the Three connotes a tension between prescription and convention in the EU, an incongruity between what is supposed to happen according to law and what actually happens in practice.

The critical components of this increasingly salient EU sphere are *informal accords*, that is, ad hoc agreements negotiated by the Three that have no

---

[33] The terms "European Union," "European Community," and "Community" will be used interchangeably throughout; in addition, the term "Treaty" shall refer to the Treaty establishing the EEC as amended by the SEA to become the Treaty establishing the European Community, which was further amended by the Maastricht Treaty on EU, the Amsterdam Treaty, and the Nice Treaty.

[34] For a similar distinction between formal and informal, see Judge et al. (1994).

[35] EU official, interview by the author, European Commission, Brussels, July 9, 2007.

legal base or third-party enforcer. Informal accords are political bargains comprised of one or more informal institutions or rules. Because they are intentionally created and bargained over, they are distinct from *informal conventions*: unintended rules derived from evolutionary patterns emerging from repeated actor interactions over time.[36] They are also different from *norms*—rules encompassing standards of appropriate behavior—which many in the literature mistakenly refer to as informal institutions or conventions.[37]

Sometimes serving to reinforce to the formal sphere, at other times to modify it, informal accords constitute the crux of the EU's "informal inter-organizational dynamics." To reiterate, if political competition can be conceived as a game, then the Three as organizational actors constitute the players and institutions constitute the rules of the game (as opposed to being actors themselves). These dynamics do not have a unidirectional causal effect, for either the Council or its weaker counterparts may be the beneficiary of reallocated powers stemming from informal accords.

Informal accords range from agreements by the Commission to inform the Parliament about its policy-making proposals early on, to agreements between the Council and Parliament to amend the formal budget-making process rather substantially. Of note, none of the rules comprising informal accords had their genesis in IGCs. For example, based on a 2001 Exchange of Letters—one of a whole range of labels given to informal accords in the EU—the Commission made several commitments to the Parliament regarding the EU's nonstandard policy-making procedure for financial securities-related legislation. These included new informal rules involving a variety of commitments, from informing the Parliament in advance of all specific legislative proposals in the securities field to sending draft legislative proposals that are at an advanced stage at the same time as they are sent to industry and Member State officials.

As is evident, the Commission does not transfer new policy-making powers to the Parliament in this particular accord. Typical of numerous informal accords the new rules here allow the Parliament to hold its counterpart more accountable, thereby augmenting its influence if not its power. On the other hand, certain informal accords may do nothing more than fill

---

[36] Weber (1978: 34) defined a convention as "that part of custom . . . which is recognized as 'binding' and protected against violation by sanctions of disapproval." Informal accords are more akin to a special kind of convention namely constitutional conventions. These too are unintentional; however, once established any breach thereof will necessarily invite retaliation in the form of political sanctions.

[37] Elster (1989: 113–20).

in the gaps in the Treaty after it is formally amended by the Member States. As will be discussed in considerable detail below, the bundles of rules comprising informal accords range across a continuum from those that transfer sovereign powers between actors to those whose rules are inert in integration terms and merely fill a gap in the Treaty. Naturally, pressure from one actor on another to negotiate an accord may come to nothing, for the causal conditions at a specific juncture may allow such attempts to be rebuffed (in which case the reversion point remains the status quo).

This book asks the following fundamental question: Given the long-standing antipathy toward the surrender of national sovereignty in Western European societies, even where "pro-European" sentiment subsists, why do the most powerful actors in the EU allow any supranational creation of new institutional rules whose effects they cannot keep under their general control? Indeed, there is a significant assortment of rules generated in the EU—laws, procedures, and policies—that not only seem to run contrary to Member State interests *prima facie*, but are also actively opposed by most Member State governments. To create informal rules of this nature, the Three must cooperate; but such cooperation is paradoxical in light of the wide disparities among them, in terms of both power and preferences. Moreover, if there is no legal third-party enforcer for what are technically nonlegal rules, why do the Three abide by them? A puzzle thus emerges.

If continued bargaining over informal accords by the Three were capable of altering the formal status quo and therein accelerate EU integration, it would seem strange for Member States through the Council to agree to them. This is the primary paradox. After all, the majority of the world's most developed nation-states are located in the EU, which features the top tier of former imperial powers. That the Member States would bestow any legitimacy on the informal sphere is odd, when conceivably they could confine any considerations of additional sovereignty transfers to the formal sphere where they have long functioned as the collective dictatress of European integration.

In this sense, the puzzle at the heart of this project is nearly synonymous with the enduring puzzle of the combined field of International Organization, Regionalism, and European integration: Why do powerful sovereign political entities relinquish sovereignty beyond their being violently coerced? This book's principal aims are first to make a general theoretical contribution by exhuming a previously obscured mechanism for institutional change, and second to explain specifically what accounts for why EU Member States brook any political activity in a sphere over which they do not exercise comprehensive control. Any potential transfer of policy-making power in the absence of a formal treaty basis demands an explanation.

A mapping of the EU's informal sphere is therefore necessary. Although a substantial portion of the EU integration outcome can be accounted for by formal EU treaty settlements, there remains a not insignificant proportion for which they cannot account. What is more, treaty contents may not be what they appear to be, for a given formal institution may not exist in its original form. Indeed, possibility turns into plausibility when one considers that a sizable number of formal treaty provisions bear more than a passing resemblance to older informal rules.

Prima facie evidence that certain formal institutions are mere reincarnations of previously extant informal institutions necessitates an examination of not only the precise numbers, but also the recursive causal process by which the informal is transformed into the formal. With verifiable evidence in hand, an adjustment in contemporary theoretical debates may be called for. The reigning theoretical contenders would be forced to grapple with the finding that seemingly new formal Treaty provisions may in fact amount to little more than an acknowledgment of a given political bargain previously arrived at in the EU's informal sphere. A further finding that certain informal institutions may not only contradict but perhaps even take practical precedence over certain formal institutions, that is, actors abiding by the informal, could make an important contribution to ongoing debates.

Parsing informal accords

Informal accords originally arose from a fairly standard scenario. When Member State governments agree to a new or amending EU treaty, they inevitably create a number of policy gray areas, as treaty language tends to specify the ends the signatories have in mind but not always the means; even the ends can be vague. Each time the Member States strike a grand bargain in the form of a treaty, they create a relatively hollow skeletal structure onto which the Three must graft the flesh and muscle of policy-making specifications.

If policy-making is to function adequately, that is, with at least a modicum of efficiency, then the structural gaps left after intergovernmental bargaining must be filled in relatively rapid fashion, preferably during a treaty's implementation phase. Without being fleshed out, treaty provisions fail to work as intended and the policy-making process becomes congested. Similarly, a treaty provision may be problematic or unworkable, in which case the Three must rectify the problem. Thus, treaties normally require not only being fleshed out, but fixed as well.

These two tasks are left to the Three which, at some point after a treaty is ratified, undertake in accordance with its provisions to establish the rules which will henceforth govern the minutiae of their interaction in the policy-making process. The Three thereby enter into varying modes of informal negotiation. In areas of EU activity where an amending treaty's language is unambiguous and the institutional configurations are acceptable to each of the actors, a rubber stamp mode of interorganizational negotiation ensues. By contrast, in areas where either the treaty language is ambiguous or the institutional configurations are not acceptable to one or more of the Three, a more contentious mode of informal negotiation ensues which goes beyond gap-filling.[38]

Informal accords also stem from a scenario, separate from treaty negotiation or implementation, in which one or more of the Three simply desire a change in the institutional framework, that is, more power. Such conditions can entice a disgruntled actor to engage in a "power-bid" strategy. The Three may very well interpret the Treaty provisions concerning a certain aspect of interorganizational relations the same way; however, one or more of them may not be satisfied with the status quo the Treaty sets out. After all, Member State principals do not give their supranational agents seats around the formal negotiating table.

If an actor becomes dissatisfied with the formally prescribed division of power or the structure of the institutional framework, it can seek to change it in one of two ways: by trying to influence the negotiations of the next formal bargaining session involving an amending treaty or by seeking to alter the division of power through informal accords. If no formal negotiations are in process or if access to these discussions is denied, a reform-minded actor is likely to opt for strategies in the EU's informal sphere.

Typically, under the second scenario the Parliament will indicate to the Council that it wishes to initiate negotiations over an informal accord of a specific nature. The Council normally responds in one of three ways: by rejecting the Parliament's informal influence attempt outright; by agreeing to discuss different options with the Parliament by setting up contacts at

---

[38] EU official, interview by the author, European Parliament, Brussels, July 5, 2007.

different levels; or by agreeing to enter into informal negotiations with the aim of brokering a deal. The deals made and bargains struck, when the first response is not in effect, take the form of informal accords.

Whereas in the 1970s and 1980s most informal accords were created in the process of a conscious effort by the Three to fill the gaps in new amending treaties, in the 1990s and 2000s this trend has shifted. In contrast, recent evidence indicates the lion share of newly created accords result from informal influence attempts by the weakest among the Three, the Parliament. Being a more powerful overall actor than it was during the early 1980s, though maintaining consistent preferences, the Parliament is better placed to bargain with the Council and Commission. It also finds greater opportunities to try to pressure its counterparts to engage in informal bargaining; this is due to the more frequent contact in the policy-making process among the Three, a factor not only of the Parliament's increased powers but also of the greater frequency of legislation being churned out of the EU's policy-making machine.

An important effect of informal accords is to restrict the freedom of action of the Three, to channel it along specific contours. These constraint-like contours may either be consistent with or divergent from the contours laid down by formal institutions. Thus, depending on what type of institutions they embody, the effect of informal accords is to support, refine, interpret, extend, and/or even alter formal treaty-based institutions. By serving these functions, their frequent effect is to render the policy-making process more operable and efficient, greasing the gears of the EU's policy-making machinery. More important still, different types of informal institutions engender different degrees of constraint. Therefore, the type of informal accord matters.

Informal accords range from simple, tacit bargains between a handful of EU officials at one end of the spectrum, to quasi-formal arrangements between the Three at the other end; it is a sizable continuum (Figure 1.1). They appear in four different types: *basic, standard, procedural,* and *substantive*. With a rather low level of formality, *basic accords* tend not to appear in written form, except perhaps in the Parliament's internal Rules of Procedure. The total number of basic accords is unknown, for by their nature they are rather esoteric and possibly completely unknown outside the narrow policy circles in which they are used. Despite the difficulty of tracking them all down, they are routinely adhered to as if at some stage they had in fact been officially codified by the Three. But there is no

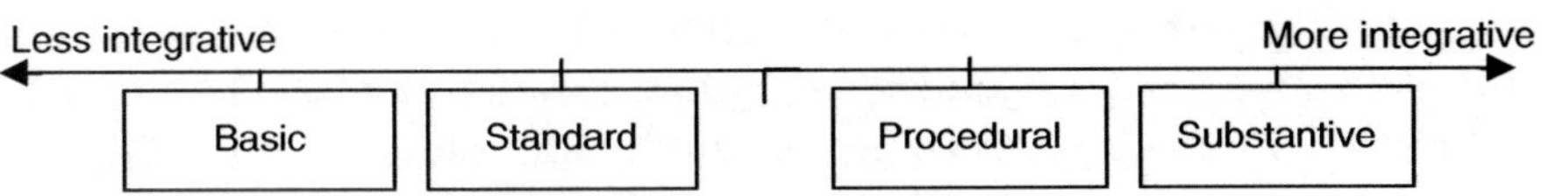

Figure 1.1 Types of informal accords: a continuum

systematic logic as to designing accords of a specific type; there are certain types for certain functions.[39]

Basic accords represent something akin to so-called gentlemen's agreements, made with the shake of a hand and the wink of an eye.[40] Depending on the circumstances, all that may be required for their creation is an individual official from one organizational actor proposing a minor procedural change to an official in one of the other Three. If the other official agrees to the change, the status quo is henceforth altered as a new informal rule of conduct is established, and altered expectations of behavioral standards come into play. For example, an understanding between a Directorate General (DG) I Commission official and an official on the Parliament's Committee for External Economic Relations that, every time the Council informally requests the Commission to introduce new trade-related legislation, the former would alert the latter by telephone, would qualify as a basic accord.[41]

With regard to relations among the Three basic accords are of little consequence, as even the Parliament gives little credence to them. The procedural changes they encompass are so marginal that no organizational leverage can be gained from them, that is, they are of such minor significance that they do not allow any actor to accrue influence at another's expense. Most of them involve few rules and rules that serve merely to codify the spirit of extant rules, formal or informal.

Of somewhat greater consequence are *standard accords*, informal accords which fall closer to the center on the (in)formality continuum. Standard accords are more widely known than basic accords, though their role is confined to fleshing out unworkable treaty provisions and filling in gaps of amending treaties. For example, the Treaty's stipulations pertaining to the old cooperation procedure were vague with regard to the timing of one of its key elements. In response to the need to resolve the Treaty's failure to

---

[39] EU official, interview by the author, European Commission, Brussels, July 4, 2007.

[40] This insensitive term remains the term of choice in EU circles.

[41] A DG is one of the Commission's bureaucratic agencies; DG I is the external (i.e., foreign) relations DG more recently known as RELEX.

establish the precise point at which the Parliament's three-month period to take action on the Council's common position actually began, after ratification of the SEA the Three met informally and determined that this juncture would be designated by the day on which the Parliament receives copies of the common position in all nine working languages.[42]

Effectively, a typically mundane standard accord does little more than establish a legislative rule or two for the purpose of filling in an obvious gap in the Treaty text: No powers or privileges are in any way altered or transferred. However, without this particular accord the Three would have been unable to agree when the clock starts ticking, as the Parliament and the Council would jockey to interpret the Treaty in a manner detrimental to the other. But with this standard accord in place conflicting interpretations of the former Article 189c were avoided, and the cooperation procedure ran more smoothly than it otherwise would have.[43]

Procedural accords represent the third type of informal accord. These accords fall to the right of center on the informality continuum. They involve more substantial changes in the rules governing interorganizational relations than either basic or standard accords. Instead of filling in gaps in amending treaties, procedural accords adjust and enhance already existing rules. Whereas standard accords create new rules—albeit entirely in keeping with the spirit of the related treaty provisions—procedural accords not only create new rules but often alter long-standing rules. Moreover, they do so in a manner that frequently serves to violate the spirit of the Treaty, that is, they organize interorganizational relations contrary to the Treaty's prescription.

Although technically correct, "violate" is perhaps too strong a term. The departures from prescription which take place as a result of procedural accords are slight, so much so that while it is clear which organization benefits from them, it is often difficult to ascertain to what degree the non-benefiting actors are aggrieved by them. The rules contained in this type of accords tend to allow weaker actors to hold their stronger counterparts more accountable, as opposed to granting them new powers to exercise clear policy-making power over them.

A classic example of a procedural accord is the 1964 Luns Procedure, the origin of which was a letter from the Council's President in Office

---

[42] There are currently twenty-three working languages of the EU, though there are only three common or 'procedural' languages: English, French, and German.

[43] Despite a smooth appearance to the outsider, from time to time disagreement over when to start "the clock ticking" have re-erupted; however, the interorganizational Neunreither Group has handled them sufficiently so as to avoid escalations of conflict in each case.

(then Dutch Foreign Minister Joseph Luns) to the Parliament, which communicated the Council's willingness to hold a discussion with the Parliament prior to the opening of negotiations for Association Agreements with non-EU countries, as well as a pledge to keep the Parliament informed of the developments throughout the negotiation. This is accomplished by an appearance of the Council's President in Office before the relevant parliamentary committees for the purpose of briefing them, confidentially, on the results of the negotiation.

There was no Treaty-based precedent for such an agreement; rather, the Parliament had for some time pressured the Council for additional information about negotiations with other governments. In 1964, the Council acceded to the Parliament's entreaties by agreeing to this accord. Typical of procedural accords, the Luns Procedure modifies the policy-making process with regard to the negotiation of external agreements in a manner unforeseen by the Treaty. The effect is in no way radical, but it does place the Parliament in a better position to influence the negotiations of Association Agreements. One would be hard pressed to demonstrate how either of the other Three explicitly "loses" in any significant way, but by the same token the Parliament has clearly gained by being in a better position to exercise influence over the Council and the Commission, and in certain cases it has done so.

In the 1990s, the Three began referring to the fourth type of informal accords—*substantive accords*—as "interinstitutional agreements." Interinstitutional agreements (IIAs) represent a quasi-formal type of informal bargain which, although more formal than the accords described above, continue to be negotiated and implemented entirely separate from either the Treaty or the EU's policy-making process. Because of their more substantive and prescriptive nature, the weaker among the Three tend to be better off as a result of this type of informal accord. IIAs have the greatest potential of the four for rearranging the status quo institutional framework.

IIAs are more consequential than the three other types of informal accords for a variety of reasons: They have a discernible political effect due to the political commitments they encompass; they deal with more substantive matters than the other informal accords; they are given considerable credence by the organizational actors; they involve specific negotiations between the Three; they attract the attention of both the press and national parliaments; and they appear in written form and are published in the *Official Journal* (OJ), the EU counterpart to the Congressional Record.

Thus, all told there exists a wide continuum of informal accords, ranging from the highly esoteric basic accords at one end and the quasi-formal IIAs at the other. This book focuses primarily on the role of IIAs, for by their nature they are more likely to have a greater impact on the changing nature of interorganizational relations. Unlike substantive accords, basic and procedural accords rarely involve rules changes of an integrative nature, that is, which serve to alter interorganizational relations in a substantial way. Standard accords involve substantive change, but not to the degree that IIAs do.

The past twenty years have provided ample evidence that IIAs have become permanent fixtures on the EU landscape.[44] Beyond any doubt they have become a viable option when the Three contemplate making changes in the policy-making process. In fact, with the advent of three amending treaties since 1992, the Parliament's increased array of formal powers has only fueled its appetite for further informal accords. The reason is not only that new treaties offer more formal treaty provisions for the Parliament to "sink its teeth into," but also because the frequency of changes in the institutional framework in which the Three interact simply feeds the integration appetite of less-powerful actors. As the Parliament's appetite remains far from satiated, its activity continues to defy the conventional wisdom that the more formal powers it receives in amending treaties, the less active it will need to be informally.[45]

In fact, in the mid-1990s, the Three brokered six new IIAs—far more in such a short period than had ever been previously agreed. As the Member States chose not to grant the Parliament all the new formal powers it had lobbied for in the run-up to the Maastricht Treaty, in the words of one official, "Maastricht wasn't enough."[46] The Parliament was not content to wait several years for the next IGC, especially given expectations at the time that the 1996 IGC (for the Amsterdam Treaty) might drag on for up to three years. The informal sphere was the obvious option for making further inroads.

Given their newfound legitimacy in the eyes of the Three, there is ample reason to believe that informal accords will continue to be opted for, if not always as mechanisms to flesh out treaties than as alternatives to treaty amendments when they prove too onerous for the Member States to negotiate and/or ratify.[47] Right up to and throughout the mid-2000s, IIAs and other informal accords have been bargained over and concluded by the Three (and further accords are in the pipeline).[48]

---

[44] EU official, interview by the author, European Commission, Brussels, July 7, 2007.

[45] EU official, interview by the author, European Parliament, Brussels, July 31, 1996.

[46] EU official, interview by the author, European Parliament, Brussels, July 10, 2007.

[47] EU official, interview by the author, European Commission, Brussels, August 1, 1996.

[48] EU official, interview by the author, European Parliament, Brussels, July 11, 2007.

Martin Westlake, an EU practitioner, offers the following interpretation of substantive accords and their significance:

> [T]reaty-based inter-institutional relations have been fleshed out by a large number of [informal] agreements with disparate scope and potentially far-reaching consequences. Though their exact legal and constitutional status remains unclear, most have resulted in generally-respected conventions, and many of these have proved important to the working of the Community's legislative procedures, particularly in the budgetary field and in facilitating the implementation of the Single European Act.[49]

He goes on to declare "it is clear that the adoption of inter-institutional agreements [IIAs] has become an indispensable element, a sort of constitutional glue, used to fill in and flesh out the bare framework provided by the inter-governmental conferences."[50] As evidenced by the increasing formality of IIA type informal accords and the increasing rate at which they are negotiated—the increased pace has remained in evidence after the Amsterdam and Nice treaties—this institutional mechanism has gained substantial legitimacy in the eyes of the Three, the Council included.

Aside from their occasional affect of redistributing power among the Three, another strong indicator of the significance of IIAs and informal accords in general is how often and to what extent the rule-based procedures they encompass are subsequently transferred to the formal sphere. This occurs when they are formally incorporated in an amending treaty, effectively a formalization or "sweeping up" process. The Maastricht Treaty was the first to formalize a large number of informal accords. All of them were originally informal institutions generated by informal accords that had been used extensively prior to being "swept up" in the amending treaty and transformed into formal laws. Thus in each case the Maastricht, Amsterdam, and Nice treaties effectively enshrined already existing practices, rules that were already in place and routinely adhered to.[51] In other words, as structural channels these rules did not change; however, their legitimacy increased dramatically as they were given greater stature and a definitive legal base. Whereas their legitimacy became based on the Treaty, previously it had been based largely on either unilateral Council declarations or the Parliament's internal Rules of Procedure.

A telling example of informal accord-based rules, procedures, and other precedents being swept up in amending treaties involves the EU's

---

[49] Westlake (1994*a*, 62).
[50] Westlake (1994*a*, 101).
[51] EU official, interview by the author, European Parliament, Brussels, May 1, 2003.

procedure for handling petitions from EU citizens. Neither the Treaty of Rome nor the SEA contained any provisions for petitions. Rather, their inception came with informal practices initiated in the 1950s by the Parliament, on the basis of its Rules of Procedure. The Commission began assisting the Parliament in this regard, and over the next couple of decades an informal procedure for handling petitions evolved. By the 1980s, it had become part of the quotidian governance of the EU, and in 1989 the Three brokered the Petitions IIA. Having imbued the procedure with additional legitimacy the Three rapidly became satisfied with this institutional equilibrium, which paved the way for incorporation in drafts of Maastricht. Then in 1991, it was formally swept up in the final text of the Maastricht Treaty itself. Why did the Council allow this? Although the Council would not have initiated this reform on its own, it found the informal procedure workable, not harmful in any way and in full keeping with democratic norms.[52]

Thus, contrary to the theory Intergovernmentalism and its assertion that the content of amending treaties is derived almost exclusively from Member State preferences, the origins—and at times the impetus—of many changes in the EU's fluid constitutional regime are informal accords. As the empirical record appears to indicate, interregnum integration in-between formal treaty-making may well be rife. A substantial number of the Treaty's provisions have informal accords as their sole source. The EU appears to have returned to a mode of regular treaty revision, thus continual institutional reform is taking place in the formal sphere which has the effect of greatly facilitating the sweeping up process by providing more opportunities for it to take place.[53]

A guide to the rest

The rest of the book is organized as follows: Chapter 2 encompasses the theoretical framework, followed by a full-fledged description of informal accords in Chapter 3. Chapter 4 parses informal accords further by examining actor strategies and their legal implications vis-à-vis such accords; this chapter functions as the beginning of the book's empirical section through an overview of public opinion evidence. The full-fledged empirical chapters comprise Chapters 5, 6, and 7, with the first of these illuminating the

---

[52] EU official, interview by the author, Council of Ministers, Brussels, August 1, 1996.
[53] EU official, interview by the author, European Commission, Brussels, July 5, 2007.

Three's strategic interaction by examining noteworthy failed attempts to negotiate informal accords. Whereas Chapter 6 examines informal accords in the budgetary sphere, Chapter 7 reviews all those that are non-budgetary in nature. The Conclusion in Chapter 8 presents the empirical findings, constructs a taxonomy of informal accords, graphs their impact, reviews the institutionalist model that underpins the book's argument, and charts the course from here.

Do informal interorganizational dynamics matter? I argue that dynamics in the EU's informal sphere do indeed engender a significant amount of integration. The evidence I will present in the ensuing chapters supports a view, contrary to conventional wisdom and a considerable body of regional integration theory, that informal accords have altered the *de facto* structure of the EU and accelerated the integration of Europe's proto-polity in the process—beyond a mere reinforcement of the formal status quo to the point of constitutional reengineering. Far from being epiphenomenal, I aver that informal strategic interaction of the Three exercises clear causal force over the nature and scope of European integration. As such, the shadowy informal sphere of supranational EU activity must be viewed in a new light.

2

A Theory of Informal Politics

No one can claim that the role of institutions is understudied in the social sciences. Although Political Science's stampede back to Max Weber commenced in the 1970s, when the state as a causal factor was brought back in, it was not until the 1980s that institutions also came in from the cold.[1] The subsequent herd of institutionalist studies was branded by March and Olsen and usefully corralled by Hall and Taylor in the mid-1990s. The trend has continued unabated under the rubric of "new institutionalism" and there is no end in sight.[2]

Throughout the 1990s economists and sociologists contributed to establishing today's troika of institutionalist approaches: Rational Choice Institutionalism (RCI), Historical Institutionalism (HI), and Sociological Institutionalism (SI).[3] Of this troika, RCI appears best equipped to explain changes in the institutional rules that the EU's political actors use to make policy. All political systems incorporate specific procedures for policy-making, for example, in the US Congress there is only one general procedure for making policy according to the law. Whereas in the EU's split legislative branch there are multiple policy-making procedures, and the institutions comprising them are both formal and informal. More so than its competitors, RCI appears capable of explaining not only how and why these institutions change, but also how some of the newly created institutions reallocate power among the EU's political actors—further integrating European nation-states in the process.

---

[1] March and Olsen (1984, 1989).

[2] Hall and Taylor (1996), Carey (2000), Diermeier and Krehbiel (2003), Helmke and Levitsky (2004) and Powell (2007).

[3] Shepsle (1989), North (1990), DiMaggio and Powell (1991), Knight (1992), Steinmo and Thelen (1992), and Pierson (1996).

Moving from the rational framework of the RCI approach to explicit theorizing, this chapter develops a transaction costs-based bargaining theory of institutional change that seeks to establish under what conditions new institutions are created in the EU's informal sphere. This account throws down a theoretical gauntlet to Intergovernmentalist theory in the debate over how and why EU Members States have increasingly pooled their individual sovereignty over the course of the postwar era. More specifically, it allows the Three to be cast as political entrepreneurs engaged in strategic interaction, the competition among whom results in the creation of consequential new institutions—an outcome different from where Member State preferences alone would have led. This bargaining theory furthermore takes HI and SI to task for their delimited ability to explain institutional change.

The rest of this chapter proceeds as follows. Initially I will review P/A theory along with the new institutionalist troika of RCI, HI, and SI. Presentation of a basic causal model of my bargaining theory of informal interorganizational dynamics will take center stage in the second section, involving the two-tiered First Stage of the argument. The next section will feature a narrative of how the weaker actors among the Three developed the capabilities to compete with the Council. Whereas the final section shall comprise the argument's Second Stage, in which the nature of the integration outcome will be further fleshed out.

Reviewing theories of institutional change

According to P/A theory, principal actors delegate a delimited degree of authority to other actors, their agents, in order to meet certain objectives or perform specific functions; this can involve the creation of new actors or an additional delegation of authority to already existing agents. In the literature, the most common principal–agent combinations tend to be the US Congress and US regulatory agencies on the one hand, and national governments and international organizations on the other. This project involves an incidence of the latter, with the twist that the agents are not entire international organizations but organizational actors within one.

Why does delegation occur? According to P/A theory, principals generally delegate authority to reduce their transaction costs. Principals may thus be motivated to delegate discretion to agents for the following specific reasons: (*a*) to utilize agents to monitor their compliance with the commitments they make to each other (and blow the whistle when they transgress); (*b*) to solve the principals' incomplete contracting problems via acting to fill in the details of contracts (that are invariably incomplete and may require other actors to create new rules as necessary, so long as they are in sync with the already framed contract); (*c*) to adopt new rules in the form of regulations that are too complex to be dealt with effectively by the principals; (*d*) to function more effectively by relying on a separate actor to initiate proposals for consideration among them and avoid the problem of cycling; and (*e*) simply to benefit from the policy expertise of agents.[4]

It would appear that the Member States, who together make up the Council, delegate policy-making powers to the Parliament and Commission at varying times for all of these reasons, particularly the Commission (though little evidence in the literature supports the fifth reason). According to P/A theory, principals are fully capable of restricting the range of behavior of their agents and reining them in when they attempt to circumvent the control mechanisms installed by the principals, potentially sanctioning them. In the EU, it is the Commission agent that is charged with the task of implementing policy, so the lion's share of EU control mechanisms is focused on supervising the Commission in its executive duties. It is fully expected that "slippage" will occur occasionally, when agents do not do precisely what their principals expect, due to the costly nature of supervising agents; however, slippage is not likely to lead to sanctioning as this type of agent behavior only involves minor deviations from the principals' expectations.

However, few contributions to the P/A literature allow for outcomes in which the agents, are capable of systematically "shirking," that is, pursuing their own preferences—and even defying principals' preferences for their behavior. In the EU, the degree of this agency loss runs contrary to most contributions in the literature. For example, whereas P/A theorists typically aver that agency autonomy varies with the efficacy of control and oversight mechanisms available to principals, the evidence presented in this book's empirical chapters suggest that the Parliament and Commission are capable on occasion of circumventing even the staunchest of such Council mechanisms. Thus, conceptualized as consistent pursuit of agents' own preferences not subject to principal constraints, I consider *defiance* behavior as a more catastrophic aspect of agency loss, beyond shirking (still generally subject to principal constraints) and slippage

---

[4] See *inter alia* Kiewiet and McCubbins (1991), McCubbins and Schwartz (1984), Weingast and Moran (1983), and Pollack (2003).

(caused by defective constraints and thus the least severe of the three types of agency loss).

While defiance is not explicitly predicted by P/A theory, I do not argue that the theory is in any way falsified. Instead, it would appear that the P/A framework could be extended to incorporate such findings. For example, Pollack's 2003 study predicts or confirms that the Commission as an agent exercises autonomy, that is, discretion as dictated by EU policy areas, each of which varies according to the Council's need for information and/or credible commitments. This type of analysis could be extended by attempting to predict the degree of agent discretion based on the costliness of oversight and sanctioning mechanisms, for on a certain level this book is about substantial agency loss. However, a significant problem would remain, namely that the Commission and Parliament occasionally team up in the EU's informal sphere, where principal-issued constraints do not exist, to pressure the Council for new policy-making powers (with intermittent success). Because of the difficulty in making *ex ante* predictions about such multidimensional outcomes, as well as the evidence pointing to intermittent success of the Parliament in getting the Council to agree to informal accords whose rules occasionally involve defiance, in this book I employ a different rationalist theory to explain the EU's informal interorganizational dynamics: institutionalist bargaining theory.

Not only is P/A theory not fully equipped to account for the phenomenon I seek to explain, but the standard versions of the institutionalist troika do not fare any better. RCI, HI, and SI each make a general claim about the process of institutional change, with RCI allegedly predicting rapid change and both HI and SI each in turn predicting more gradual change—highly gradual in the case of SI. In *prima facie* terms however, it would appear that each standard version does more to describe this phenomenon rather than explain what causes it. While a narrative about the rate of change is associated with each, at first glance it seems that none fully specifies the conditions under which institutional change will be causally generated.

Thus, whether change is alleged to be more revolutionary or evolutionary, concepts like punctuated equilibrium and increasing returns often serve as little more than metaphors standing in for more complete explanations. Without question the institutionalist troika represents a series of advances over earlier understandings, but standard versions of each leave a certain explanatory precision to be desired. According to the godfathers of modern day institutionalist theory, March and Olsen, "[m]ost theories of institutional change or adaptation . . . seem to be exquisitely simple relative to the reality of institutions that is observed."[5]

This trend is particularly prevalent with HI and SI. Moving to the other end of the institutionalist theory continuum—which impressively cuts across a wide variety of more specific theory—the assumptions and predictions of SI theory are simply not conducive to explaining a wide variety of political outcomes, let alone the EU empirics examined in the ensuing chapters. One of the underlying assumptions of SI posits that actors design and comply with institutions not as a result of rationalist cost–benefit calculations, but rather out of considerations of the "appropriateness" of specific institutional arrangements.[6] In this sense, institutions reflect shared understandings of what actors perceive as legitimate, efficient, or modern.[7]

Consequently, institutions according to SI are characterized by a high degree of durability and thus stability, particularly in light of its assumption as to how difficult it is to change normative or ideological "investments." However, because the causal mechanism involves the evolution of different shared understandings among two or more actors, the rate of change is predicted to be fairly slow—in poor comparison with a wide variety of political phenomena involving rule changes. Highly related is the degree to which SI underpredicts how frequent institutional change often is in politics; more conducive to the study of internal aspects of organizations, SI fares less well in accounting for how political actors pursue and achieve rule changes.

SI thus cannot account for the frequency of institutional change as evidenced *inter alia* by informal interorganizational dynamics in the EU. Despite its prediction of considerably less change *ceteris paribus* compared to RCI, SI does actually grapple with the notion of institutional change. It does so by emphasizing the prominence of norms in defining actor predispositions and, as such, norm-prominence constitutes a key condition for affecting actor behavior and outcomes.[8] However, a key set of flaws in SI accounts of change—beyond its inability to explain "big bang" change— involve a general difficulty not only in explaining how norms emerge in the first place, but also in identifying the conditions under which certain norms will be infused with prominence by norm coalitions or

---

[5] March and Olsen (2006: 13).
[6] See March and Olson (1984, 1989).
[7] See DiMaggio and Powell (1991, intro chapter).
[8] To reiterate, *norms* are defined not as standard rules but as standards of appropriateness.

entrepreneurs.[9] As such, SI proves fairly deficient at explaining how and why norms change, let alone how often and how frequently institutions are altered.

In-between RCI and SI resides HI theory. If RCI is supposedly the most "at ease" with institutional change or breakdown and SI most at ease with the persistence of institutions, what can HI add to this picture? In terms of institutional change at least, standard HI actually bears a considerable resemblance to SI: it is fairly proficient at explaining institutional stasis, or inertia, as opposed to change. The high degree of institutional persistence observed in HI studies appears neither to serve any functional purpose nor to provide the optimal solution to a specific problem.[10] HI actually endeavors to explain why institutions persist even in the light of highly volatile technological, social, economic, and political environments. This persistence or path dependence allegedly stems from several factors: the degree to which increasing returns lock in specific institutions and practices, the uncertainty of risk-averse actors about the future payoffs produced by new institutional rules and practices, the number of institutional veto points, and specific preference constellations.[11]

In HI, the likelihood of institutional change is expected to increase with lower levels of an institution's "return on investment," where there is relative certainty concerning the prospective effects of institutional reform, where the institutional provisions for change are permissive, and where preferences of change agents converge on the reform option. As such HI sets a fairly high mark for institutional change attempts to be successful. Moreover, akin to SI institutional change is projected to be incremental rather than radical, as well as reflective of processes of layering (new institutions being created on top on change resistant institutions) and conversion (old institutions being remodeled for new purposes). Although HI is fairly proficient at explaining the lack of change, due primarily to the buildup of increasing returns and the switching costs attached to them, it struggles to predict when the threshold at which the benefits of change outweigh the costs for actors is reached. While HI's explanatory power is arguably stronger than SI's, its attempt to account for institutional change amounts to a sort of theoretical tinkering.

[9] Institutional adaptation or change occurs when prevailing norms are superseded or replaced by others through the activities of "norm entrepreneurs" (Finnemore and Sikkink 1998) or "transnational advocacy networks" (Keck and Sikkink 1998) via mechanisms of persuasion and socialization (Checkel 2001).

[10] See the foundational HI works of David (1985) and Arthur (1994), *inter alia*.

[11] See Pierson (2000*a*, 2004), for a comprehensive elaboration of the HI approach.

Therefore, not only do HI and SI by and large start with a lack of microfoundations related to the precise mechanisms that account for the creation of change in institutions, they end with a shared inability to theorize conflict among actors with competing interests thereby connoting difficulty handling distributional concerns. In fact, the nature and interests of individual actors are almost entirely absent from HI and SI approaches, as the emphasis is far more on structure than it is on agency. These approaches focus nearly exclusively on the role of institutions to a fault, namely how they constitute actors, determining appropriate actor behavior, for roles often conflict. Therefore, not only do they by and large fail to account for competition, but even more glaringly they fail to account for actor behavior at least insofar as explaining specific outcomes is involved. One should note also that the rate of change issues is to a certain extent secondary for these theories, as timing is conditional and primarily a function of the causal force of independent variables (IVs) such as increasing returns.

The standard variant of the RCI approach has problems of its own, largely related to accusations of a failure to account for suboptimal behaviors or outcomes, the changing nature of actor preferences, or the role of power in the interdependence of actors in a given social arena. As such, the Williamson and Northian variants of RCI do not go far enough.[12] Instead, I seek to extend the traditional RCI variant derived from New Institutional Economics (NIE) to develop a full-fledged bargaining theory of institutional change à la Knight. My bargaining theory RCI variant involves a carefully specified theoretical incorporation of the concepts of power, intentionality, strategic interaction, distributional motivations, and conflict.[13] Moreover, it is theoretically agnostic regarding the degree of constraint of any extant institutions, while emphasizing in particular the endogeneity of institutions. Incorporating these critical theoretical building blocs as assumptions and variables allows me to rely on the RCI approach to construct a viable theory. As opposed to being a mere approach, it is thus able to generate tight predictions and account for specific outcomes in social life such as institutional change.[14]

RCI thus employed seeks to build on the standard institutionalist troika's attempts to explain change by simultaneously compensating for a prevalent set of weaknesses, for example, RCI's alleged inability to account for

---

[12] Williamson (1985) and North (1981, 1990).

[13] Knight (1995).

[14] Crudely stated, an *approach* constitutes a theoretical project comprising assumptions, whereas a *theory* constitutes a project comprising not only assumptions but also specific hypotheses.

gradual change and both HI and SI's inability to account for rapid change—much less any type of change. However, it is not at all inherent in the RCI approach that slower rates cannot be accounted for, as indeed most RCI work has the opposite problem, namely an inability to theorize rapid change!

It is puzzling why the major scholarly proponents of RCI do not often employ it to explain change, choosing instead to explain other types of outcomes in arenas of institutional stasis. Here I speak largely about the body of work by Shepsle et al. that comes under the rubric of structure-induced equilibrium that is centered on institutional exogeneity.[15] The Structure Induced Equilibrium (SIE) variant of RCI made serious advances beyond the pioneering early work of social choice theorists like Riker and McKelvey *inter alia*, whose work highlighted problems of instability, cycling, and chaos all related to the inability to predict stable equilibrium outcomes and the propensity for multiple equilibrium predictions.[16] While Shepsle has gone on to produce work more focused on the endogeneity of institutions, it has been more centered on tabula rasa institutional design or the use of extant procedures in legislative assembly arenas as opposed to power-based competition among actors over institutional change.[17] SIE ultimately has considerable difficulty predicting change.

Pushing off from SIE, Diermeier and Krehbiel make a strong abstract case that RCI theories are in fact equipped to explain a variety of changes in institutions. Using their terminology, the theory proffered below is both an institutionalist theory and a theory of institutions:

> The focus of a theory of institutions is to explain why some institutional features come into existence, and persist, while others are either nonexistent or transient. The defining characteristic of a theory of institutions is that some of the essential contextual features that were assumed to be constraining in the foundational institutional theory become objects of choice within a somewhat more general theory of institutions. The necessarily partial endogenization of institutional features is what distinguishes a [theory of institutions from an institutional theory].[18]

Although I use the following terms differently in my own model, these authors deem second-order institutions as exogenous and first-order institutions as the objects of choice in a theoretical framework like mine.

---

[15] Shepsle (1979, 1986).

[16] See *inter alia* Riker (1962) and McKelvey (1976).

[17] See *inter alia* Shepsle (2006).

[18] Diermeier and Krehbiel (2003). There is far more HI-based work on generation of institutions in the literature; however, see Acemoglu and Robinson (2006) for a recent formal RCI theory of different types of institutional change.

However, it is in close contrast to HI and SI where the understanding that RCI of the three is best placed to predict rapid change becomes clear, for much of the modern historical work under the RCI aegis has emphasized institutions as Pareto optimal and fairly stable, due to concepts such as logrolling and reciprocity—all in arenas involving legislative assemblies. However, when RCI models incorporate strategic interaction and asymmetrical power allocations among actors, it becomes apparent that the RCI approach can equally be deployed to explain varying rates of institutional change.

As will be clear in the introduction of my bargaining theory below, the concept of incomplete contracting is connoted. Numerous NIE and RCI scholars have written about this, namely the notion that any agreement among actors is incomplete because the contracting parties cannot foresee all eventualities. Thus, there are gray areas—or gaps as I refer to them—that need to be filled in by the agreeing parties, which as theorized in the EU occurs in the implementation phase of the agreement in accordance with the preferences of the actors. Because of transaction costs, as part of the intended delegation the principal transfers a delimited amount of discretion to its agents that involves this key element of filling in the gaps that were too costly for the principal to fill itself.

In this book, newly created informal accords are literally part of the implementation phase of the formal institutions agreed to in EU treaties, or the implementation procedures established in secondary legislation regarding comitology. Andrew Moravcsik actually seeks to incorporate this concept into his competing explanation of integration in the EU; however, the contract does not get completed as intended by the Member State principals for the agents have a different agenda that they are fairly successful in pursuing.[19]

The first stage: a rationalist theory of bargaining

As far as the degree of institutional constraint is concerned, unlike any of the standard troika my own rendition of RCI assumes that institutions are neither uniformly thick nor thin: some are thick, some thin, and others vary in thickness over time. Despite how it is most often used in political arenas characterized by stasis, the bargaining theory I employ is capable not only of accounting for different rates of institutional change, but also of

---

[19] See Moravcsik (1998: 73).

40

specifying the conditions under which a probable change in the institutions is predicted.

The theory stipulates that actors engage in strategic interaction within a framework of rule-based institutional constraints. However, in a slight departure from both SIE and NIE, while constrained by institutions the actors nonetheless seek actively to alter them or create new ones. This dynamic entails a vigorous competition whose political outcome often takes the form of new institutions, which in turn restructure the next round of the competition. Institutions, therefore, are endogenous to the qualitative model I construct below.

Furthermore, the institutions that "lock in" equilibrium payoffs crucially affect the distribution of the benefits of joint activity. Selection among institutional alternatives is thus a bargaining competition among the actors over the various alternatives.[20] The change trigger in this theory occurs at a precise threshold, specified by the point at which the most powerful coalition in a given arena makes a crucial calculation—that the benefits of a potential change would accrue to it outweigh the buildup of increasing returns for the status quo set of institutions—and moves to make it happen. At this point the catalyst for change is provided, with the built-in strategic interaction assumption that if a contest over the institutions were to occur the most powerful coalition of one or more actors would prevail. Anticipating the reactions of others, the actors make their determinations with consideration of the reversion point or the best alternative to a negotiated settlement (any altered or newly created institutions become part of the reversion point in the next round of the game).

In sync with a bevy of standard RCI assumptions—the unitary actor assumption, methodological individualism, and perfect information—my bargaining model posits that actors are rational: They perceive their interests, determine strategies and rank them in terms of preferences, and maximize their utility by choosing the strategy of action they have ranked highest in terms of the means to their desired end. Institutional change is induced by a change in constraints on the actors, for example, in distributional implications of existing institutions or modifications in the bargaining power of the actors. Changes in constraints function as causal mechanisms in my model, which as Elster reminds us are crucial.[21] The model generates outcomes via holding the preferences of the Three constant while allowing their constraints to vary.

---

[20] Knight (1995: 108).
[21] Elster (1989).

However, in further relaxing the comparative statics assumption, even weak actors can cause problems for powerful actors over time. With a temporal assumption operating, actor strategies will tend to militate in favor of tit for tat rather than defection in a prisoner's dilemma.[22] As such, the likelihood of bargaining thereby increases, for weaker actors may have leverage based on their intermittent ability to obstruct if not compel; powerful actors may therefore have incentives to bargain in order to mitigate the obstructionist motivations of their weaker counterparts.

The key here is not leaving structure in the lurch while privileging agency. As emphasized by Knight in his distributional variant of RCI, despite asymmetrical power disparities weaker actors will not be consistently vanquished.[23] Of critical importance here is Knight's notion of bargaining power, which may be temporary. While most actors will survive for future rounds of the game, even though stronger actors tend to win more rounds of the competition weaker actors will occasionally fair well in skirmishes. This is because bargaining power amounts to a condition in which a given actor has other options beyond that immediately facing it in conjunction with another actor.

Such an eventuality fits with a cogent take on the order-change issue by Lieberman, whose so-called multiple order approach gets at this quite impressively. In this perspective, an "order" effectively comprises a constellation of institutions that structure social life in a particular place at a particular time.[24] As these constellations are the products of political deals, to varying degrees they are fraught with instability, incoherence, and jury-riggedness, so long as actors are not satisfied with the status quo equilibrium. Lieberman actually posits layers of orders, one on top of another. Moreover, old orders are rarely jettisoned in full; rather, certain elements of them are reconnected and reconfigured, influencing events into the future. It is the friction between these layered orders where Lieberman finds the seeds of change for a given order.

Expanding slightly on the stochastic tendencies of his assumptions, actors may themselves be the source of this friction—intentionally generating change via the pulling and hauling of politics. For example, an elusive constitutional settlement in the EU can be viewed as a source of friction in the EU's legislative process via motivating the weaker actors to push for greater powers and rules *ipso facto*. Non-status quo actors can be expected to

---

[22] See Axelrod (1984).
[23] Knight (1992, 1995).
[24] Lieberman (2002: 702).

press for change and, indeed, to bargain for it; in scenarios where they have something to offer the more powerful status quo actors, old institutions may be altered or replaced. Indeed, as close as he gets to this variation on his theme, Lieberman states "institutions also create strategic opportunities for purposive political actors to further their interests, and they shape political opportunities for the mobilization of social interests."[25] Thus, not only do orders clash, but political actors can readily be relied upon to do the same.

Institutional equilibria are thus likely to be at least somewhat persistent, but not ineluctably so. As institutions are assumed to be neither too thick nor too thin in my theory, it compensates equally for standard RCI's putative inability to theorize persistence and for HI's putative inability to theorize change. The aim of my model is to explain endogenous change in the EU, treating institutions as dependent variables (DVs).

I employ the following bargaining model of informal interorganizational dynamics based on the RCI approach. This qualitative model is comprised of three basic components:[26] (*a*) specifying the preferences of the actors, (*b*) identifying the constraints these actors confront in the pursuit of their preferences, and (*c*) generating outcomes in terms of changes in the constraints that they face. Given a set of actors, their specific preferences, and the constraints they encounter in the attempt to achieve their preferences—contingent upon the constraints and preferences of the other actors—specific outcomes result from their strategic interaction in the context of shifting constraints. The pace of institutional change in the outcome is dictated by the pace of shifts in the constraints.

Of course in social life no strategic environment can truly be "held constant," for on some level each is always affected by strategic interaction. However, in the EU the preferences of the Three have remained quite consistent just as the model assumes. In the EU's structural milieu, a given institutional design outcome gets fed back into the constraints that structured the previous outcome; in so doing they become a novel constraint that will structure the next round of agent competition. Thus, even in an arena in which agents and their structure codetermine each other, agency is more pervasive than structuration as agents continue to compete over potential rule changes that further their own stable set of preferences. Such a dynamic entails a broad feedback loop in this qualitative model.

---

[25] Lieberman (2002: 709).

[26] For a similar attempt at modeling EU outcomes in the legal sphere, see Mattli and Slaughter (1998).

Figure 2.1 A bargaining model of the EU's informal sphere: actors, preferences, and constraints

	The Council
Preferences	To retain its large share of legislative powers To ward off the Parliament's bid for coequal status
Constraints	Pressure to decrease the EU's "democratic deficit" Pressure on states to achieve successful Presidencies

	The Commission
Preferences	To maintain its sole right of legislative initiative power To obtain a modicum of additional powers
Constraints	Power bids would undermine its precarious legitimacy Avarice would jeopardize retention of its current powers

	The Parliament
Preferences	To eke out as many additional legislative powers as possible To retain any power or influence previously obtained
Constraints	The more powerful Council's antipathy toward coequal status The lack of expertise and skill of its members and staff

The tables in Figure 2.1 set out specifications of the model in terms of identifying the EU's primary organizational actors, their preferences, and the constraints each faces in their competition to enhance their allotment of policy-making powers in the EU's policy-making process.[27] The model holds preferences of the Three constant while allowing their constraints to vary, akin to formal models insofar as some rules are exogenously given and other rules are endogenously chosen. Instead of ranking preferences, I assume that the Three prefer the institutional outcome that maximizes their influence on future policy-making and/or policy implementation outcomes.

It is important to note that I am examining strategic interaction of the Three only in the EU's informal sphere, not the formal sphere in which each of the actors is highly constrained by formal rules in the Treaty and secondary legislation in the policy-making games the Three play.[28] I do recognize, however, that some of the constraints above function also as part of the utility functions on other actors in making their own decisions; this affects the elegance of the model, but I defer to the empirical reality here in terms of what actually constrains these actors in their real world interactions.

Not surprisingly the Three prefer to augment and/or preserve their individual allotment of powers in the EU policy-making process.[29] The Parliament, feeling squeezed by the Commission and the Council, prefers to garner practically as much power as it can; in light of how impotent it is compared to many national parliaments, this is not an exaggerated assumption. More specifically, the Parliament is desirous of achieving co-equal powers with the Council in all policy areas under EU competence (at present it possesses this status only in certain policy areas).

Another salient example of the Parliament's aims is to obtain the power to initiate individual pieces of legislation, which would necessarily impinge on the Commission's historically unique and at present sole possession of

---

[27] The preferences of the Three were derived deductively and adjusted based on a series of interviews with officials from each organizational actor; the constraints were derived inductively. Interviews of EU officials were conducted on six occasions spanning 1994 to 2007.

[28] One might assume that formal rules act as constraints in the EU's informal sphere, but as the empirical chapters will indicate there are in fact instances where the creation of an informal rule actually contradicts an extant formal rule; in every instance of this, the Three in fact abide not by the formal rule but by its informal "replacement."

[29] On the issue of policy-making powers, individual officials and politicians within each of the organizational actors share preferences (i.e., the aggregation of their interests at the next level is smooth), whereas individual preferences consistently splinter on policy issues (hence, regarding policy outcomes, a unitary actor assumption would be fallacious). Interview by the author, official of the European Parliament, Madison, May 31, 2001; interview by the author, official of the European Parliament, Madison, June 1, 2001.

this power. In essence, having already "gained" substantial powers relative to its earlier days as an unelected and largely consultative body, the Parliament is intent on procuring an additional array of powers that would place it on par with the Council. As the only supranational actor with full democratic legitimacy, it views this as something akin to a birthright.

The Council is highly intent on precluding any parceling out of powers. With most of the cards in its hands already, its chief objective is to limit the Parliament's would-be capture of more cards for itself. Over time, the Council's Member States have obviously relinquished some of their power to the Parliament; however, its ethos (as represented by the officials in its Brussels secretariat) is to retain the most important and prolific policy-making powers for itself, for example, in the areas of taxation and foreign policy. While certain Member States like Germany favor increased powers for the Parliament (which would come at the Council's expense), as evidenced by the Amsterdam and Nice treaties it is far from clear whether a majority of like-minded Member States will be assembled in the foreseeable future.

Although the Commission would prefer to increase its powers—particularly in the area of monitoring and enforcement—it is highly unlikely to obtain virtually any substantial gains beyond the power of being the primary agenda setter of the EU (neither the Council nor the Parliament can propose legislation). Because its sole "right of policy initiation" is unique among executive bureaucracies the world over, the Commission is already perhaps the most powerful executive bureaucracy in modern history. Hence, it is mostly concerned with holding onto this atypical and therefore potentially precarious power, as opposed to seeking further powers at the expense of its counterparts. In fact among EU officials there is practically no expectation whatsoever that the Commission will be able to augment its policy-making powers in either the near or long term. Because of this the Commission is somewhat less central to the model than are the Council and the Parliament.[30]

The constraints on the Three are fairly straightforward and stem partially from a priori deductions and partially from the inductive source of interviews with policy-makers, though I acknowledge that they occasionally sound like anticipation of other actors' behavior. As indicated, the Commission is highly constrained by its historically unique possession of power as an executive bureaucracy. Already capable of exercising far greater

---

[30] Regarding implementing and oversight powers, the Commission does indeed harbor aims of gaining greater influence, for example, with respect to comitology and new policy competences—but in terms of the policy-making process, its primary preference is to maintain its monopoly power of policy initiative.

legislative influence than any bureaucratic counterpart in any other political system, the Commission is constrained from attempting to garner additional powers; this is largely a matter of legitimacy. Seeking to procure new, additional powers would risk the wrath of its organizational counterparts and put its present power allotment in jeopardy. Moreover, being the so-called "conscience of the Community" (a formal dictate from the Treaty), it is partially in the Commission's interests for the Parliament to grow in legislative strength—also because its own ability to influence policy legislation would grow proportionately. However, the downside for the Commission is how the Parliament would also be able to hold it more accountable, not to mention maintain greater political sway over it.

The Parliament is constrained by the Council's general unwillingness to relinquish further power to it. While a few Member States are occasionally inclined to strengthen the Parliament's powers via future treaty revision—most notoriously Germany, but also the Benelux countries—the majority of them are not; moreover, as borne out by numerous interviews, Council civil servants have a staunch antipathy for what they tend to regard as an upstart organizational actor. For roughly half of its existence, the Parliament has encountered a lack of organizational legitimacy in the eyes of the public, which resulted in general inefficacy stemming from the lack of expertise and largely deficient political strategizing commensurate with Members of the European Parliament (MEP)'s former unelected status. With little power and almost no legitimacy, the Parliament simply did not attract talented staff or MEPs and the ambition that traditionally accompanies them. Largely for historical reasons pertaining to its *sui generis* evolution, in capabilities terms the Parliament has not been as well "endowed" as its interorganizational counterparts. Case in point: across the EU it remains more prestigious to attain legislative office in Member States' national parliaments than in the European Parliament.

The final constraint on the Parliament is the general lack of formal institutions, which constitutes a specific feedback loop in the model. As will become clearer in Chapter 3, one of the primary sources of informal accords is the post-treaty ratification implementation phase in which informal rules are often needed to make formal rules work in practice. The fewer formal treaty institutions there are—as well as the fewer treaty implementation phases there are, that is, batches of formal institutions—the fewer opportunities there are for the Parliament to use them as the basis to demand something from the Council on the side, as it were. An important source of informal accords is the need of the Council to make sure the policy trains run on time. When the Council comes to the Parliament and asks for an understanding of when to mark the start of, say, the time in which the Parliament has to make amendments to a Council common position, an instance of informal interorganizational dynamics ensues.

In essence, any agreement of this sort creates an informal rule, and it is precisely at this point when the Parliament has at least a modicum of bargaining leverage in which to launch an influence attempt for new informal rules that go beyond making the trains run on time actually to constructing new tracks. As will be analyzed later in the book, at times the Member States choose to formalize existing informal rules, thereby inserting them into the Treaty. Thus, greater informal institution creation over time, via this feedback loop in the model, begets still greater informal institutions creation; for some though not all informal institution creation is conditional on the presence of formal institutions on which the Parliament can launch its influence attempts. As such, the recursive nature of informal interorganizational dynamics becomes apparent, for the line of separation between the EU's formal and informal spheres is as thin in the abstract as it is in practice.

The Council is constrained chiefly by not only the EU's so-called democratic deficit, but also the penchant among Member States at the Council's six-month helm for achieving individual success at the expense of the group, that is, occupation of the EU Presidency. The Council has traditionally been dogged by the accusation that it is an undemocratic bastion run by technocratic officials who are not directly accountable to EU citizens. Although Member State cabinet ministers make the Council's most important EU policy-making decisions—normally members of voter-supported governments and directly elected themselves—due to the fact that legions of low-level decisions are made by civil servants, the Council has encountered difficulty in shedding this widespread perception. Indeed, its counterparts have often attempted to exploit this vulnerability in the court of public opinion.

In addition, Member States occupying the six-month rotating Presidency regularly engage in what seems like a never-ending bout of one-upmanship to the detriment of the overall body.[31] Member State governments robustly compete with each other in terms of which of them is able to achieve the most "successful" six-month term at the helm of the Council as occupant of the EU Presidency. "Success" can be operationalized in terms of how many pieces of EU legislation each Presidency is able to shepherd through

---

[31] Some have argued that the Parliament's ability to be fairly obstructionist in the course of the EU policy-making process qualifies as a third major constraint. There is some legitimacy to this claim, for it has demonstrated a disposition for sporadically dragging out and interrupting the policy-making process on those occasions in which it feels the Council has dismissively ridden roughshod over its policy preferences.

the EU policy maze—as well as achievements of comity in relations with its counterparts—any Member State in the Presidency must broker a fair amount of legislative deals with the other actors, the Parliament in particular. This can involve relations in the informal sphere and the Council's proclivity for reaching informal accords with the Parliament. Thus, the pressure and preference to succeed militate against the Council's preference to protect its power prerogatives, and thereby functions as a significant constraint on the Council.[32]

The following comprise the model's hypotheses regarding ultimate causes, that is, those that postulate changes in constraints necessary to generate changes in outcomes. I hypothesize that three particular changes in constraints largely account for the generation of new institutional rules, which may result in further integration:

Hypothesis 1: If the pressure on the Council to further democratize the EU either remains significant or increases, then the Council will accede to at least a modicum of the Parliament's influence attempts and the number of informal accords will increase (as will their integrative content).

Hypothesis 2: If the pressure on Member States occupying the EU Presidency to succeed either remains significant or increases—making the Council situationally more likely to compromise with the Parliament—then the number of informal accords will increase (as will their integrative content).

Hypothesis 3: If the advent of direct election of the Parliament's MEPs occurs—in turn triggering an increase not only in the competence of MEPs, but also the quality of the Parliament's political strategizing—then the number of informal accords will increase (as will their integrative content).

Hypothesis 4: If the number of formal institutions increases, then the number of informal accords will increase.

---

[32] One might expect that the level of intra-Council agreement or discord should matter when the Council is interacting with the Parliament in the EU's informal sphere, that is, the more consensus among the Member States that exists the more likely the Council will do a deal with the Parliament. However, to a surprising degree, informal relations with the Parliament are dealt with by Council civil servants and diplomats from the Council Presidency without the input of other Member States. This is partly surprising, given instances of power and authority transfer, but there are no Council decision rules when it comes to the informal sphere dynamics. Thus, Council civil servants are often left on their own, with only the occasional involvement of Presidency officials. When the Presidency does get involved, say for reasons involving *Hypothesis 2*, the Presidency tends to act as a chairman operating on its own. Other Member States do not get involved unless the issues involved are highly salient.

Hypothesis 5: If the constraints on the Commission remain the same or decrease, then its positional status will only change insofar as the Parliament may prove more able to hold it accountable.

The predicted change in outcome stemming from the first four postulated changes in constraints is the creation of new informal rules, bundled in more frequent and more integrative informal accords. This in turn should render the Parliament better off vis-à-vis both the Council and the Commission, that is, in possession of a more powerful organizational position via increased policy-making powers. Whereas the final hypothesis does not predict increased power for the Commission via informal interorganizational dynamics; rather, the Commission may lose power due to the third hypothesis.

The principal *alternative hypothesis* to be tested by the assembled evidence stems from P/A theory: If the Council remains significantly more powerful than its counterparts, then notwithstanding such potential constraint changes, the number of informal accords will not increase as a form of prevented shirking. As the formally more powerful actor, the Council should be able to ward off the influence attempts of its counterparts in the informal sphere. Evidence as to whether or not these hypotheses are confirmed or falsified will be discussed in the ensuing chapters and then definitively assessed in the Conclusion.

The DV associated with Figure 2.2 consists of the incidence of informal accord creation as well as the substantive content of these accords. I postulate above that certain constraint shifts will lead not only to a greater frequency of informal accord creation, but also a higher integrative nature of the institutional content of the accords. In other words, these hypotheses predict greater integration as a result of informal interorganizational dynamics in terms of new rules that reallocate power from the Council to either the Parliament or the Commission. The ensuing chapters will test these hypotheses.

However, in order to account more fully for the variance in new informal accord creation, an additional order of IVs must be introduced; this necessitates drawing a distinction between ultimate causes and proximate causes. To reiterate, ultimate causes are those factors or explanatory variables that involve somewhat deep, structural changes in actors' environments, which exercise their causal effect on the DV over the medium to long term. Whereas proximate causes involve changes of a more fleeting nature; their effect has a more immediate quality, thereby exercising something approximating a short burst of causal influence over the short term.[33] While ultimate IVs exercise their

---

[33] The distinction between different types of causes is similar to the distinction between general causal laws and causal mechanisms (Elster 1989: 4–10).

Figure 2.2 Hypotheses of ultimate causes: postulated changes in the model's constraints

	Constraints on the Council
Changed	Then: pressure for successful 6 month. EU Presidencies Now: ⇑ pressure for success (i.e., ⇑ legislative output)
Changed	Then: pressure on the Council to democratize the EU Now: ⇑ pressure to decrease the "democratic deficit"

	Constraints on the Commission
Unchanged	Power bids would undermine its precarious legitimacy Avarice would jeopardize retention of its current powers

	Constraints on the Parliament
Unchanged	The Council's antipathy toward coequal status with the Parliament
Changed	Then: traditional lack of expertise associated with unelected MEPs Now: direct elections: ⇑ member expertise and ⇑ strategic acumen
Changed	Then: low number of treaties and formal institutions within them Now: increase in the number of treaties and formal institutions

causal effect indefinitely, the effect of proximate IVs is more ephemeral in that they often soon revert to their status quo position prior to varying. The three postulated constraint changes outlined earlier, which have the character of ultimate causes, are necessary but not wholly sufficient to achieve full-fledged covariance in the model. In order to meet this important theoretical requisite, several proximate causal factors must be incorporated for the model to attain a priori causal sufficiency.

In light of the puzzle motivating this inquiry—why more powerful actors relinquish power and/or control in spite of an explicit long-standing preference to retain their allotment of policy-making power—the ultimate causal factors in this model are not sufficient to account for why the Council capitulates to certain Parliamentary influence attempts and not others. In other words, despite the significant shifts in the institutional framework that structures agent interaction in the EU's quotidian policy-making process, a zealous and predominant actor like the Council may still repel the influence attempts of its counterparts in the informal sphere; indeed, empirically speaking, it would appear this is an intermittent occurrence. While the Council may occasionally ascertain that brokering informal accords with the Parliament is in its interests—which it hardly would in the absence of constraint shifts—additional factors are necessary to gain full leverage on the variance in outcome.

Therefore, the model also comprises three IVs that exercise proximate causal force in the EU's informal sphere: actor preference intensity, actor time horizons, and issue linkage. In terms of the model, variation in these proximate IVs are considered second-order constraint changes—first-order constraint changes being shifts in the model's ultimate IVs—which are necessary for explaining informal institutional change, this study's outcome or DV. I aver that both the first-order and the second-order constraint changes together are sufficient for explaining i.e. the DV.

To begin with, political actors tend not only to hold general preferences, but they also hold some preferences more strongly than others. In other words, actors desire certain policy outcomes more than others; in addition, these policy preference intensities vary over time. Time horizons are somewhat akin to actor preferences in that certain actors tend to care largely about achieving certain policy outcomes in the short term, while others are more patient and thus open to achieving their policy aims over the long term. Like preferences, time horizons vary; moreover, they can vary across policy issues or vary more according to individual policy issues. For example, governments may have short-term time horizons for economic growth but long-term horizons for military security; likewise, in peacetime or an environment lacking in threats, a government may have a weaker preference for security than it does when threats are clearly evident.

Issue linkage as a proximate IV is also fairly straightforward. If the Parliament can manage successfully to link a piece of legislation desired by the Council to one of its own attempts to broker an informal accord, then agreement over a new (or amended) accord is likely. In order to employ this strategy successfully, the Parliament, for example, must credibly commit to rejecting the Council's preferred legislation, if in fact the latter does not agree to what the former seeks. In the absence of such credibility, the Council can effectively call the Parliament's bluff, in which case there will be no accord. For example, the Parliament may communicate to the Council its desire to negotiate a new informal accord, say, to grant it increased power in the financing of any Common Foreign and Security Policy (CFSP) initiatives of the Council. As the more powerful actor, the Council may reject this attempt due to its differing preference. However, a newly negotiated external trade agreement between the EU and the Baltic states may come up for ratification in the Parliament. In such a scenario, the Parliament may threaten to reject the agreement unless the Council agrees to do an informal deal on CFSP financing. If the Parliament can do so credibly—successfully persuading the Council it will make good on its threat—then the Council is likely to enter into negotiations with the Parliament over such a potential accord.

In a separate and more general hypothetical situation, holding strong preferences and having short time horizons tend to make an actor vulnerable vis-à-vis others with clashing preferences—particularly if the others possess, say, weak preferences and long time horizons concurrently (similar preference intensities and time horizons tend to cancel each other out with regard to bargaining outcomes). In terms of ultimate IVs, the Council may be persuaded that over the long term it is in its interests to share more power with the democratically elected Parliament, and the holder of the Council Presidency may strongly desire to be judged a success at the end of its six months in office—while the Parliament may at the same time be vigorously pursuing its preferences in strategic fashion; however, the more powerful Council may not actually capitulate to a specific demand of the Parliament to negotiate an informal accord unless the proximate IVs are in operation.

Staying with this proximate IV hypothetical, if the Council's time horizons at a given juncture are long and its preferences weakly held, it is not likely to capitulate knowing that it still has a considerable period of time in which to pursue its interest in ameliorating the EU's democratic deficit and likewise its Presidency occupier's desire to achieve success. Under such a constellation of circumstances, a successful bargain with the Council, for example, is not likely for the Parliament. Whereas under different circumstances, an informal accord is more likely. If the Council were to possess short time horizons and desire greatly for the Parliament to cooperate on a given piece of legislation (and perhaps also being susceptible to a Parliamentary strategy of issue linkage), it would likely enter into negotiation over an informal accord intentionally—and via bargaining thereby transfer an allotment of policy-making power to the Parliament, gaining democratic kudos in the process and possibly more. It might additionally garner Parliament's cooperation on a salient piece of legislation or much sought after policy-making peace.

For either the preference intensity or time horizon IVs to compel the Council and Parliament to broker an informal bargain in proximate terms—that is, dictating the timing of an accord, with both actors already inclined to do a deal based on variation in one or more of the ultimate IVs—a specific causal combination must be in evidence. For the Council's strong preference for a certain piece of legislation to have an effect on the outcome of its interaction with Parliament, the Parliament must have weak preferences on the legislation. Thus, if it were also to possess strong policy preferences, this would cancel out the causal effect of the Council's preference intensity.

Likewise, short time horizons on the part of the Council regarding a piece of legislation must be matched by long time horizons on the part of the Parliament; otherwise, a Parliament's matching time horizons would cancel out key shifts in a factor influencing the Council. In terms of issue linkage, for this IV to exercise proximate causal force there need not be a reciprocal quality on the part of the other actor; all that is required is for the Parliament to credibly link an issue before it (one for which the Council desires Parliament's cooperation) to one of its own attempts to persuade the Council to negotiate or amend an informal accord.

The issue of credibility is important for issue linkage attempts, for when it is lacking the Parliament can be stymied in its informal influence attempts. In a 2001 empirical example of considerable salience, the Parliament attempted to influence the Council to broker an informal accord in the area of comitology (the system of administrative oversight of the Commission's executive activities, long dominated by the Council). In doing so, the Parliament employed a strategy of issue linkage, seeking to link its comitology influence attempt with legislation for the creation of the first proposed directive on EU-wide financial services. With so much riding on this directive from the Council's perspective—the keystone for EU efforts to integrate European capital markets—the Council possessed an intense preference for winning its approval by Parliament.

However, the outcome was largely one of Parliamentary capitulation, for it was influenced so heavily by the media and a bevy of interest groups that its own preference for the financial services directive grew quite strong before the termination of its interaction with the Council. As such, because this change canceled out the Council's strong intensity and in the process rendered the Parliament's issue linkage attempt incredible, no negotiations of a new or amended accord regarding comitology took place; and all the Parliament secured was a commitment by the Council to revisit the issue in the near future.

Thus, there would appear to be an intermittent spur for the Council to capitulate to the Parliament and/or Commission particularly when a given policy issue generates intense preferences and short time horizons for the Council, matched by weak preferences and long time horizons by one of the others—not to mention successful issue linkage. Once one or more of these temporary second-order variations ensue and the Council in turn develops a predilection for doing an informal deal, the prospects for advantageous outcomes for its counterparts even increases to the degree that they can offer something for the Council to receive in turn. The Council may desire cooperation from them on a different piece of legislation, or less obstructionism in some specific regard, or perhaps an ad hoc commitment that will advantage it at their expense. Rarely if ever does a given informal

Figure 2.3 Proximate hypotheses: postulated changes in the model's second-order constraints[34]

Proximate hypotheses
1 – The stronger (weaker) Actor A's preference intensities for the passage of a piece of legislation relative to Actor B's preference intensities, the more (less) likely Actor A will agree to an informal accord with Actor B.
2 – The shorter (longer) Actor A's time horizons relative to the Actor B's time horizons, the more (less) likely Actor A will agree to an informal accord with Actor B.
3 – An actor is more likely to reach its objectives with regard to the adoption of an informal accord if it credibly links such an outcome to the passage of a piece of legislation.

[34] Because on occasion the Parliament and the Commission bargain with each other over the prospect of creating or altering an informal accord, similar dynamics are hypothesized about the outcome between them.

accord not hand the Council something in return for any allotment of power or responsibility it relinquishes to its less powerful counterparts.

This shift in first-order constraints is a necessary causal factor, but not a sufficient one—these make the change in outcome probable but cannot fully account for the timing of specific instances of this change. Despite the Council's becoming more disposed to informal accords—and the Parliament's becoming more sophisticated in their pursuit—as a direct consequence of first-order constraint changes, full explanatory sufficiency remains elusive. To this end, I maintain that the causal requirement for explaining the consequential creations of new institutional rules in the informal sphere is met by shifts in second-order constraints (Figure 2.3).

Cooperative outcomes are nonetheless paradoxical, for on paper the Council and the Member State principals it subsumes should theoretically be able to fend off the influence attempts of its far weaker agents. Cooperation should be unlikely not only because the Council is more powerful (due to the distribution of policy-making powers via long-standing institutions), but also because its preferences are hawkish. In addition to the barrier of power asymmetries, the Parliament in particular has more intense preferences than the Council and is willing to go to greater lengths (i.e., give up more) to achieve at least some form of cooperative agreement (i.e., at least achieve an informal accord, if not one with a rules content as beneficiary to it as it would prefer, *ceteris paribus*). Thus, cooperation is prohibitive also because of the greater preference intensities of the supranational actors.

In spite of these obstacles to cooperation, as embodied by new informal accords, accommodation among the Three is theoretically achievable. I argue that shifts in the model's first and second-order constraints interact to provide the conditions in which informal accords are created. These two orders of IVs—combining ultimate and proximate causes—interact to predict specifically when the Council will accede to the Parliament's entreaty to negotiate a new informal accord, namely one that advantages the Parliament while also meeting specific Council interests. Thus, either the first or second-order constraints in and of themselves are insufficient to predict the timing of cooperation, but their interaction does in fact prove sufficient. If this were a large-N project and statistical analysis could be employed, I would be testing for interaction effects of these two types of constraint changes.

I maintain that while the Council is pressured to close the EU's democratic deficit, it does not acquiesce to every single influence attempt by the Parliament. Nonetheless, I argue that the latter achieves its aims when it gets the Council "over a barrel," for example, when it successfully links an informal influence attempt to a separate issue on which the Council has short time horizons and intense preferences. For example, the Parliament may threaten that it will not ratify a highly important external trade agreement until the Council capitulates on a proposed informal accord.

In temporal terms, there are two phases involved in operationalizing the timing of new informal accords. The first phase involves how long it takes a weaker actor like the Parliament to get a stronger actor like the Council over a barrel. For example, if the Council has highly intense preferences either over a potential informal accord (e.g., if the Presidency needs a deal to brag about) or over a proposed piece of legislation (that the Parliament has linked to its influence attempt), then subject to normal transaction costs change in the form of a new informal accord is rapid (time horizons operate in the same manner). Or it may be sufficient that the Parliament successfully engages in issue linkage in the absence of either short time horizons or intense preferences on the part of the Council. However, change is predicted to be more gradual if the process of issue linkage by the Parliament takes longer than two to three weeks, or if the Council only gradually develops intense preferences.

Thus far the discussion about timing assumes normal transaction costs, that is, several weeks of negotiation between the actors to hammer out a deal for an informal accord. When a second-order constraint shift occurs, either a single shift or in combination, negotiating the contents of an accord that is relatively devoid of inter-actor conflict normally takes three to four weeks. However, if the conflict level is high then a second timing phase is postulated. Relaxing the assumption of normal transaction costs, the negotiation phase may take longer than one month and potentially up to a year. However, once an informal accord is agreed new institutions are *ipso facto* generated, right on the spot. Because the arena under study here is the EU's informal sphere— not that of an IGC or the EU's policy-making process—there is no third phase, which would involve either ratification in Member State capitals or all the normal hoops that secondary legislation goes through in the formal sphere.

Therefore, in terms of the rate of change, how rapidly or gradually the process of generating new institutions is predicted to be is determined by the rate at which the proximate causes occur, that is, how quickly or slowly the model's second-order constraints shift. This is consistent with the fact that RCI theories are capable of explaining outcomes of either institutional stability or institutional flux, unlike its HI and SI counterparts. I will present evidence in the ensuing chapters in seeking to confirm the argument underpinned by my bargaining model. Prior to that, the second stage of my argument seeks to frame the explanatory outcome of the book in a larger context.

The second stage: an argument about integration

Whereas the first stage of the argument employs an RCI bargaining model to explain an outcome of informal institution creation in the EU, the second stage attempts to interpret this outcome. In what may appear as transitioning from endogenizing institutions in the first stage of the chapter to exogenizing them in the second stage, instead this section attempts to shed light on the operationalization and measurement of this project's DV. The second stage actually is an exercise in interpretation of the DV, rather than a successive explanation further down the causal chain.

In terms of interpretation, an ancillary question to this book's primary question asks whether the outcome generated by my model of informal interorganizational dynamics results in *institutionalization, integration,* or *disintegration,* that is, institutional rule creation in the EU's informal sphere which reinforces the formal Treaty-based status quo, reconfigures it by parceling powers away from the Council, or reconfigures it by parceling powers to the Council. As set out in Chapter 1 and to be further elaborated in Chapter 3, the Three negotiate an array of different types of informal accords, some of which reinforce the status quo and adhere to the spirit of the Treaty, and others of which alter it by creating new informal rules of conduct for the day-to-day policy-making that have the potential of swinging the pendulum of legislative power allocation in either direction.

Under the guise of this empirical question I hypothesize that informal accords, the crux of informal interorganizational dynamics, engender both institutionalization *and* integration, but not disintegration. *Institutionalization* refers to the reinforcement of extant Treaty-based or secondary legislation-prescribed rules via the ongoing entrenchment of normal, expected, routinized behavior of the actors consistent with the *acquis.* This process is operationalized in terms of the creation of new rules that reinforce the status quo equilibrium underpinning the previously existing rules; institutionalization is in evidence when new rules leave the spirit of the Treaty intact and the interorganizational balance of power unaltered. New informal rules à la institutionalization do not represent the kind of change that could effect substantively different outcomes—only mirror what was already taking place prior to their creation, perhaps enhancing the previous status quo but not fundamentally altering it.

As such, the new but inert rules merely serve to fill in the incomplete contract of the Treaty, that is to do one of the following: to flesh out, streamline, or render the status quo formal rules more efficient. For example, Article 251 of the Treaty encapsulates the codecision procedure. The formal rules for the operation of this decision-making procedure are laid out in the provisions of this treaty article. However, the Three have seen fit to codify a host of their informal practices regarding the practical application of the formal rules, which had accumulated from the early period when the Maastricht Treaty was ratified. In 1992, the Three had to find ways to implement EU law regarding this procedure, in order to make use of it as intended (or, from the Parliament's perspective, to extend its powers). But the formal rules did not address or encompass all of the necessary aspects of working out the codecision procedure in practice. Hence, in 1993 and again in 1999 and 2007 the Council and the Parliament resorted to an informal accord to meet the need of practical application, and they negotiated a specific informal accord in each of these years.

Part of the 1999 accord provides an illustration of the institutionalization dynamic, as distinct from integration (and disintegration). There are references throughout Article 251 to different periods of time within which certain actions must take place, for example, three months for the Parliament to propose amendments to the Council's common position or to reject it. Nowhere among the formal rules is there an allowance for any deviations from the strict timelines they prescribe. However, the Three recognized that circumstances would arise in which some form of extensions might be needed. Thus, in the 1999 accord one finds an informal rule stating:

> Should the European Parliament or the Council deem it essential to extend the time limits referred to in Article 251 of the EC Treaty, they shall notify the President of the other institution and the Commission thereof.[35]

As is self-evident, this informal rule in itself in no way alters the decision-making prerogatives or actual Treaty-prescribed legislative powers of either actor. It does change the parameters of allowable behavior, technically speaking, but its purpose and effect are merely to make the formal prescriptions more practicable. Thus, it amounts to an institutionalization of relations between the actors, reinforcing—indeed, improving—them, but without any fundamental alterations.

Institutionalization connotes an "inert" result of institutional change, that is, an informal means of reinforcing the EU's rule-based structure. The type of new institution creation comprises only minor adjustments to the rules of institutional behavior—for example, an informal accord that alters the timing of a particular legislative procedure. Such an accord alters the

---

[35] Joint Declaration on Practical Arrangements for the New Codecision Procedure, 1999.

specifications of that procedure but leaves unchanged the substance of the procedure, thereby adhering to the spirit of the law. Most crucially, accords like this do not alter the power allocation among the Three; procedural practice does not diverge from constitutional prescription in such instances. The inert balance of interorganizational power outcome stands in contrast to one involving integration.

Integration is defined as a transfer of specific allotments of sovereignty, that is, politically or legally binding policy-making powers, to supranational actors.[36] Integration is operationalized as the creation of new rules that alter the status quo by swinging the pendulum of power away from the Council. It is in evidence when changes in the rules change the spirit of the Treaty and produce a discernible shift in the interorganizational balance of power—redistributing power from more powerful organizational actors to less powerful ones as from the Council to the Parliament. In other words, a gain in one of the weaker actor's powers must come at the expense of the ability of at least one of the other actors to dictate the policy-making process according to its designs. In such an instance, *de facto* reality diverges from *de jure* constitutional prescription.

Integration thus differs from institutionalization in that it involves changes in the rules of everyday organizational conduct—encapsulated in informal accords—that do not cohere with extant provisions of the Treaty and the spirit undergirding them. Although the formal law remains the same, the rules prescribed by law become altered by new informal rules. Dynamics in the informal sphere thereby modify the formal *acquis*. In this manner, integration as a product of informal interorganizational dynamics actually changes the EU's quasi-constitution, albeit outside the formal sphere.

Disintegration is defined as the devolving of specific allotments of sovereignty, that is, politically or legally binding decision-making powers, to actors at a lower level of governing (e.g., from actors at the regional and supranational level to actors at the national level). This is operationalized in terms of the creation of new rules which also alter the status quo, but in the opposite direction of integration. Disintegration is in evidence when changes in the rules governing actors' behavior produce a shift that redistributes power from less powerful organizational actors to more powerful ones, for example, from the Parliament to the Council.

I argue that informal accords have, contrary to expectations and a bevy of EU-specific theory, resulted in accelerated integration among EU Member

---

[36] For other definitions of "integration," see *inter alia* Haas (1958), Lindberg (1963, 1970), Pinder (1970), Haas (1971), Lindberg and Scheingold (1971), Pentland (1973), March and Olsen (1989), Wallace (1990), and Laffan (1992).

States, understood as the redistribution of policy-making powers from either the Council to the Parliament or the Commission to the Parliament (the Commission has only made one failed influence attempt aimed at the Council in the informal sphere). The theory of Intergovernmentalism as well as certain RCI and HI theories predict that such an outcome should not occur. However, it now appears that LI theory in particular has to contend not only with potentially falsifying evidence from the legal sphere of the EU, but also from the informal sphere of the EU's policy-making process.

Typically, the study of sovereignty transfers in the EU focus almost exclusively on treaties between the Member States—opportunities to effect history-making integration. I contend that interregnum integration also occurs, that is, the transfer of national sovereignty to the EU in ways that do not depend on formal bargains between states. I further contend that informal accords amount to the creation of new rules that not only re-inforce the treaty-based status quo, but also intermittently alter, and in certain cases even replace, formal treaty provisions. Bargaining theory from the RCI approach therefore offers a progressive research program in the study of regional integration.

In terms of a clear set of expectations for the rest of the book, I argue that the EU's informal accords are explained by strengthened constraints on the Council, a weakened constraint on the Parliament, and a particular con-stellation of preference intensities, time horizons, and issue linkage scenar-ios. I furthermore maintain that a significant number of the newly created informal institutions therein serve to redistribute power among the EU's supranational actors, thereby further integrating the EU's now twenty-seven Member States. As the empirical chapters to follow will show, not all institutional contents of informal accords are integrative. However, a fair amount of those that do exercise this effect have subsequently been for-mally swept up into the Treaty, demonstrating that a variety of EU laws are directly traceable to the EU's informal sphere.

3

Describing Informal Accords

Rearrangements of the EU institutional configuration are carried out in response to particular needs or changed circumstances. Normally, such rearrangements take the form of amending treaties negotiated by the Member State governments. However, these formal bargains are not the sole means of effecting institutional change; bargains in the mode of informal accords offer an alternative mechanism for change. Whereas formal bargains tend to reorganize interorganizational relations in an obvious manner in full public view, informal accords perform the same function—only more subtly, esoterically, and haphazardly. But beyond the notion that informal accords alter interorganizational relations, how do they get created? Where do they come from? What functions do they perform?

This chapter sheds greater light on informal accords, dragging them in from the scholarly shadows. The first section delves into what it is about the EU that allowed the informal sphere to develop and shows how accords fit into the EU institutional architecture. The next section describes the form and function of informal accords. Thereafter, the third section discusses the sources of informal accords, while the fourth explores the legal base of informal accords. The chapter's fifth section illuminates the critical role of the Parliament's "Rules of Procedure," that presages the final section's focus on the derivation of the Parliament's political strategy.

The interorganizational context

After roughly four decades of academic efforts to ascertain "the nature of the beast"—that is, the European Economic Community (EEC), the European Community, and now the EU—it may come as something of a surprise that virtually the only nonlegal scholar who seems to have shed light on the EU's dimly lit informal sphere is a historian. Keith Middlemas captures the essence of informal interorganizational dynamics in the following passage from *Orchestrating Europe*:

> The Treaties lay down what has been agreed by the sovereign players and what therefore will be. But that is a higher fiction: in the gaps between what the law says and what actually takes place, between the public version of how authority operates and the reality, lie the [EU's informal dynamics].... Although its *acquis* builds up steadily, it is not a true community and its institutions have constantly to renegotiate large areas of their authority if the *acquis* is to be fully binding—that is, to be *internalized* in patterns of thought and behavior.... Informal activities, and the rules and conventions which control them, have a greater impact at the Community level even than in nation states, where political systems have matured over centuries.... This was true from the beginning, and informal characteristics have become a Community hallmark.[1] [Emphasis in original]

Although vague at times about what he means by informal, Middlemas captures the crucial notion that by focusing solely on the formal aspects of European integration, EU observers are destined to misconstrue this colossal chameleon and thus fail fully to explain it.

Aside from the obvious fact that the constituent parts of the EU are nation-states instead of subnational regions or county-like districts, one of the few remaining fundamental distinctions between the EU and national political systems involves how the functions of the two primary branches of government—executive and legislative—are split unevenly between three distinct organizational branches, as opposed to being discharged by only two in the national context. As a result, the milieu of interorganizational relations in the EU is qualitatively different.

The 1986 SEA, the 1992 Maastricht Treaty, the 1997 Amsterdam Treaty, the 2003 Nice Treaty, and the 2009 Lisbon Treaty significantly and formally altered the EU's interorganizational balance of power, but it continues to be tilted toward the Council. In the context of recurrent changes in the allocation of power among them, triangular relations among the EU's organizational actors are marked by fragility and discord; the recurrence of this dynamic is more frequent than the conventional scenario in national political systems. Although interorganizational relations in most advanced industrial nation-state are by their very nature cacophonous, at the national level a considerable degree of continuity of practices,

---

[1] Middlemas (1995).

procedures, and other varieties of institutional rules is the norm. Quite simply, interorganizational relations have become firmly embedded in the *modus operandi* of their respective political systems, in some cases over centuries.

By contrast, at the supranational level of the EU, relations between the executive and legislative branches of this political system remain embryonic, as they have yet to congeal in a manner akin to their national counterparts. By all accounts, this proto-polity is not a finished product. On the one hand, to a certain degree this is due to the system's relatively short-lived existence, while on the other hand, the flexible nature of the treaty-based institutional framework allows ample room for maneuvering by political leaders. Still more important, however, is the fact that EU interorganizational relations have not only been constitutionally recast on five occasions between the mid-1980s and the late 2000s, but they continue to evolve and could well be recast again if the failed Reform Treaty were to be successfully revived at some stage.

The pattern of Member States gathering together recurrently to broker a formal amending treaty has engendered the expectation that interorganizational relations will be altered *de novo* on a fairly regular basis. Because treaties tend to reallocate legislative and administrative power, less powerful political actors are conditioned not only to expect change, but to exploit all political and legal means available to maximize their policy-making powers in-between formal bargains.[2] Concurrently, more powerful actors are conditioned to be acutely sensitive to the need to defend their respective bases of authority and ward off the power bids of others.

As national constitutions tend to be formally amended in this manner only on rare occasions, this same dynamic is virtually absent at the national level. National political actors, lacking realistic expectations that they will have new powers distributed to them on even an infrequent basis, thus generally do not maneuver in the informal sphere in order to eke out more power in-between formal constitutional amendments. Rather, they tend to accept the status quo, making the most of the powers already in their possession; change in policy-making routines does occur, but it is gradual and mostly occurs at the margins. In contrast, the EU's weaker actors, cognizant of the pace of formal changes of the Treaty, are emboldened to

---

[2] The only other obvious exemplar of such dynamics are so-called failed states, where opportunities for wholesale change in the domestic political system occur far more frequently than in older more stable nation-states.

attempt to change the status quo allocation of power. However, because the pace is not expeditious enough for the Commission and especially the Parliament, they tend not to wait around for the Member States to negotiate the next grand formal bargain. Instead, they are motivated to take matters into their own hands and try to broker informal accords with the Council and each other.

The EU's conflict-ridden interorganizational milieu stems quite simply from disagreement among the Three about how Europe's supranational political system should be organized—that is, who should possess a particular policy-making power. In fact, the chasm between actor perspectives remains wide enough that even a general degree of agreement about the proper state of their relations continues to be elusive. Without a constitutional settlement in hand, non-status quo actors have ample incentives to keep up pressure in part by brokering informal accords, especially knowing that some of their informal institutions not infrequently find their way into the Treaty. According to a key strategist in the Parliament, "We decided to become strategic as an actor."[3] However, as evidenced by this comment from a high-ranking official, the Council is highly resistant to this: "At the end of the day in the Council we have to act like little Ayatollahs who have to keep an institutional memory and keep up our role as arch defenders of the institution."[4]

Notwithstanding this intrinsic discord, in the *ex ante* belief that institutional configurations are likely to change in the future, EU officials among the Three share a general verisimilitude that, in the course of formal reconfigurations, the Parliament's power will gradually increase, while the power of the Commission, as well as the Council, will gradually decrease.[5] Although it would be folly for the Parliament to entertain prospects of becoming as or more powerful than the Council, as will become evident there is considerable pressure on the Council to capitulate to at least some of the Parliament's demands.

Instead of waiting idly for the next formal intergovernmental bargain, the Parliament believes it has everything to gain and little to lose from using all means at its disposal to actuate transfers of power *in-between* formal bargains: "We always want to progress institutionally, whether there is formal progress or not."[6] During the 1970s and early 1980s, prior

---

[3] EU official, interview by the author, European Parliament, Brussels, July 5, 2007.

[4] EU official, interview by the author, Council of Ministers, Brussels, July 6, 2007.

[5] EU official, interview by the author, European Commission, Brussels, July 17, 1998; EU official interview by the author, Council of Ministers, Brussels, July 25, 1998.

[6] EU official, interview by the author, European Parliament, Brussels, July 5, 2007.

to the so-called relaunch of European integration, the Parliament and the Commission in fact had little confidence that Member States would soon engage in substantial revision of the Treaty. They viewed such as a rather arduous prospect, involving protracted negotiations and a tortuous ratification process that often proves too prohibitive. Hence, given their desires for altering the EU's constitutional framework, the informal route appeared more auspicious.[7]

Because intergovernmental treaties recur on average only once a decade, informal accords thus offer a means of garnering increased influence within the *existing* framework, by going beyond the Treaty but not radically contradicting it. As will be discussed below in greater detail, the inception of direct elections for MEPs in 1979 emboldened the Parliament to become more strategic and politically astute. According to Jorg Monar, "it is the growing assertiveness and political role of the European Parliament which has paved the way for IIAs to become a standing feature of the Community system."[8] The Parliament is the prime mover behind informal interorganizational dynamics.

The function of informal accords

To reiterate, informal accords constitute nonlegal, unofficial agreements to arrange particular aspects of the EU's policy-making process in particular ways. Their contents include one or more informal institutions that are intentionally created by political actors. In the EU informal accords are negotiated by the Three and are binding insofar as the organizational actors decide to uphold them. As opposed to being legally binding and enforced via legal sanctions, the penalty for noncompliance is political sanctions from aggrieved actors. Informal accords in the EU appear in a variety of forms: tacit understandings, oral bargains, unilateral declarations, exchanges of letters, joint communiqués, and negotiated documents that appear in published form: IIAs.

In the course of the Three's incessant strategic interaction in the informal sphere, when a power game outcome among the Three cannot be fed into a current set of IGC negotiations for a new amending treaty, they take the form of new informal accords.[9] The intermittent result of each round of

---

[7] EU officials, joint interview by the author, European Commission, Brussels, July 11, 1998; EU official, interview by the author, European Parliament, July 27, 1998.

[8] Monar (1994: 695).

[9] At times, even if negotiations in the informal sphere are coterminous with Member State negotiations in an IGC, the Three may prefer that newly created institutions take their place in

this competition is a bundle of new institutional rules, which then feed back to become part of the institutional framework that structures the next round—the altered set of institutions being what the actors comply with in making their subsequent strategic choices. These new institutions affect both the ability of the Three to achieve their own preferences in ensuing policy games *and* the ongoing reallocation of policy-making powers among them. But despite how important they have become, it is unlikely that all of these informal institutions—which range in the hundreds—will "come out of the shadows and get codified" because there is value to their informality."[10]

Depending on a given accord, the effect of informal institutions is to support, refine, interpret, extend, and perhaps alter aspects of the EU's formal sphere. In addition to rendering various aspects of EU policy-making more operable and efficient, they occasionally create new areas of EU policy-making in the course of filling gaps in the Treaty; they also provide a flexible and creative means of bringing about desired changes in the institutional setting and are frequently used as a mechanism for solving problems in the policy-making process; finally, they serve to reduce tension and interorganizational conflict. This last function is particularly pertinent from the perspective of conflicting preferences among the Three, as informal accords offer a pragmatic solution to the seemingly never-ending dissension among them.

First, informal accords offer the Three a convenient tool for increasing the efficiency of the EU policy-making process. Not surprisingly, from time to time the policy-making machinery requires an adjustment of some sort in order to keep the engine running smoothly. For example, a timing stipulation from one of the Treaty's policy-making procedures—like codecision's stipulation that the Parliament has three months to perform its second reading—might be rendered more efficient if an informal institution was created to start the clock ticking on the day the Council's common position is translated into English and French, instead of waiting for it to be translated into each and every official EU language. By relying on a specified rule rather than mere custom, actors have greater confidence that an agreed alteration in their policy-making activities will be abided by and likely become fully routinized over time.

---

the informal sphere rather than become formal provisions in the Treaty. Informal institutions offer greater flexibility to the Three and are adhered to as if they were more formal then they are. EU official, interview by the author, European Parliament, Brussels, May 1, 2003.

[10] EU official, interview by the author, European Commission, Brussels, July 4, 2007.

Second, the very ability to use informal interorganizational dynamics to increase efficiency stems from a second function of informal institutions and accords, namely that of flexibility. Because these entities are not formal—that is—created by formal policy-making procedures and subject to judicial oversight—they can be made and unmade with minimal transaction costs. At any given time, two or three organizational actors can agree to a new institutional rule (the only prohibitive factor involves the issue of enforcement, see below). Likewise, at any time the actors can call a deal off, however long the rules created by the deal have been in existence (assuming mutual acceptance). This flexibility stems from the lack of any need to go through lengthy policy-making proceedings, intra-actor debates, and judicial review. Indeed, it has proved so useful that even the Council has found this facet of the informal sphere occasionally worthwhile.

Third, related to the efficiency and flexibility functions is that of necessity. Quite often, as seen in the next section, the Treaty's formal institutions simply lack what the policy-makers may need at a given juncture; in other words, the Treaty is riddled with gaps. Without filling the gaps, the Three cannot adequately perform their policy roles. To use the previous example, the Treaty may not have even stipulated when the clock starts for various stages of the codecision procedure. Thus, apart from any designs among the Three to gain new powers through an informal accord, new informal institutions are necessary after the ratification of each new formal amending treaty. The appropriate analogue here is the federal office in a national system that writes the rules subsequent to the passage of any parliamentary legislation; the difference in the EU is the lack of any analogous body, thereby leaving this task to the activities of the Three in the EU's informal sphere.

Fourth, beyond filling gaps and other not so problematic functions, informal accords are also used to solve problems. Occasionally, the Three will either stumble across a problem shared by all of them or perhaps simply by one of them (for whom the others have some sympathy). For example, a committee in the Parliament may not be able to perform its work in a first or second reading until it can have a pertinent dialogue with an official from the Commission or the Council. If private or ad hoc meetings become prohibitive to schedule, due to competing routines in other organizations, such a problem may be solved via an agreement that the Environment Commissioner will appear in the Parliament's Environment Committee, say, twice a month. Such an informal institution may take the form of an exchange of letters between the Presidents of the Commission and the Parliament.

Fifth, informal accords in the EU also function to provide an arena in which to sort out conflicting preferences among the Three about their allocation of policy-making power. Beyond an incomplete contracting role, as suggested by P/A theory, agents like the Parliament and Commission occasionally go beyond shirking against their Member State principals and actually try to alter the formal status quo allocation of power among the Three. As predicted by my bargaining model and confirmed in the ensuing empirical chapters, certain informal accords create new institutional rules that serve to reallocate power among the Three. Normally, they do so without gaining headlines in the press, but it is the aggregate effect of the more integrative types of accords—namely the substantive and procedural accords—that will be crucial to the primary hypothesis test of this book.

Finally, some would argue the most useful function of informal accords is to reduce tension and interorganizational conflict in the policy-making process. Limited adaptations of procedures and gradual shifts in the policy-making process achieved by informal accords serve to reduce tension among the Three by ensuring more constructive cooperation.[11] Perhaps the best way to conceive of cooperation between two or more political actors is in terms of their mutual adjustment—each altering its behavior in exchange for the other doing so. The EU's formal sphere allows for little flexibility or creativity, except in areas not covered by the Treaty's provisions. But even in such unmarked areas, iterated cooperation is difficult to establish without the advantage of rule-based precedent. Though of dubious legal status, the contents of informal accords—whether a single institutional rule or many—can establish precedent.

One of the fundamental operating premises of governance is that political actors on the whole need to avoid excessive conflict, for conflict is costly; it impedes the achievement of the political actors' aims and augments transaction costs. Specific conflict among the EU's organizational actors has *inter alia* led to the rejection of several annual budgets, the derailment of important policy reforms, and the delay of numerous international agreements between the EU and third parties. The ability of informal accords to redirect, channel, isolate, and eliminate conflict between the organizational actors has served to reduce this cost. *Ipso facto* informal accords function as lubricants for reducing the inevitable friction when different parts of the policy-making machine come into contact. The EU policy-making machine thus relies on them in order to operate more smoothly than it otherwise would.

---

[11] Monar (1994: 695–6).

In a different sense, informal accords act as the cement that binds the formal blocks of the EU's overall institutional structure, while occasionally acting as building blocks of their own—adding on a new block every so often or simply fortifying current ones. In terms of the functional roles of informal accords, both the lubricant and cement metaphors are applicable. However, without a legal base of their own, the cement-based fortifying and lubricant-like greasing qualities of accords do not derive from law; rather, enforcement of their institutional rules content derives from a different source.

How do informal accords fulfill these six functional roles? What are the mechanisms inherent in them that explain their success in fulfilling these functions? In essence, the institutional rules they contain act as two types of mechanisms for such: the first as a provider of information and the second as a provider of enforcement. On the one hand, the institutional contents of accords provide information about the choices and strategies of an actor's counterparts, while on the other hand they provide an incentive structure involving threats of sanctions imposed by the counterparts in the event of one's noncompliance.[12] Through these mechanisms, informal accords serve to structure the strategic interaction of the Three so as to produce equilibrium outcomes—along with the rules for the EU policy-making game found in the Treaty.

The provision of information helps to alleviate the uncertainty inherent in the interaction of any political actors in social life. Institutions help to structure social interaction via their information about the probabilities of future actions by other actors, which attests to the self-enforcing nature of institutions due to the decrease in uncertainty. Specifically, this information alters the expectations attached to the possible strategies of the other actors involved in a given interaction. In rational choice terms, the distribution of probabilities an actor formulates for the actions of others affects its feasible set and limits the strategies that can help the actor attain its preferred outcome.

Whereas provision of information by institutions is the steady, primary source of compliance among actors in a given environment, institutional constraints are solidified by an additional enforcement mechanism involving reputation and political goodwill. The EU's organizational actors are bound to the commitments underlying informal accords by the degree to which they value political goodwill. Operation of the pressure to ensure at

---

[12] Knight (1992: 54).

least a modicum of goodwill among actors is crucial for understanding how informal accords play an ancillary role in the self-enforcing nature of bargaining among actors connected to each other in a framework of strategic interdependence.

In effect, political goodwill is nothing more than the equivalent of being able to rely on another actor giving its word to you, as opposed to signing a legal contract. If an actor breaks its word, then those to whom it was given are unlikely to trust it enough to enter into a future agreement. If actors were to only play their game for one round, as in noncooperative game theory, it would not be rational for actors to rely on goodwill; however, under conditions of indefinite rounds to the game, iterative interaction engenders goodwill. The so-called shadow of the future looms large, and the actors do not heavily discount it. The same dynamics operate in the EU's informal sphere. By entering into an informal accord, the Three signify their intent to abide by the commitments expressed therein, whether in oral or written form.

In essence, breaking an interorganizational bargain, however informal it might be, is politically costly. This cost is measured in the loss of political goodwill, which prevents an organizational actor from deriving the benefits that would accrue from the future bargains now precluded by the goodwill squandered in the course of breaking an agreement. Loss of political goodwill has two effects. First, by losing the trust of its counterparts, an actor incurs reputational costs. Without a reputation for compliance such an organizational actor is less likely to be able to persuade its counterparts to agree to a similar type of informal accord in the future—even if both actors find a potential accord to be in their mutual interest.

Second, noncompliance with informal accords commonly induces political sanctions that are more significant than reputational costs and critical to the success of self-enforcing cooperation. The principal effect of political sanctions is to diminish the value of noncompliant behavior, which is what allows them to bolster the rules that are actually spelled out.[13] Actors tend to violate the rules either because of an incomplete understanding of them or because they find it is in their interests knowingly to do so, in which case they would likely have a preference for a change in the rule-based status quo. To be successful, sanctions need to be sufficiently harmful to the violator to the point that "defection" no longer is a dominant strategy. Instead, tit for tat tends to prevail, itself being incumbent upon actors

---

[13] Knight (1992: 59).

interested in cooperation where their environments possess elements of iterated team production games and lack the tethers of formal institutions.[14]

A given strategic actor's cost–benefit analysis of a potential strategy is affected by the possibility of sanctions enforcement. Knight offers a useful overview of the general workings of political sanctions:

> In the strategic decision-making calculus, these sanctions serve as costs of employing a particular strategy. Suppose that an actor knows the expected value of a potential strategic choice, given the choices of the other actors.... [If a rule exists] that penalizes that strategy, the actor must take into account the potential costs when assessing the utility of that choice.... The more likely it is that the sanction will be enforced, the higher the weighed probability will be.... The potential costs make the prohibited strategies less attractive to those who face those sanctions. If the costs are sufficiently large and the enforcement is sufficiently probable, we may have to revise the preference ordering of our strategies. What was once an optimal strategy for us may become an unacceptable alternative.[15]

Except in situations in which sanctions are not enforced, the unwritten rules of sanctions that define the relative payoffs to the actors always affect their strategic decision calculus. In this manner, sanctions are best viewed as the costs of implementing particular strategies.

Political sanctions among the Three involve one actor intentionally causing difficulties for another by delaying or blocking an individual piece of legislation it otherwise would have supported, or linking a stand-alone piece of legislation to another thereby introducing additional hurdles to passage—all tits for tats. Actors invite this form of retaliation when they violate informal accords. Relative to the EU context, political sanctions are less easily applied by states to other states, for states are not as closely tied together in the same sort of tight structural policy-making nexus that the EU's organizational actors are; interstate interactions simply are not as iterative as interorganizational interactions tend to be. Approximate equivalents to political sanctions among state actors are private diplomatic complaints or public demarches, or economic sanctions.

In terms of enforcement, without a definitive legal base informal accords cannot be enforced by the ECJ; hence, the organizational actors are forced to rely on informal political sanctions. In practice, because of the Parliament's ardent efforts to ensure the other organizational actors comply with their

---

[14] See *inter alia* Axelrod (1994); Bianco and Bates (1990*a*, 1990*b*).
[15] Knight (1992: 61–2).

informal accord-based commitments, noncompliance is rare enough that the question of whether the degree of costliness is proportional to the degree of formality is relatively minor, if not inconsequential. Enforcement involves one of the Three engaging in the following: communicating its expectation that another comply with its commitments to it, threatening a sanction (i.e., not to live up to its own commitments until the other does so), and/or carrying out a threatened sanction. For example, the desire on the part of the Council and the Commission to maintain congenial relations with the Parliament (which is increasingly capable of upending their policy aims) explains why this means of enforcement is effective.[16] Policy issues are easily and sometimes instantaneously linkable in the EU's interorganizational nexus.

The efficacy of sanctions-based enforcement among the Three is considerable. However, it would be inaccurate to imply that accords are largely complied with for negative reasons. Indeed, the positive side of compliance, the expectation of benefits from the creation of new institutions plays a still greater role. Clearly, the Three find the option of informal interorganizational dynamics a useful way in which to accomplish the aforementioned functions, as they continue to negotiate new bi- and trilateral accords. In fact, informal accords have become such a familiar fixture on the EU's institutional landscape that an occasional EU official will forget that, technically speaking, accords are not formal entities.[17]

Intriguingly, on occasion the Parliament will use an accord in a new policy area as a foundation for striking additional informal accords, with further modifications of the EU policy-making process being the result. Indeed, by continually making still more demands—sometimes immediately on the heels of having its demands accommodated—the Parliament has gradually ratcheted up its influence (see below for a discussion of the "ratchet effect"). In other words, the Parliament appears to have developed a strategy of making an excess of demands for new informal accords, with

[16] The Parliament's zeal for "reminding" its counterparts of their commitments stems from its being the chief beneficiary of informal accords.

[17] Several officials interviewed have come to view informal accords, at least the *substantive* type, as formal—due to several accords appearing in the latest printed volumes that include the Treaty and other "selected instruments" (published by the EU's Office for Official Publications). Although they acknowledge when pressed that technically informal accords lack a legal base and are not subject to judicial oversight, they base their views on the fact that the Three operate in the context of formal and informal rules and treat them similarly in practice. EU official, interview by the author, European Parliament, Brussels, January 24, 2002; EU official, interview by the author, European Commission, Brussels, January 25, 2002.

the expectation that its counterparts will feel pressured to at least capitulate to a modicum of influence attempts.

The source of informal accords

Informal accords generally arise from the following scenario: When Member State governments agree to a new or amending EU treaty, they inevitably create a number of policy-making cavities, as formal treaty language tends to specify the ends the signatories have in mind but not always the means—even the ends can be vague. Each time the Member States strike a grand bargain in the form of a treaty, they create a somewhat hollow skeletal structure onto which the Three must graft the flesh and muscle of policy-making specifications, that is, the legislative rules.

If policy-making is to function adequately then the structural gaps left after intergovernmental bargaining must be filled in relatively rapid fashion, preferably during a treaty's implementation phase. Without being filled in with additional institutional rules, a treaty's formal institutions fail to work as intended and the policy-making process becomes convoluted. Similarly, a formal treaty provision may be problematic or unworkable, in which case the Three must rectify the problem. Thus, treaties normally require not only being filled in, but fixed as well. As indicated earlier, informal institutions constitute a viable option.

These two important tasks are left to the Three who, after a treaty is ratified, undertake in accordance with its provisions to establish any additional rules and routines that will henceforth govern the minutiae of organizational interaction in the policy-making process. In the course of agreeing to a workable policy framework post-ratification, the Three enter into varying modes of informal negotiation. In areas of EU activity where a treaty's language is unambiguous and the institutional configurations are acceptable to each of the organizational actors, a rubber stamp mode of interorganizational negotiation ensues. By contrast, in areas where either the treaty language is ambiguous or the institutional configurations are not acceptable to one or more of the Three, a more contentious mode of informal negotiation ensues.[18]

Informal accords also arise from a scenario in which, separate from any questions of ambiguous or inapplicable treaty language, one or more of the Three desire a change in the institutional framework. Such conditions can

---

[18] Less powerful actors tend to try to lean on their counterparts to interpret ambiguous formal institutions in the manner most advantageous to them.

entice a disgruntled actor to engage in a "power-bid" strategy. The Three may very well interpret the formal treaty provisions concerning a certain aspect of interorganizational relations in precisely the same manner; however, one or more of them may not be satisfied with the status quo as set out by the resulting cumulative Treaty—after all, the principals in the Council do not give their supranational agents seats around the formal negotiating table.

If an organizational actor becomes dissatisfied with the formally pre-scribed division of power or the structure of the institutional framework, it can seek to change it in one of two ways: (*a*) by trying to influence the negotiations of the next formal bargaining session involving an amending treaty and (*b*) by seeking to alter the division of power through informal accords. If no formal negotiations are in process or if access to these discussions is prevented, a reform-minded actor is likely to opt for strategies in the EU's informal sphere.

Typically, under the second scenario the Parliament will indicate to the Council that it wishes to initiate negotiations over an informal accord of a specific nature. The Council normally responds in one of three ways: by rejecting the Parliament's informal influence attempt outright, by agreeing to discuss different options with the Parliament by setting up contacts between different officials, or by agreeing to enter into informal negotia-tions with the aim of brokering an informal accord. The deals made and bargains struck take the form of informal accords.

The legal base

The multiple functions and increasing importance of informal accords generate an obvious question concerning their legal status. If the Three treat them as fairly binding and tend to behave in accordance with their rule-based contents, might some or all informal accords be in any way legally binding? In other words, might they possess a legal quality as in a legal base? As informal accords are obviously brokered by the EU's organi-zational actors, there can be no question that broadly speaking accords constitute "Community acts." However, they do not qualify as one of the types of Community acts as specified in Article 249 of the Treaty. Nor are they appropriated an ad hoc legal status elsewhere in the Treaty. As a consequence, their legal status is generally regarded as somewhat ambigu-ous and fairly dubious.

One factor lending to their dubious legal status is the multiple types of informal accords found in the EU; indeed, they vary considerably in form, content, and impact on the EU's policy-making process and its constitutional makeup. Although they all fit into this book's general classification of informal accords, their variation is nonetheless considerable. The early informal accords of the 1970s were mostly "exchanges of letters" between the Presidents of the Three, which committed them to conducting their activities in certain ways. Others took the form of unilateral declarations, primarily issued by the Council in response to pressure from the Parliament. In the 1980s, the Three began concluding "joint declarations," which have greater stature in that they were negotiated albeit informally— and also because they were published in the C series of the *Official Journal*. To reiterate, in the 1990s the specific term "interinstitutional agreement" (IIA) has been applied, primarily in recognition of the fact that the formality of general accords has been growing steadily (IIAs constitute substantive accords). Informal accords such as the 1999 IIA on budgetary discipline and others since have been published in the L series of the *Official Journal*.

In principle, mere declarations and resolutions are not legally binding; however, they may nonetheless have a certain legal standing.[19] To add to the confusion, presumably IIAs would seem to be more legally binding than the other types of accords, though not necessarily in direct correlation to their degree of formality. Interestingly, several IIAs are derived directly from the Treaty, for example, those formal provisions governing the Parliament's right of inquiry and the Parliament's decision on the regulations governing the Ombudsman's duties.[20] The Maastricht Treaty added new provisions to the old Article 138, which call for the Three to determine together how the EU should proceed in relation to both of these matters. Basically, during the negotiation of Maastricht the Member States could not agree on more detailed prescriptions in either case, so they decided to proceed based on the general aspects over which they could agree (e.g., that the EU should provide recourse for citizens aggrieved by its activities,

---

[19] Wellens and Borchardt (1989: 297).

[20] Monar contends there are two other instances in which the Treaty calls for informal accords, but in the case of the Treaty Establishing a Single Council and a Single Commission, the informal accord called for has never materialized as the two actors have simply worked out their relations informally. Moreover, although the language of old Article 203(9) stipulates that the Council and Parliament fix the maximum rate of increase "by agreement," it does not specifically call for the negotiation of an informal accord. The 1988, 1993, and 1999 IIAs on budgetary discipline did not stem from this Treaty provision (Monar 1994: 697).

as well as the capability of dealing with maladministration) and issue a specific formal charge to the Three to fill in their incomplete contract. Member States considered these two matters innocuous enough to have allowed the Parliament a major role in shaping their final content.

As far as their legal status is concerned, it may appear that by virtue of the fact that these particular accords stem directly from Treaty language stipulating some form of common understanding among the Three, the resulting IIAs are legally binding *ipso facto*. Yet, although there is a modicum of plausibility to this view, whether or not they—or the vast majority of informal accords stemming from other sources—have an explicit legal base in the Treaty or secondary legislation remains a matter of considerable doubt. First, the ECJ has yet to rule directly on their legality. Second, old Article 138c stipulated that the "detailed provisions governing the exercise of the right of inquiry shall be determined by *common accord* of the European Parliament, the Council and the Commission" (author's emphasis), not necessarily via an informal accord.[21]

Third, in the case of the Ombudsman, Maastricht did not call for an accord of any kind. Old Article 138e simply stated that the regulations and conditions of the Ombudsman's duties are to be determined by the Parliament on the basis of a Commission proposal and the Council's assent by qualified majority vote.[22] And fourth, the Maastricht provisions cited above do not represent the first occasion on which the Treaty has called for some common understanding among the Three. Article 218, unaltered since the Treaty of Rome, stipulates that the "Council and the Commission shall consult each other and shall settle by common accord their methods of cooperation." Yet, the Council and Commission have never proceeded to do so. Instead, they have simply worked out their relations pragmatically and informally over the course of the ensuing decades. Therefore, although the ECJ would presumably be more likely to deem these unique informal accords legally binding (compared to those that cannot claim even an implicit legal base in the Treaty), enough gray area exists as to cast a fair amount of doubt over whether in fact it would.

The vast majority of informal accords are on even shakier legal ground. Essentially, nowhere does the *acquis*—let alone the Treaty itself—specify their legal status. Not only do they lack a legal base in the Treaty, but in most cases

---

[21] That the Three chose to specifically broker an accord in this situation further demonstrated the importance they had begun to attach to this method of organizing and refining their relations in the wake of the SEA.

[22] Treaty of European Union, Article 138.

the intention of the organizational actors to comply with the provisions of the bargains they conclude are couched in rather obscure language. In addition, formal enforcement mechanisms are essentially nonexistent, and specified sanctions in the event of noncompliance are absent altogether. One might surmise that the technically more formal substantive types of accords theoretically have a more pronounced legal status than less formal accords, but neither is this necessarily the case. The only possible exceptions are the 1988, 1993, 1999, and 2006 budgetary IIAs, each of which stipulates that the agreement "is binding on all the institutions involved for as long as the Agreement is in force."[23] But even these examples do not provide for ample enforcement, that is, sanctions in the event of noncompliance.

Thus, *prima facie* it would appear that informal accords are essentially informal nonlegally binding political agreements between the organizational actors. Based on their answers to a 1977 written question from the Parliament, the Council and Commission appear to share this view. In response to being asked what legal effects they imputed to the 1975 Joint Declaration accord, the Council labeled the provisions "political undertakings," while the Commission declared it a "political declaration of intent constituting a political and moral commitment."[24]

Monar takes issue with this view, contending that such legal interpretations are too restrictive. In his view, at minimum informal accords all share certain elements that militate in favor of a legal obligation:

1. They are entered into by subjects that have the legal capacity to enter legal obligations in accordance with their internal procedures. Although under the Treaties only the Community is vested with the legal personality, it is generally acknowledged that its institutions equally have this capacity within the limits of the tasks conferred on them by the Treaties.

2. They establish rules or principles of conduct for the institutions who are parties to them. The intensity and exactness of these rules or principles differs, for example, a "declaration" addressing in fairly general terms the problems of racism and xenophobia or an "agreement" establishing precise budgetary ceilings. However, all IIAs establish rules and principles which—if effectively complied with—will limit the future freedom of action of the institutions.

---

[23] *Official Journal* 1988, L 185/33; 1993, C 351/01; 1999, C 172/01.

[24] *Official Journal* 1977, Annex Debates C 180/18 and C 259/4–5 (Written Questions No. 170/77, Commission, and 169/77, Council).

3. By entering an IIA, the respective institutions acknowledge the authority of the rules or principles established therein and express their willingness to comply with them. Again, the intensity of the formal acknowledgment that obligations have been entered varies considerably from one IIA to the other, but it is never totally absent.

4. IIAs also have an impact on the conduct and the political posture of the respective institutions. In the case of the IIAs on budgetary discipline, the impact is a decisive one with respect to budgetary ceilings and some aspects of the budgetary procedure, whereas in the case of the "joint declarations" on fundamental rights and against racism and xenophobia, the impact will be limited to the establishment of a common platform of principles to which each institution can refer when proposing, adopting, or debating Community measures.[25]

Although not sufficient to establish the existence of strict legal obligation, based on these four characteristics, one can speculate that informal accords at least partially meet several legal obligations. Presumably therefore, they possess a legal status somewhat beyond mere political undertakings. They may constitute Community acts that "fulfill some but not all of the necessary ingredients for establishing a binding legal obligation under the Treaties, thereby having a legal status somewhere 'in between' a political undertaking and a plain legal obligation."[26]

Driessen both concurs and takes issue with such analysis. He argues simultaneously that those accords stemming directly from the Treaty "fall within the purview of the Community's judges ... [yet] it is difficult to make a general statement that interinstitutional agreements are of a legal nature."[27] He goes on to argue that "in some cases the Treaties and secondary law provide a legal basis for interinstitutional agreements and, where these are sufficiently concrete, they are certainly enforceable. For many other arrangements, however, there is no such legal foundation."[28]

These diverging assessments take the argument into the nebulous territory of "soft law." Wellens and Borchardt define soft law as rules of conduct that are not legally enforceable but nonetheless have a legal scope in that they guide the conduct of the organizational actors, the Member States, and

---

[25] Monar (1994: 698–9).
[26] Monar (1994: 699).
[27] Driessen (2008: 552).
[28] Driessen (2008: 554).

individuals in their various undertakings.[29] Abbott and Snidal define soft law as arrangements weaker than hard law on one or more of the following dimensions: obligation, precision, and delegation. In their view, "softening can occur in varying degrees along each dimension and in different combinations across dimensions.... Soft law offers many of the advantages of hard law, avoids some of the costs of hard law, and has certain independent advantages of its own."[30]

Assuming that actors act purposively in their specific arenas, they are likely to try to choose specific soft law institutional arrangements as means for solving the quotidian problems they encounter. Compared to hard law, which features an array of drawbacks and costs, soft law by contrast can lower transaction costs (several facets of negotiation are mitigated in the soft law realm), lower "sovereignty costs" (avoiding binding indefinite legal obligations is often attractive), reduce uncertainty (not as much as hard law, but more so than mere political commitments), and facilitate compromise (flexibility is advantageous, particularly in multilateral negotiations when actor power is asymmetrical) among actors, much as I described earlier.[31] Hence, there are advantages to informal accords and their soft law status, not only for weak actors but strong ones as well.

Actors with different preferences who are engaged in iterative interaction share the need for cooperation, at least with regard to establishing regularized mutual behavior and stable expectations. The informality that stems from soft law offers a device for minimizing impediments to cooperation.[32] Agreements of a more informal nature are less constraining, can be concluded more quickly, are less public, and more easily abandoned than their formal counterparts—all of which facilitate cooperation. Thus, the necessity and desirability of speed, simplicity, privacy, and flexibility explain the frequent use of informal agreements among political actors of all types.[33] Although less than formal agreements, informal agreements like the EU's informal accords also raise the political cost of noncompliance.

Soft law in the EU comes into play in areas of discretion that legislative acts either fail to cover or do not cover sufficiently. These areas of discretion are often clarified by informal accords, which quite considerably appear to

---

[29] Wellens and Borchardt (1980: 285).
[30] Abbott and Snidal (2000: 422–3); see also Weil (1983).
[31] Abbott and Snidal (2000: 434).
[32] Lipson (1991: 500).
[33] Lipson (1991: 500).

be instruments of soft law.[34] Because informal accords seem to possess a legal quality despite their lack of legally binding provisions, the concept of soft law is relevant in this context. Basically, soft law involves measures that may or may not be legally enforceable but nonetheless serve to guide the rule-based institutions, procedures, and general activities of the Three. Given its diffuse nature, soft law can be difficult to distinguish from hard law at one end of the continuum and purely political onetime arrangements at the other. In the view of one seasoned EU observer, "soft law is perhaps the principal means of operationalizing policy principles outside the domain of the supranational treaties."[35]

Informal accords tend to vary considerably in their degree of "softness" and "hardness," terms that are basically analogous to "informality" and "formality." As mentioned earlier, informal accords span a wide continuum with *substantive* accords occupying the more formal end and *basic* accords occupying the less formal end. Hence, for the purposes of this project, primary and secondary EU legislation and all formal Treaty provisions constitute hard law; informal accords (including *substantive, procedural,* and *standard* accords) constitute soft law; and highly informal *basic* accords, which are akin to gentlemen's agreements, possess a nebulous legal standing. For example, the Council's 1968 pledge to reconsult the Parliament represents a *basic* accord, the 1990 Code of Conduct between the Commission and the Parliament represents a *procedural* accord, and the 1988, 1993, 1999, and 2006 budgetary accords represent *substantive* accords somewhat akin to hard law.

Having established that soft EU acts have prospective legal effect, can informal accords be considered to have binding legal effects under EU law? Although they have no strict legal base in the Treaty, Monar contends they are "so closely related to the institutional and legal framework of the Treaty that they can be regarded as a direct emanation from it."[36] Informal accords are agreed to by actors defined in and/or created by the Treaty; they are aimed at the activities of the Three within the framework of the powers conferred on them by the Treaty; they are based on and often clearly refer to policy-making procedures provided for in the Treaty; they are circumscribed by the Treaty in that accords cannot legally alter its content; and they are necessary institutional instruments in order to ensure harmonious cooperation and smooth operations of the EU, as is actually called for in the

---

[34] Bulmer (1994: 367).
[35] Bulmer (1994: 368).
[36] Monar (1994: 700).

1982 Joint Declaration.[37] In light of these factors, Monar concludes that informal accords are an expression of an obligation of loyal cooperation, which is deducible from Articles 7 through 11 (old Articles 4 and 5) of the Treaty.[38]

While Monar's conclusion appears to slightly exaggerate reality, the factors he highlights lend a certain amount of credence to speculation that the ECJ might at some stage bind the Three to upholding the informal accords they enter into. However, the ECJ has yet to rule directly on the legality of either *substantive* accords or other types. Its only related stipulation holds that soft law acts cannot modify provisions in the Treaty, which does not indicate whether they can be binding beyond it. The ECJ's case history provides only a minimally more precise indication of its future rulings regarding the relationship between informal and formal provisions of the Treaty.

In its reply to the aforementioned parliamentary question, the Council did not preclude the possibility of the ECJ ruling in favor of legally binding effects. Although it labeled the informal accords in question "political undertakings," the Council admitted that "it would be for the Court of Justice to assess their legal implications."[39] The ECJ has deliberated that it possesses the power to annul measures outside of Article 249 (old 189).[40] In the ECJ's view, it is inconsistent with the aim of old Article 164 "to interpret the conditions under which the action [of annulment] is admissible so restrictively as to limit the availability of this procedure merely to the categories of measures referred to by Article 189."[41] One can therefore assume that informal accords are possible objects for annulment rulings by the ECJ. In the same case, the ECJ declared that annulment action must "be available in the case of all measures adopted by the institutions, whatever their nature or form, which are intended to have legal effects."[42] Therein lies the crucial legal criterion: An informal accord must provide a

---

[37] Monar (1994: 700).

[38] While the previous Article 4 of the Treaty did little more than name the organizations, Article 5 stated: "Member States shall take all appropriate measures, whether general or particular, to ensure fulfillment of the obligations arising out of this Treaty or resulting from action taken by the organizations of the Community. They shall facilitate the achievement of the Community's tasks. They shall abstain from any measure which could jeopardize the attainment of the objectives of this Treaty."

[39] *Official Journal* 1977, C 259/5.

[40] The previous Article 136 in the Treaty stated: "The Court of Justice shall ensure that in the interpretation and application of the Treaty the law is observed."

[41] Case 22/70, *ERTA* [1971] ECR 263, at 277.

[42] Case 22/70, *ERTA* [1971] ECR 263, at 277.

clear indication that the parties of the agreement intend to commit themselves to be bound by its provisions.[43]

The ECJ has ruled that unilateral declarations (one form that the different accords types can take) are not detrimental to the objective meaning of EU law; however, in the same case it declared "they cannot be relied upon for the interpretation of Community measures."[44] In other words, they do not constitute law in and of themselves. It is nonetheless possible for informal accords to be binding without being direct measures of law. According to Wellens and Borchardt:

> [I]t seems sustainable...that the European Court attaches more value to unanimous declarations of the Institutions...with regard to its methods of interpretations in connection with problems which are not directly important to the individual but which do have a more constitutional or institutional character. The institutions...are after all well aware of these declarations as they are taking part in the decision-making.[45]

Grabitz concurs in asserting that "indirect legal effects, if they create the conditions necessary for further measures or where the Community institution which drew them up binds itself, the consequence of which may be to create a situation of legitimate expectation.[46]

Two ECJ cases are of particular relevance to this issue. In the *ERTA* Case that dealt with British contributions to the EU budget, the ECJ found that "the discussion of March 20, 1970 could not have been simply the expression or the recognition of a voluntary coordination, but was designed to lay down a course of action binding on both the institutions and the member-states, and destined ultimately to be reflected in the tenor of the regulation."[47] In the second, the ECJ ruled that a particular Council decision taken outside the strict treaty framework did have legal effect, although the Advocate General was of the opposite opinion.[48]

Case 81/72 dealt with the question whether the Council legally bound itself by a March 1972 Decision regarding its salary scheme that allegedly lacked a sufficient legal basis. In its deliberations the ECJ noted that the Council orally declared itself bound by its decision, and on that basis it declared that the Decision bound the Council in its future action. This ruling

---

[43] Wellens and Borchardt (1989: 306).
[44] Case 143/83, *Commission vs. Denmark* [1986] 46 C.M.L.R. 1, 44.
[45] Wellens and Borchardt (1989: 307).
[46] Grabitz (1983: 87–8).
[47] *ERTA Case*, paragraph 53.
[48] Case 81/72, *Commission vs. Council* [1973] E.C.R. 575, at 3342.

is indicative of how the ECJ has been proceeding cautiously with regard to non-treaty based acts by emphasizing the principle of legitimate expression, that is, the extent to which said parties demonstrate a clear intention to be legally bound by their decision. It also emphasized the factual context within which agreements are made. Thus, some claim a reasonable extrapolation could be made that this principle may apply also to informal accords.[49]

In addition, it would appear that there is potential for informal accords to be reviewed under Article 230, which provides for judicial review of joint organizational acts. According to the Treaty, one organizational actor could presumably bring charges against another (alleging infringement of an informal accord). If a clear intention of the organizational parties to bind themselves legally to the accord in question can be established, then it is not implausible that the ECJ could declare an interorganizational act illegal on this basis. Therefore, if a legal obligation for the Three to cooperate were to exist, then even an accord not explicitly prescribed by the Treaty could be deemed an expression of this obligation and accordingly be subsumed under EU law.[50] Under such circumstances, violation of an informal accord could be considered an infringement of interorganizational cooperation, and thereby illegal.

In reference to the actual accords in existence, however, it appears that only a number of them would actually meet these criteria. The 1988, 1993, 1999, and 2004 budgetary IIAs, for example, would appear to meet this criterion through their stipulation that each "is binding on all the institutions involved for as long as the Agreement is in force."[51] A statement to this effect is lacking in almost every other accord, which forces one to conclude that the majority of accords, strictly speaking, lack legal force:

> When this intention to a legal commitment can be demonstrated, then the legal consequences envisaged in the interinstitutional field can be established and defined by the European Court. When this intention cannot be demonstrated or the drafters have made it clear that they do not want to commit themselves then we are dealing with purely political commitments and consequently it is not community soft law.[52]

Considering the credence the Three continue to give to informal accords and the increasing use the Three make of them as EU instruments,

---

[49] Wellens and Borchardt (1989: 308).
[50] Bieber (1984: 521).
[51] *Official Journal* 1988, L 185/33; 1993, C 351/01; 1999, C 172/01.
[52] Wellens and Borchardt (1989: 317).

the EU's principal organizational actors certainly appear to consider them binding—for, if nothing else, infringement of them has been incredibly rare.[53] If certain accords are merely political commitments—note, until the ECJ rules on them directly one cannot be sure which ones can be considered legally binding and which ones cannot—then the basis for their binding effect must derive from the earnestness of the Three and their interest in maintaining cooperative relations, and we return full circle to self-enforcing cooperation.

Continued adherence to the institutional rules of informal accords appears to be based more on political goodwill and tit-for-tat strategies than on more abstract notions of legal effect. In Case 204/86, the ECJ held that interorganizational relations are subject to "the same mutual duties of sincere cooperation" that govern relations between the Member States and the Three.[54] Informal accords are effective because ultimately they are in the mutual self-interest of the Three. As such, the basis here is much less legal, that is, based on the threat of legal enforcement if the Three breach the rules, than it is political, that is, based on goodwill among the organizational actors and the threat of informal sanctions. At times, the ECJ appears inclined toward this approach, while at other times its rulings appear to militate in favor of the principle of intention to be bound. In Case 34/86 regarding an interorganizational dispute over the distinction between compulsory expenditure and noncompulsory expenditure, the ECJ held that as this distinction is the subject of the conciliation procedure created by the 1982 Joint Declaration accord, such a dispute is capable of being resolved in that context.[55]

In essence, regarding the EU's informal sphere the ECJ has not proceeded as far as a host of legal scholars suggest it has. The ECJ effectively has very deliberately stayed out of the political conflicts of the Three in terms of informal interorganizational dynamics. In several early judgments, it first ruled that the obligation of loyal cooperation operates not only from Member States toward the Three but also among the Three themselves, and it came close to ruling on the legality of informal accords (in particular the 1982 Budgetary informal accord). But subsequent to these early pronouncements, the ECJ has quite clearly backed away; indeed, it appears to have decided that relations in the informal sphere are mostly about policies,

---

[53] EU official, interview by the author, European Parliament, Brussels, January 21, 2002.

[54] Case 204/86, *Greece vs. Council* [1988] E.C.R. 5323, at 5359.

[55] Case 34/86, *Council vs. European Parliament* [1986] E.C.R. 2155, at 2212.

leading it to shy away. Indeed, this holds true even for informal accords that the Treaty has prescribed or secondary legislation has prescribed. As such, informal accords continue to have an ambiguous legal base at best.

Whatever the eventual determination of the legal base for informal interorganizational dynamics, the rules comprised by informal accords are clearly as much a part of the day-to-day *de facto* code of interorganizational conduct as are the rules comprised by formal provisions laid out in treaty form. Despite their unofficial, ambiguous status outside the Treaty, in practical terms informal accords function as crucial components of the overall institutional framework, clearly connected to the *acquis* if not strictly apart of it. In essence, practically speaking, they are adhered to as if they were in fact a part of the *acquis*, and for all intents and purposes the Three behave as if they are (rarely pausing to ponder their legal status). In the course of every day policy-making, the Three rarely make distinctions between those procedures and practices that stem directly from the Treaty and those that have an informal accord as their source. All the contentious claims concerning their legal force aside, based purely on their practical and political effects, informal accords constitute a crucial element not only of the EU's policy-making process, but also its *de facto* constitution.

Rules of Procedure

The results of informal negotiations are fully codified in the Parliament's Rules of Procedure, though not at all in the Rules of Procedure of the Council and Commission. The Treaty calls on each of the organizational actors to adopt its own "rules of procedure" but does not specify how such entities should be constructed or what their contents should include. The constitutional spirit of this formal institution would seem to call for each organizational actor to create its own internal guidelines which would be set out in one's Rules of Procedure.

The Council and the Commission have conformed to this apparent intent, as each of their Rules of Procedure pertains exclusively to internal matters, for example, personnel and administration. The Parliament, however, has fashioned its Rules of Procedure in accordance with its general strategy of constantly seeking to alter the EU's interorganizational balance. From the Parliament's perspective, Rules of Procedure have an important purpose: to govern an individual organizational actor's interaction with the other organizations in the policy-making process, thereby having relevance to each one of the Three.[56]

The Parliament's Rules not only mention the other two actors, but they also repeatedly call on them to perform specific tasks and act in accordance with the procedures suggested by the Parliament's Rules. As one might imagine, these rule-based procedures do not always strictly conform to the letter or spirit of the Treaty; in fact, on occasion they dramatically diverge from it. For example, a recent version of the Parliament's Rules of Procedure called on the Commission automatically to introduce any legislative proposal that the Parliament specifically requests; whereas nothing of the kind is found in the Treaty.

Changing its "internal" Rules can be viewed as the Parliament's own unilateral undertakings of sorts—one of the forms that its influence attempts take. The key question is whether the other actors will conform or dismiss such an overt influence attempt. Under such circumstances, it is almost as if the Parliament assumes that the status quo already reflects its desired changes in policy-making procedures. As predicted by my bargaining theory, where the model's constraints change so does the outcome of the influence attempt; put differently, under conditions in which the Parliament is situationally strong and the Council and/or Commission is situationally weak, the latter will agree to the former's desire to create new institutional rules—the precise result depending on the precise nature of the constraint changes in the IVs. The Parliament's "openly declared aim to maximize its formal and informal powers can involve imaginative use of its rules to extend or elaborate upon existing Treaty provisions."[57]

The Council and the Commission are actually under no formal obligation to conform to the Parliament's Rules. In fact, publicly they claim to discount them thoroughly. In reality, however, both are intimately aware of what the Parliament's Rules say. As much as the Council in particular likes to claim that the Parliament's Rules have no legal base—or "absolutely no basis in reason"—both actors have at various times given direct credence to a quasi-binding quality they possess.[58] One of the more notable examples is the occasional ironic insistence of the Council and the Commission that the Parliament must be bound by its own Rules—if ever the Parliament is caught not abiding by its own rules—as if they stemmed directly from the Treaty. As Westlake asserts, "Community processes involving the

---

[56] As the Council and Commission's Rules of Procedure do not perform this function, the Rules of the Three do not even relate to each other, much less complement each other.

[57] Westlake (1994*a*: 74).

[58] EU official, interview by author, Council of Ministers, Brussels, Belgium, July 6, 2007.

Parliament are 'fleshed out' by the Parliament's own rules, which in practice (though not necessarily in principle) the other organizations largely accept [when they remain largely within the scope of the Treaty]."[59]

The Parliament frequently employs the tactic of including an advantageous procedural mechanism in its Rules as a means of putting pressure on the others to cede some legislative power. In many areas of interorganizational relations, the practical realization of the Parliament's powers depends to a considerable extent upon the way in which it has drafted its Rules. Where it manages to garner even a "meager" concession, for example, simply an additional meeting or point of contact, the Parliament amends its Rules and augments its organizational standing.[60] This "creative" use of its Rules is directly derived from an overall political strategy that the Parliament initiated and then honed from the late 1980s forward.

The Parliament's strategy

Aside from changes in its Rules, the Parliament's strategy also takes the form of a request directly communicated to the other actors. In either form, this strategy has realized measurable dividends in that any form of compromise by the other actors necessarily leaves the Parliament better off than it was before. Its use tends to involve calling for changes that do not conform to the letter of the Treaty and may even constitute clear departures from it. Moreover, by effectively "shooting for the moon" and demanding a surfeit of changes, the Parliament has discovered that the Council and Commission are often hard pressed not to at least concede to its demands in some way.[61] This is primarily due to the democratic legitimacy the Parliament is deemed to possess by its counterparts.[62] See Chapters 5–7 for examples of seemingly small concessions by the Council turning out to be significant gains for the Parliament.

Given that the Council and the Commission continue to impinge on the "traditional" parliamentary role sought by the Parliament, the latter has committed itself to an ongoing struggle for a legislative role germane to its

---

[59] Westlake (1994*a*: 4).

[60] Westlake (1994*a*: 90).

[61] EU official, interview by author, the European Parliament, Brussels, Belgium, July 21, 1994.

[62] EU official, interview by author, the Council of Ministers, Brussels, Belgium, January 22, 2002. EU official, interview by author, the Council of Ministers, Brussels, Belgium, May 4, 2003.

direct election-based legitimacy. Critical to its success is the shoot-for-the-moon strategy, for the Parliament appears to expend nearly as much effort attempting to augment its organizational position via this strategy as it does performing its day-to-day legislative role. The Parliament thereby plays politics on two different levels; on occasion it attempts to leverage between these levels by sparring with the Council over specific policy conflicts for the particular purpose of improving its overall organizational position, that is, garnering greater influence and policy-making power.

The Parliament's preference for increased powers—both informal and formal—is not simply a matter of the sheer political avarice that tends to characterize most political actors. Although there is a substantial element of this, MEPs base a portion of their interorganizational agenda on the principle of democracy, namely that decisions affecting the lives of citizens must be made and/or participated in by their elected representatives. As the only EU officials with direct democratic legitimacy aside from national ministers, MEPs demand policy-making powers on par with the unelected civil servants that constitute the vast majority of their counterparts in the Council and Commission. Intermittently, they have been hard pressed to resist.

One senior Parliamentary official prefers the analogy of "coalition government" when discussing the vicissitudes of the Three taking part in the policy-making process.[63] Such resolute preferences elicit the question of how the Parliament has fared in its quest. Clearly, at present it remains some what far from its coveted position vis-à-vis its counterparts. However, stretching back to the early 1960s, the Parliament's progress in the informal sphere has been marked by a series of *petites pas*, that is, securing small advances by way of wringing accord-based concessions from the other organizational actors. The Parliament's shoot-for-the-moon strategy can thus be further characterized as one of "small steps," for its maneuvering has resulted in expanding its influence bit by bit—notwithstanding its gains from formal treaty amendments by the Member States. However, the means it has employed in this regard involves nothing less than a steady bombardment of demands on its organizational rivals. In other words, whereas the Parliament would prefer to take great leaps—and, indeed, has attempted to do so—its grandiose gambits often result in little more than small steps.

It is as if, at least in the informal sphere, the Parliament has been standing on one side of a river with its two counterparts on the other more enviable

---

[63] EU official, interview by the author, European Parliament, Brussels, July 13, 1994.

side, where it would like to be also. Informal accords are thus akin to floating planks of wood that the Parliament has collected and fastened together, one by one in makeshift fashion. First it erected a bridgehead. Gradually, as more informal accords were negotiated, the Parliament collected enough flotsam to build a pontoon bridge permitting minor interorganizational incursions. In time, with still more informal accords to solidify its position, the Parliament may be able to construct a sturdy permanent fixture, a bridge that would considerably improve its ability to influence the outcomes of interorganizational relations.[64] One might argue that the Parliament has at long last crossed its Rubicon, with the advent of codecision in many policy areas, the right to a roll-call vote on the Commission President nominee, and its recent procurement of a callback power in comitology—the latter two based on informal institutions.

It is however true that its Member State-granted formal powers amount to the source of most of the Parliament's gains over the years. Although the Parliament has no direct control—and very little influence—over the outcomes of treaty negotiations, one must not forget the salient fact that numerous formal treaty-based institutions stemmed directly from informal accords; rather than create new rules out of thin air, during IGCs Member State negotiators frequently pluck the fruits of viable informal institutions. Thus, informal accords act as the primary tool by which the Parliament seeks to augment its influence beyond the scope of the Treaty.[65] As arrangements that alter the status quo, by their nature informal accords tend to favor the Parliament.[66] In fact, the Parliament views informal accords as preparatory arrangements for revising the Treaty.[67] Hence, they constitute an essential part of its political strategy.

According to Guy Peters, the Parliament is engaged in two concurrent and interconnecting games.[68] The first involves influencing specific policies in the legislative process in accordance with its powers as prescribed by the Treaty; whereas the second involves attempting to directly assert its own powers and prerogatives vis-à-vis the Council and Commission, which the Parliament engages in because of its limited ability to achieve its aims in the first game. If it succeeds in the second, it will increase the likelihood of

---

[64] I gratefully acknowledge John Fitzmaurice's suggestion of this metaphor.
[65] EU official, interview by the author, European Commission, July 27, 1994.
[66] EU official, interview by the author, European Commission, July 27, 1994.
[67] EU official, interview by the author, European Parliament, Brussels, July 14, 1994.
[68] Peters (1992).

90

succeeding in the first, but not necessarily vice versa. Alternatively, if it becomes mired in bickering and self-obstruction, it will fail in both games. This project pertains to the second game and shows how on successive occasions the Parliament has succeeded, albeit haphazardly, in winning intermittent rounds of the game. By brokering informal accords with the other organizational actors in the informal sphere and altering the rules of the policy-making game in the process, the Parliament can augment its organizational standing in seemingly marginal but significant ways.[69]

How has the Parliament achieved this? Part of the explanation lies in the Parliament's increasingly shrewd conduct stemming from the changes ushered in from the advent of direct elections of its members in 1979. Since 1986, it has not only attempted to broker a bevy of informal accords; it has attempted to do so after the entrance into force of every single formal legislative procedure agreed by the Member States. Partly by not missing any opportunities and partly by both proposing the negotiation of informal accords and actually presenting draft accords or Rules of Procedure-based influence attempts (thereby eliciting a responses it otherwise might not have received), the Parliament's efficacy and authority have grown considerably. While the Council and Commission tend to lie back, the Parliament stakes out territory, readies its strategy, and draws the battle lines for any ensuing negotiations.[70]

In addition, the Parliament in part is the fundamental source of the two major constraints on the Council's behavior namely the pressure to democratize the EU and the predilection of Council Presidents in office to achieve substantial legislative success.[71] On one hand, MEPs clamor incessantly for greater authority in correlation with their perceived direct election-based legitimacy, much more so than either the press or academia is aware.

On the other hand, crucial to the success of this somewhat abstruse means of improving the Parliament's position is the increasingly less conflictual manner in which it has recently sought to effect interorganizational change. Traditionally, the Parliament has fomented most of the EU's interorganizational conflict, which allows it to use offers to curtail this behavior as bargaining chips in interorganizational negotiations. In fact, by offering the

---

[69] EU officials, joint interview by the author, European Commission, Brussels, July 11, 1994; EU official, interview by the author, European Parliament, Brussels, July 12, 1994.

[70] EU official, interview by the author, European Commission, Brussels, July 20, 1994.

[71] Of course, the Parliament's increased political shrewdness stemming from direct elections does not explain all of its success, as the Council's interests and activities must also be taken into account. See Chapter 7 for a full discussion of the Council's role in informal interorganizational dynamics.

prospect of either substantially reducing or effectively channeling interorganizational discord, the Parliament achieves more success by inducing the Council to enter into negotiations of informal accords than it does by rejecting the Council's common positions under Article 252. All of this assists Member States occupying the Presidency to achieve their short-term aims.

Indeed, in the eyes of the Council and Commission, not long ago the Parliament began to behave overall in a more responsible manner.[72] One example is the hurdles the Parliament has erected for itself in the legislative process.[73] Regarding its self-declared right of legislative initiative (not recognized by the other organizations because it has no Treaty basis), in the past the Parliament typically made a deluge of requests of the Commission to initiate legislative proposals reflecting the Parliament's policy aims.[74] But in the wake of the SEA, *inter alia* the Parliament made a change in its internal Rules that raised the threshold of votes required in plenary sessions to approve motions for making requests of the Commission to initiate formal legislative proposals.

The effect of this change has been to garner some respect from the Commission and Council, whereas on the other hand it has enabled the Parliament to apply greater pressure on the Commission; though the opportunity presents itself less frequently, with a far larger number of MEPs voting in favor of such motions in its plenary sessions it is more difficult for the Commission to reject the Parliament's requests. Another self-imposed hurdle involved the Parliament's power to amend legislative proposals under the old cooperation procedure. In similar fashion, the Commission came under greater pressure to adopt the Parliament's proposed amendments because the latter increased the threshold of plenary votes required to table them. Both these important changes naturally were included in the Parliament's Rules of Procedure.

The Parliament actually includes all informal accords in its Rules of Procedure, not to mention still unresolved influence attempts; whereas informal changes do not appear at all in the Rules of Procedure of either the Council or the Commission. From the Parliament's perspective, its Rules have not one but several purposes: to lay out internal guidelines, to specify how the Three will implement the Treaty, to indicate the legal rules of the EU as a whole, to govern interorganizational interaction in the policy-making process, and to act as a political statement of how the

---

[72] EU official, interview by the author, European Parliament, Brussels, July 6, 1995.

[73] EU official, interview by the author, European Parliament, Brussels, July 20, 1994.

[74] Only the Commission can initiate legislative proposals in the EU.

Parliament wishes to conduct itself. However, their most important purpose is to act as a formidable negotiating instrument.[75] The Parliament's attempt to maximize its formal and informal capabilities involves imaginative use of its Rules to extend or elaborate upon existing Treaty provisions.

According to one Parliamentary official, various sections of the Parliament's Rules of Procedure act as draft accords.[76] They are a sort of "trial and error" measure, or a series of shots across the bows of the other actors, so to speak. These instances can be viewed as the Parliament's own unilateral undertakings of sorts, the only question being whether the other actors will conform to their designs. In fact, the Commission acknowledges that the Parliament's Rules function as "soft accords" which first initiate informal interorganizational dialogue, then lead to more formal discussions, and eventually take the form of specific informal accords; "if the Council and the Commission don't say 'no' it means 'yes'."[77] Perhaps the best testament to the importance of the Parliament's Rules is that many of them have found their way into the Treaty. Hence, the Council is at minimum giving credence to the Parliament's Rules on an occasional basis.[78]

The shoot-for-the-moon strategy was once little more than a crapshoot, but with the Parliament's increased political acumen this once quixotic stratagem has become a time-tested mechanism for reorganizing relations with the Council and Commission—particularly the allocation of policy-making powers. The targets of this strategy are fully cognizant of the Parliament's motivations; nonetheless, they continue to respond to it even on occasion to the point of capitulation.

Indeed, the Council and Commission appear to value consensual interorganizational relations over strict adherence to the letter of the Treaty. They choose to offer the Parliament a few meaty bones to chew on rather than have it constantly snapping at their heels. However, as has been made clear, the more bones the Parliament gets, the more confidently it snaps at the heels of its counterparts, and the more scratched and bruised the Three become from the dogfight of EU policy-making. The difference in the view of the Council and the Commission is that snapping is less problematic than what might be worse, for it is interorganizational bloodletting that they seek above all to avoid.

---

[75] As the Council and Commission's Rules of Procedure do not perform this function, the Rules of the three organizations do not even relate to each other, much less complement each other.

[76] EU official, interview by the author, European Parliament, Brussels, July 14, 1994.

[77] EU official, interview by the author, European Commission, Brussels, July 25, 1994.

[78] EU official, interview by the author, European Commission, Brussels, July 27, 1994.

4
Explaining Informal Accords

This chapter is the first of four chapters that present the evidence for testing the theory. Prior to this it is important briefly to discuss methodology and construct a comprehensive test of the predictions of my model. After beginning with a brief recapitulation of the argument, the next section will comprise a taxonomy of the EU's informal accords, presenting some of the book's most compelling evidence. This section will take stock of the cumulative effect of informal accords, providing part of the capstone evidence necessary to evaluate the primary hypothesis test before I go on to introduce comprehensive case study evidence in the ensuing chapters. The third and fourth sections will evaluate the evidence for the first-order changes predicted by the model.

Reviewing the argument

The Three are engaged in a bilevel political competition at the supranational level of European governance. On one level, using the policy-making powers bequeathed to them by the Treaty, each organizational actor vies to shape the content of policies generated by the EU's legislative process in accordance with its own (aggregated) policy preferences. On a second level, the Three are attempting to attain and retain policy-making powers that directly account for their capability of realizing their policy preferences on the first level. The bulk of the analysis in this book is devoted to the second, higher level, on which the Three vie to change the institutional rules of behavior—formal and informal—so as to better position them to influence policy outcomes on the lower level. As the formal side of this struggle has been widely documented, this book is concerned with shedding light on the undocumented informal side.

The bargaining theory presented in Chapter 2 is in many ways a basic model of bureaucratic politics. It involves the ways in which EU versions of national government branches fight it out for influence in the policy-making process (i.e., the distribution of legislative power, as opposed to the specific content of policies). More specifically, its aim is to generate tight explanations of the impact of informal interorganizational dynamics on what is conventionally viewed as the EU's "stop–start" integration phenomenon. How the model's constraints on the actors have changed, why they have changed, and the consequences in terms of outcomes of this tripartite political competition are fleshed out in this chapter.

I argue that the power-altering informal accords among the Three stem from changes in constraints on them as actors—furthermore, that these changes account for a significant proportion of the outcome of increased integration. In ultimate causal terms, I postulate that the following three changes in the model's IVs generate a series of integrative informal accords: increased pressure on the Council to democratize the EU, increased pressure on individual Member States to achieve successful six-month presidencies, increased political acumen of the Parliament's MEPs, and increased activity in the EU's formal sphere as in a greater number of formal institutions. I argue that without these three shifts, increased EU integration in the form of integrative informal accords would not occur; that is, they are causally necessary for the outcome predicted by the model.

Each element of this quartet of IVs on its own accounts for a not insignificant proportion of the outcome's variance. Operating in conjunction, however, together they account for the preponderance of the DV's variance—the lone exception being the timing of informal accord creation. The remainder of variance, in terms of why an informal accord gets created by strategic interaction of the Three at any given point and time, is accounted for by causal factors more proximate to the creation of informal accords than the quartet. Thus, I argue that integration in the EU's informal sphere is explained not only by my four *ultimate* IVs, but also by three *proximate* IVs, namely the intensity of the policy preferences of the Three, the time horizons of the Three, and the degree to which there is issue linkage among issues the Three care about. Prior to one or more of the proximate causal factors accounting for when a given informal accord is produced, one or more of the ultimate causal factors must already be exercising causal force on the interaction of the Three.

Regarding the ultimate IVs, pressure on the Council's Member State governments to democratize the EU and its organizational forerunners has increased over time. While this IV has certainly also contributed to why the Member States have progressively transferred greater formal sovereignty to the supranational level of the EU—thereby engendering greater history-making integration—I argue it has also had a significant effect on interregnum integration. As formal treaty-amending opportunities are rare in incidence, the informal realm of potential interregnum integration is thus a more convenient arena for pursuing opportunities to behave as "good democrats" and therein respond to public and elite opinion alike. At some stage, in order to infuse the EU with greater democracy, logically speaking the Parliament must be made politically stronger. This IV predisposes the Council to transferring sovereign powers to the Parliament, at least in theory, even if countervailing preferences to maintain its preponderance of power constitute the norm in practice.

Second, the political acumen of the Parliament's MEPs has also grown over time. The degree to which an actor possesses political savvy has a direct effect on its ability to bargain and compete successfully with other actors. With the advent of direct elections of MEPs in 1979, the Parliament began to attract higher caliber MEPs with greater political ambitions for the organization. As such, during the 1980s the Parliament began to develop targeted political strategies for pursuing both policy and power preferences, including using the previously anodyne informal sphere as an arena where it might be able to augment its paltry policy-making powers prior to the next IGC. In beginning to bargain overtly with the Council over potentially more integrative institutional rules in informal accords, this change—in conjunction with one of the other IVs—made it more likely that newly created accords would fit into the *procedural* and *substantive* categories—rather than fitting into the *basic* and *standard* categories, as almost all informal accords prior to the mid-1980s had.

Third, as opposed to influencing the Council from the outside, the pressure on the Council to achieve successful EU Presidencies emanates from inside the Council. Separate from pressures from the supranational level—the Commission or Parliament—or pressures from the national level—citizens, parties, or the media—Member State governments in the 1980s began to compete among themselves to see who could achieve the most "successful" EU Presidencies. Indeed, the issue has actually become one of competing for bragging rights, a matter of my-residency-was-more-successful-than-yours one-upsmanship. Whether fueling or following the trend, journalists in newspapers influential in Brussels—like the *Financial Times*—now regularly rate the efficacy of EU Presidency occupants and compare them with past occupants.

As the reputational importance of the six-month tenures at the EU's helm became more important to the Member States, the preferences of the EU Presidency occupant began to diverge from the general Council preference. Whereas the latter remained generally disinclined to capitulate to the Parliament's influence attempts, the government occupying the EU Presidency began to search for ways in which to increase the overall legislative output during its tenure—this being the primary criterion by which "success" of different Presidencies is measured. In order to achieve high levels of legislative output, the cooperation of the Council's organizational counterparts is important—particularly that of the Parliament. As such, the occupant of the Presidency has a compelling incentive to cooperate with the Parliament.

Finally, the Parliament is capable of initiating influence attempts at any time. However, thinking strategically it knows it has somewhat more leverage *ceteris paribus* when formal institutions from a fresh amending treaty are being implemented. Procedural informal institutions are needed by the Council to allow the newly minted formal institutions to operate adequately in the formal policy-making process. In the course of bilateral discussions over devising new procedural rules, with more leverage than normal the Parliament uses this as an opportunity to demand additional influence in the form of integrative rules of one of the other three types. Indeed, beginning in the mid-1980s, the EU began to experience more regular amending episodes with constellations of new formal rules in the amending treaties. Every seven or eight years the Parliament has had more to work with so to speak.

To reiterate, although the shifts in this quartet of causal factors represent what has to change in order for the probability of interregnum integration to increase—thereby accounting for the bulk of the outcome—the four ultimate IVs do not account for the timing of informal accord creation. While variation in these IVs is necessary for the integration outcome to ensue, in and of themselves they cannot account for why any given informal accord gets successfully negotiated precisely when it does; hence, they are necessary but not sufficient to explain 100% of the outcome's variance. As such, the remainder of the DV's variance is accounted for by three more proximate IVs.

In bargaining power terms, I further argue that such bargains occur specifically when the Council is temporarily weak and the Parliament is temporarily strong. Thus, in terms of proximate causes—the ultimate

variables enumerated above having already exercised their causal force—
I aver that the Parliament entices the Council to bargain away powers (in
the form of an informal accord) under one of three situational scenarios, or
any combination thereof: when the Council is holding intense policy
preferences, when the Council has short time horizons, and when issue
linkage is in evidence. Effectively, the Parliament becomes temporarily
more powerful than the Council in bargaining power terms when it has
other options.[1] In exploiting this intermittent but ephemeral set of circumstances, the Parliament also supplies the Council with something in return;
hence, the bargaining outcome for the Council allows it to meet its own
interests, just as the Parliament does in becoming the beneficiary of newly
created rules in the form of an informal accord.

Under these proximate circumstances—or combinations of them—the
Parliament in essence has the option of waiting to achieve its preferences.
While they expand the Parliament's avenues for pursuing its aims, they
narrow the Council's. When these proximate IVs vary, the Parliament gains
the ability to wait out the Council, thereby allowing it to bargain with
its normally more powerful counterpart on the same playing field. Intense
preferences for a particular piece of legislation, short time horizons for
sewing up a particular piece of legislation, and a situation in which the
Parliament links a particular piece of legislation to one of its informal
influence attempts each renders the Council more vulnerable. The Parliament is able to exploit these scenarios, each of which provides the Council
with incentives to act to achieve its long-term interest of a more democratic
EU when it otherwise would be more likely to behave in accordance with its
short-term policy and political interests. Therefore, the integration outcome ensues when the equally necessary ultimate and proximate variables,
in conjunction, serve sufficiently to account for the creation of new and
more integrative informal accords.

Constructing a taxonomy

In terms of methodology I do not present a formal model; instead,
I underpin my bargaining theory with a qualitative model that nonetheless
bears a certain similarity to formal Rational Choice Institutionalism (RCI)
models. My original intention was to employ a different type of formal

---

[1] Knight (1992: 126–7).

98

methodology, namely statistical analysis in the form of least squares regression of maximum likelihood estimation analysis. However, I encountered a lack of data surrounding influence attempts in the EU's informal sphere up until the mid-1990s. This limited my ability to generate at least 100 data points, my view of the very minimum required for using quantitative analysis. The archives essentially consist only of the agreed upon rules in informal accords, but no data about the negotiating dynamics surrounding them and no data about failed influence attempts. Leaving my N under 100, I have proceeded instead to construct a test of my qualitative bargaining model in the form of a taxonomy of informal accords that will allow me to measure whether informal interorganizational dynamics have increased European integration.

The major limitation involved in the case study aspects of the book relate to the difficulty of uncovering the negotiation dynamics surrounding informal accords, particularly those that were created prior to the 1990s. There simply are no historical records compiled by the Three about informal accords, aside from the terms of the agreements themselves. Because many of the early accords were not even written down—also because of their very informal nature—a culture developed around informal accords that militated against a paper trail. Thus, the vast majority of the evidence surrounding informal accords of whatever era comes from interviews of officials among the Three that were involved in their negotiation or creation. Because most all officials involved with earlier accords are retired or deceased, this study is limited insofar as presenting the desired evidence in these instances.

This also means that failed influence attempts by the Parliament and failed negotiations from prior to the 1990s are especially difficult to dig up. For obvious reasons I am interested to shed light on the dynamics surrounding both accords and so-called non-accords, but this is highly difficult to accomplish in light of this ineluctable limitation. For this reason, ahead of the later empirical chapters, Chapter 5 will present evidence about some recent non-accords as well as only marginally successful accords. The reason for this is an attempt to compensate for the above limitation by presenting full evidence for a time period for which complete evidence could be collected, the sooner the better. Whereas some of the accords presented in Chapters 6 and 7 can only be subjected to content analysis, those presented in Chapter 5 will be subjected to a more comprehensive analysis that also encompasses the negotiation dynamics surrounding both the accords and non-accords.

The primary reason for constructing a taxonomy is to impose a sense of order and tidiness on a confused or chaotic set of circumstances or evidence.[2] Given the maladroit manner in which the EU's organizational actors have transacted informal accords, the wide-ranging terminology used to refer to them, and their many differences in form, content, and purpose, a proper analysis necessitates introducing a certain degree of imposed order. Furthermore, because the meager amount of academic studies of informal accords in the EU approaches the issues involved from a largely legal perspective, there is a general need for a precise classification and analysis of them.[3] While Monar's study is useful, a more rigorous classification will allow one to arrive at a clearer assessment of the impact of accords in the EU's informal sphere.[4]

The taxonomy of informal accords presented here shall consist of three categories. Category III is comprised of *substantive accords*.[5] The key to Category III accords is that they create new procedural rules that alter the interorganizational balance of power, however subtly or significantly. Thus, they occupy the far right segment of the (in)formality continuum—hence their inclusion in the *Official Journal* (OJ).[6] (See Figure 2.2.) These accords represent "quasi-formal" accords, in that the only reason they are not considered "formal" is that they have not actually been formalized and thereby subsumed under the Treaty. Hence, for this reason they must be characterized as informal—being neither legal nor subject to the purview

---

[2] A taxonomy is an intermediate means of ordering things, something in between a *classification* and a *typology*. A classification orders items according to a single criterion, whereas a typology orders items according to two or more criteria, as in a two-by-two table. A taxonomy orders items by more than one criteria but less than two. For example, in my taxonomy I order informal accords by their degree of formality (i.e., how integrative they are) and the year in which they were created (not quite a second criterion, because time is not really a substantive means by which to order things). For a discussion of these matters, see Sartori (1976).

[3] Westlake (1994*a*: 63).

[4] Monar (1994).

[5] For a review of accord types, see the discussion in Chapter 1.

[6] Whether or not an informal accord is published in the *Official Journal* (OJ) (the EU's version of the US Congressional Record) is decreasingly valuable as an indicator of its level of formality. Whereas up until the late 1980s or so, anything that appeared in the OJ was considered to be relatively formal, this is no longer necessarily the case. The Council normally tried to avoid publishing an informal bargain or accord in the OJ, for fear of setting precedents. Around this time, the Parliament discovered it had always had the legal right to have things published in the OJ and, for precisely the same reason the Council wished to avoid doing so, thereafter began to exercise the right as often as possible. Hence, now accords, irrespective of which of my categories they fall under, are likely to be published in the OJ, instead of only those in Category III and some in Category II.

of the ECJ—but in practice they are adhered to by the organizational actors as if they were in fact formal.

Category II also comprises *substantive accords* that overhaul previous sets of rules, but Category II accords affect a smaller degree of change than Category III accords. They do not involve discernible shifts in the interorganizational balance (see Figure 2.2); the distinction is slight but important. Category II accords occupy a segment of the (in)formality continuum to the immediate left of Category III accords, that is, they are more informal by direct comparison. Category II accords sometimes create but more often simply adjust institutional rules; they serve more to *enhance* the Parliament's current powers, as opposed to expanding them. While these accords do not transfer new powers from a stronger organizational actor to a weaker one, they do engender a change in the specific ability of the latter to hold the former more accountable.

For example, an accord in this category may mandate a new meeting between the Council and the Parliament at the conciliation stage of the codecision procedure—a meeting not prescribed by the Treaty and not requiring any specific outcome, but a mandated meeting nonetheless. As such, Category II accords enhance the authority of the weaker organizational actor party to such an accord, if only because they force the stronger actor to have to deal with its weaker counterpart; indeed, listening to and having to interact with another actor consistently over time augments the legitimacy of the weaker in the eyes of the stronger. Category II accords are also afforded a considerable amount of respect and adherence by the Three, which is reflected in their inclusion in the OJ.

Whereas Category II accords have less substantive importance in the eyes of the Three than Category III accords, the organizational actors are more committed to adhering to Category II accords than those in Category I. Category I consists of *procedural accords*, which are less integrative than Category II and Category III accords in that they involve less significant changes in the rules (see Figure 2.2). They do not so much overhaul and adjust interorganizational rules of conduct as slightly adapt and recalibrate them. Changes in rules are effected by this type of accord, but they do so entirely in accordance with the spirit of the Treaty's formal provisions. In other words, Category I accords neither enhance the authority of weaker actors nor transfer new policy-making power to them; rather, they simply fill institutional gaps in the Treaty and further institute the status quo.

Category I accords occupy the center of the (in)formality continuum, further to the left of Category II and III accords but to the right of *basic* and *standard accords* (both of which represent little or no consequential change). In fact, many Category I accords cannot be considered true "agreements" in that they are accords resulting from unilateral declarations by the Council or the Commission. Whereas Category II and III accords are brokered by at least two of the Three (and more likely three), Category I accords normally take the form of either Council resolutions or exchanges of letters between the Presidents of the Three. As they are afforded less legitimacy in the eyes of the Three—and involve little if any substantive changes—they are not included in the OJ. *Basic* and *standard* accords are so informal that they are not even included in the taxonomy, for the changes they engender are not only rather slight but furthermore do not alter relations among the Three in any discernible way.

My methodological test is straightforward but comprehensive nonetheless. Informal interorganizational dynamics matters when newly created informal accords possess integrative content—i.e. new informal institutions that augment the influence of weaker actors in the EU such as the Parliament. When new institutions transfer either power or authority from strong actors like the Council to weaker actors, integration occurs. Thus, we can evaluate the predictions of the theory by counting the number of informal accords in Category II and Category III. Category III accords transfer power, and Category II accords augment authority. Category I accords do neither; they merely reinforce the formal status quo, perhaps improving it by making formal rules more efficient but not substantively altering the *acquis* in a discernible manner. Thus, they demonstrate institutionalization, whereas accords from the other two categories demonstrate integration.

While this chapter and the three chapters to follow will present additional empirical evidence that confirm my model's predictions by elucidating causal mechanisms, the figure and tables presented in this section perform the crucial test. Indeed, Figure 4.1 and Tables 4.1–4.3 indicate that dynamics in the EU's informal sphere do indeed involve an outcome of integration. While the evidence will show that informal institutions act as the source of, and therefore directly account for, a series of formal institutions in the Treaty, numerous institutions residing in the EU's informal sphere achieve further integration of the EU and thus make an important contribution to explanation of the overall EU integration achievement.

Table 4.1 Categorization of informal accords

(a)

Category III
2007 Codecision IIA
2006 Comitology IIA
2006 Budgetary Discipline IIA
1999 Codecision IIA
1999 Budgetary Discipline IIA
1994 Comitology IIA
1993 Budgetary Discipline IIA
1988 Budgetary Discipline IIA
1982 Budgetary Joint Declaration
1975 Budgetary Joint Declaration

(b)

Category II
2005 Framework Agreement
2003 Better Lawmaking IIA
2000 Framework Agreement
1999 Anti-Fraud Office Investigations IIA
1995 Code of Conduct
1995 Commission Investiture
1994 Committees of Inquiry IIA
1994 Codification IIA
1993 Codecision IIA
1993 Subsidiarity IIA
1993 Ombudsman IIA
1993 Declaration on Democracy/Transparency/Subsidiarity
1989 Petitions IIA

(c)

Category I
2005 Impact Assessment IIA
2001 Recasting Technique for Legal Acts IIA
1998 Quality of Drafting IIA
1994 Codification of Legal Texts IIA
1991 Transmission of Documents
1990 Code of Conduct
1990 Immigration/Free Movement Meetings
1990 Multilateral Surveillance Agreement
1988 Comitology Committees (Plumb–Delors Procedure)
1984 Council Resolution re: budgetary relations
1983 Stuttgart Solemn Declaration
1981 Council Resolution re: Council—Parliament Relations
1977 Council Declaration re: budgetary collaboration with the Parliament
1977 Luns–Westerterp II Procedure
1973 Improvement of Council—Parliament Relations
1973 Luns–Westerterp Procedure
1973 Improvement of Commission—Parliament Relations
1970 Council Resolution re: budgetary collaboration with the Parliament
1964 Luns Procedure

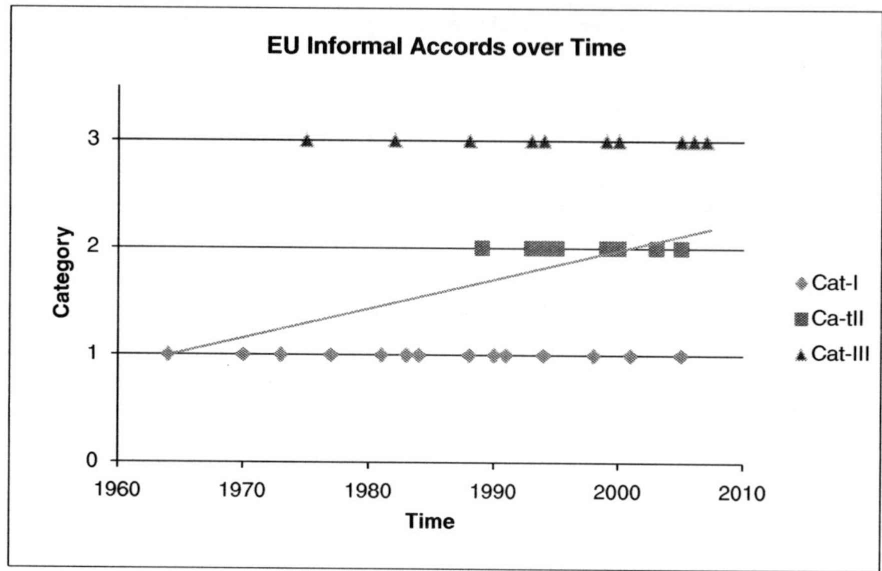

Figure 4.1[7] Trend line of the EU's informal interorganizational dynamics

As indicated in Tables 4.1a–c, there are ten accords in Category III, thirteen in Category II, and nineteen in Category I.[8] By itself, this information reveals a considerable amount; clearly the Three have been integrating the EU informally. Figure 4.1, however, shows a clearer trend in the EU's informal sphere. Basically, the pattern in evidence provides an unambiguous indication that accords have taken on increasing importance for the organizational actors. Over time, the Three have increasingly brokered a greater number of accords and with greater frequency—as demonstrated by Table 4.2—while Table 4.3 demonstrates that the substantive nature of informal accords in the EU has become increasingly integrative. Thus, not only has the number of accords increased over time, but their number over comparable units of time has also increased; and most significantly, a

[7] The curve in Figure 4.1 is generated by Excel according to level of formality, which is represented on the graph as Category I, II, or III (each data point on the chart often represent clusters of accords, that is, more than a single accord—see other tables for precise count).

[8] Although it is unlikely that all existing *basic* (and possibly *standard*) accords are accounted for in this study—due to their highly esoteric nature—all informal accords that fit into one of the taxonomy's three categories—*procedural* and *substantive* accords—are in fact accounted for.

Table 4.2 Informal accords by decade

Decade	Number of accords
1960s	1
1970s	7
1980s	7
1990s	19
2000s	8

Table 4.3* Informal accords by decade

Decade	Categories II and III
1960s	0
1970s	1
1980s	3
1990s	13
2000s	6

* The number of accords in the 2000s would most certainly be higher—of all types—were it not for the unique circumstances in the run up to the Lisbon Treaty. Officials in the Three held off from pursuing and/or negotiating a host of potential accords in expectation that the desired institutional changes may have gotten created by Lisbon, thereby obviating the need, post-2005, for any new accords but those that were acutely necessary in the eyes of at least one of the Three

specific trend is discernible in how the content of accords over the course of the 1990s has transferred more power and authority away from the Council and the Commission to the Parliament. In other words, informal accords have become more likely to alter interorganizational relations among the Three by making the weakest EU actor stronger and better able to hold stronger actors more accountable on a consistent basis.

The most conclusive evidence that increasingly formal informal accords are making a discernible impact on EU policy-making is found in Figure 4.1. Subsequent to 1987, soon after the SEA came into force, the number and the degree of formality of accords increased. Likewise, following mid-1993, soon after the Maastricht Treaty came into force, again both the number and degree of formality of the accords grew. Of particular importance, however, is the change in accord type over time. The increase in the degree of formality—that is, how integrative an accord is—indicates that many in the recent surge of informal accords have been brokered for purposes other than merely filling in the Treaty's gaps and making slight improvements in the policy-making process (the numerous basic and standard informal accords not included in the above figure and tables accomplished these mundane tasks).

According to the trends illuminated by the figure and tables, informal interorganizational dynamics are playing an increasingly important role in EU policy-making, both in terms of their growing number and their growing ability to shift the balance of interorganizational relations among the Three. Whereas in the 1960s and 1970s, scholars of European integration could ignore the significance of informal accords, in light of how these bargains in the EU's informal sphere have gradually transformed the EU's policy-making framework over the course of the 1980s and 1990s and 2000s, they can no longer do so. So as to better observe the details of what the EU's informal accords consist of and the details surrounding their negotiation, let us proceed to the empirical evidence so as to better elucidate causal mechanisms and further confirm the hypotheses generated by my theoretical model.

Bringing in additional empirical evidence

In arguing that changes in EU institutions are dictated by strengthened constraints on the Council, a weakened constraint on the Parliament, and a particular constellation of preference intensities, time horizons, and issue linkage scenarios, I make no claim that all *prior* changes in the EU's institutions that allocate power among the Three have been accounted for by these same factors—certainly not all of the EU's formal institutions. On the contrary, historically speaking a considerable amount of these changes— particularly those prior to the SEA—have been effected in the formal sphere by a combination of bargaining among the Member States, the factors influencing this bargaining, and the effects of unintended consequences. Once the Parliament and Commission gained a modicum of actor independence, however, they themselves became capable of effecting changes in the EU's institutional rules, specifically via strategic interaction in the informal sphere (i.e., new informal accords) and the "sweeping up" of informal rules into the formal sphere (i.e., reappearing as treaty provisions).

Prior to the onset of informal interorganizational dynamics, practically the sole source of sovereignty transfers and new policy-making powers for the EU's organizational actors were the treaty-based outcomes of Member State bargaining, that is, history-making integration in the formal sphere of the EU. For the reasons discussed earlier, at various junctures some of the Member State principals preferred to allocate new powers to the agents at the supranational level, and the formal bargains they arrived at included new rules encapsulating these allocations. Indeed, with considerable regularity though to varying degrees the Member States have devolved powers to the Commission and especially the Parliament in every amending treaty up to present day, most recently in the Lisbon Treaty (and attempted in the Reform Treaty).

Concurrently, when the Commission and Parliament began to assert their incipient quasi-independence in the mid-1980s and behave contrary to Council interests and intentions, it became puzzling why the Council-based principals did not rein in their supranational agents. As the Council's counterparts began to pursue their own divergent preferences—resulting in agency loss in the form of slippage, shirking, *and* defiance—one would have expected the principals to monitor and sanction the agents, especially by curtailing their powers. Why have the EU principals failed to prevent these occurrences, thereby allowing their agents if not necessarily to "run amok" then at least to achieve mild success in realizing their preferences? I maintain that the expectation of successful sanctioning of EU agents by their principals did not transpire in the formal sphere for quasi-path-dependent reasons—though not path dependence as conventionally understood.

As Pierson and others have asserted, institutions can sometimes be "sticky," that is, difficult to alter even when it is in one's interests to do so. Due to increasing returns, that is, a gradual accumulation of exit costs for switching to a previously or theoretically plausible alternative—the political sovereignty transferred by Member State principals to their supranational agents via formal treaties has "locked in." This is to say that over time the Member States have found that relative benefits of intermittently transferring additional sovereignty increase in sync with a concomitant increase in exit costs. Indeed, the increasing returns to this well-trodden path have grown so staunch as to render alternative paths highly prohibitive—for example, retrieving previously transferred sovereignty or withdrawing from the EU altogether.[9]

However, path dependence does not possess sufficient explanatory power to account for the autonomous activities of supranational agents in the EU's informal sphere, which have allowed the Parliament and Commission intermittently to go beyond mere slippage and shirking in order to exercise an independent effect on bargaining—the outcomes of which have arrogated additional policy-making powers to them. In such instances, these actors are autonomously defying principals' preferences in full view of the Council. Instead of either pursuing their own preferences within constraints laid down by the Council's Member States or taking advantage of any perverse incentives of the institutions it bequeathed—aka shirking

---

[9] In addition to Pierson, see Gourevitch (1999), Marks et al. (1996), and Sandholtz (1993*a*).

and slippage—the Parliament and Commission have proved capable of defiance, in terms of competing with the more powerful Council in the informal sphere and eking out additional allotments of powers to augment their prior policy-making capabilities.

Although the Council as principal is responsible for creating a substantial portion of the EU's formal institutional framework, institutional change from non-principal sources has become possible, even probable (note: one must not lose sight of how often informal institutions turn into formal institutions via being swept up). This eventuality has come to pass because of the Council's strategic interaction with the Parliament and Commission and their penchant for challenging it within the institutional constraints in which the Three interact. Through their bargaining in the EU's informal sphere, current institutional rules can be changed and new ones created, the practical effects of formal and informal rules being virtually indistinguishable as both are considered binding.[10]

Much more than the Commission, the Parliament has been the prime mover behind informal interorganizational dynamics. Once it received a modicum of autonomous policy-making power, as a result of the infusion of democratic legitimacy stemming from the advent of direct elections in 1979, the Parliament began to develop shrewder strategies for pursuit of its power-related preferences. With the increasing divergence of its preferences vis-à-vis those of the Council, subsequent to the SEA the policy-making interaction of these two actors was transformed from a strict P/A type of interaction into more strategic interaction based on their incipient bargaining. No longer something akin to deference, their relationship became more adversarial.

By this point, the actor preferences that I hold constant in my model had fully congealed. Prior to the agents surmounting the threshold of quasi-independence, when any divergence of preferences did not amount to much, informal accords in the EU were all cases of institutionalization—putting flesh on the bones but not altering the interorganizational balance of power (the Council successfully repelled the influence attempts of its counterparts with relative ease). However, I argue that the subsequent change in outcomes—new informal rules of greater consequence—has been generated primarily from the change in constraints posited in the model.

---

[10] In the EU, politicians, civil servants, committees, etc. do not in the course of their day-to-day activities and interactions pause to consider the origin, formal or informal, of a given rule; instead, they simply abide by it. EU official, interview by the author, Council of Ministers, Brussels, January 22, 2002.

Evidence in favor of informal interorganizational dynamics abounds; where it is tied directly to my argument's hypotheses is revealing. In terms of the first hypothesis, the postulated change in constraints involves an increase in the public pressure on the Council to democratize the EU. The pressure on the Council to infuse the EU with greater democracy has grown over time, but particularly after the Parliament's MEPs became directly elected in 1979 (this pressure also accounts for why the Member States have gradually granted the Parliament greater formal powers in successive amending treaties).[11] This constraint has changed in sync with the gradual decrease in the popularity of the EU with its citizens. As the EU has felt increasingly distant to its citizens, calls for it to increase in terms of the tandem of democracy and transparency have grown apace. Clarion calls to erase or decrease the so-called democratic deficit have grown more pronounced, with many of these individuals and groups nearly making the assumption that a stiff injection of democracy would be a panacea for the lion's share of EU woes. This pressure has not dissipated, despite the fact that the Member States have in fact given the Parliament significant new formal policy-making powers in the last four amending treaties.

As my interview evidence will further indicate in later chapters, individual officials in both the Council and national capitals are often compelled to increase Parliament's modicum of powers largely for philosophical reasons; in other words, the majority possess values maintaining that any organizational entity devoid of election-based representational legitimacy is antithetical to deeply held European ideals. Although these national officials and their supranational cohorts in the throes of EU policy-making are loathe to do anything granting the Parliament a greater ability to compel them to do what they otherwise would not, a substantial core of Member State officials are committed at least in theory to greater policy-making authority for the Parliament. This perspective renders the Council, as a collective actor, vaguely in favor of the long-term advancement of the Parliament but not the short term. In the short term, a catalyst is necessary. When a second-order catalyst is operational, the Council may relinquish modest allotments of authority, in the process burnishing its credentials as a "good democrat." This eventuality is more likely when the Council can

---

[11] The literature on public opinion with regard to the EU has gotten increasingly sophisticated in the 1990s and especially the 2000s, examining an array of dependent variables. See *inter alia* Eichenberg and Dalton (1993), Nidermayer and Sinnott (1995), Gabel (1998), Gelleny and Anderson (2000), Nelsen and Guth (2000), and Rohrschneider (2002).

garner something in return, bargaining with the Parliament instead of simply capitulating to it.

Regarding the second hypothesis, the postulated change in constraints involves pressure on the Council President-in-Office to succeed.[12] This particular cause connotes intra-Council competition—a change more endogenous than exogenous. Prior to the 1980s when any specific Member State government held the Council's reins via occupying its Presidency, it viewed this role as important if largely for policy reasons. Indeed, specific policy and ideological bents of the different Presidency occupiers have always made a difference in terms of policy output. However, as more national policy competences were transferred to the EU, and as the EU began to produce larger amounts of legislation, the Council Presidency began to take on great importance as a result. Indeed, it eventually became crucial for the overall good of the EU—and certainly the Council as well— for the Presidency occupant to be an effective coordinator, a weaver of numerous legislative threads into a coherent overall piece of policy fabric.

As such the Member State leading the Council as the Presidency occupant began to be watched closely—by both its peers and the press—and evaluated as to how solidly it managed the EU for its six months as *primus inter pares*. Early on in this process, criticism in elite circles of poor performers generated a desire among Member State governments not so much to succeed as to avoid "failure," and one's tenure in the Presidency became an opportunity to augment (or harm) one's reputation.

"Success" in this regard certainly could have come to be defined in numerous ways; ironically, the primary indicator of success actually became the number of EU laws the EU Presidency occupant steered through the policy-making process to their fruition—despite the presumed preference of stemming the EU's legislative tide, not only of the Council overall but also of many individual Member States. Thus, as the Parliament's contributions to EU legislation grew concurrently, the Council became more vulnerable to its adversary's informal influence attempts— particularly as a consequence of the desire of its current "chairman" to push through sizable amounts of legislation.

Regarding the third hypothesis, the postulated change in constraints is that of a substantial increase in the competence and political adroitness of

---

[12] A variety of interesting work has been performed about the Council Presidency in recent years, some of which gets at the "pressure for success" aspect that I focus on. See *inter alia* O'Nuallain (1985), Kirschner (1992), Wurzel (1998), Kollman (2003), Meerts and Cede (2004), and Schalk et al. (2007).

the Parliament over time stemming directly from the exogenous change to direct elections of MEPs in 1979.[13] The expectation here is that, *ceteris paribus*, when the Parliament has members and staff with improved skills and political savvy that were hitherto lacking, the likelihood of its achieving its preferences (i.e., more power via informal accords) is increased. Originally, the Parliament was a lame duck body of political appointees and low skill civil servants that rarely outmaneuvered the Council politically, partly because it lacked legitimacy and partly because it lacked the means to do anything about its preferences.

Upon the advent of direct elections, however, the skill level of the average MEP gradually increased along with the political strategizing of its civil servants; this furthered its concomitant desire to procure more prolific policy-making powers. MEPs prior to 1979 possessed strikingly little of this, as they were appointed to the Parliament and tended to be either national parliamentary aspirants who did not "have what it took" or older politicians whose careers were nearing an end. Thus, not only did they lack ambitious preferences for advancing the potency of the Parliament, but the few who fancied such an outcome also faced the bleak reality of the EEC era of the EU, namely little likelihood that the formal status quo division of powers among the Three would change.

Understanding that IGCs were fairly rare and furthermore that it had no political leverage in IGCs, the Parliament began to act on the notion that informal accords were potential devices for transferring small increments of policy-making power. Though *basic* and *standard* informal accords were originally fairly technical tools for making the policy-making process more efficient, the Parliament began to act on the notion that accords could also be used to bargain for increased policy-making power. In this way, it would not have to wait in vain for its principal to act; as an agent the Parliament could attempt to shirk, and perhaps engage in excessive shirking to the point of defiance via the informal sphere.

By the time the SEA was ratified, the Parliament had received enough power to exercise a certain degree of autonomy. Although not entirely independent, it had become capable not only of getting its counterparts to take it more seriously, but also of being occasionally obstructionist. Due only in part to additional formal powers, it developed increasingly

---

[13] A number of works on the Parliament, examining the organizational actors from a variety of perspectives, also weigh in and support my contention about the increase in the expertise of MEPs: see *inter alia* Bryder (1998), Franklin and Scarrow (1999), Kreppel (2002), Scully (2005), and Hix et al. (2007).

avaricious preferences and an incipient independence from its principal (as dependent on its altered identity as on its allotment of policy-making power). As a consequence, the Parliament's chief constraint of political inefficacy shifted—set in motion by the abrupt exogenous shift from being a body of appointed members to one of elected members.

With the advent of direct elections, the Parliament experienced higher MEP competence and the concomitant development of a political strategy for achieving its preferences. The newfound strategy for exploiting opportunities in the informal sphere, as well as the greater political skill set of more competent members, increased the likelihood that informal inter-organizational dynamics would achieve greater success than previous influence attempts had. As this constraint has become less pronounced and the Parliament's strategy has experienced some success, it is likely cooperation among the Three in the informal sphere will grow still more common.

To the degree to which the Council may be sensitive to incipient pressures—that it views democratic and legislative kudos as being in its interests—it nonetheless seems unlikely to capitulate on every occasion in which it interacts with the Commission or Parliament (or every time these actors subject it to an informal influence attempt). Rather, it is likely to be playing a longer strategy of trying to appease its detractors enough over time to keep the game going while repelling a certain number of influence attempts by its agents in the interim; still more likely, the Council appears to require a more proximate "nudge."

Evidence: a deeper cut

Recalling my argument's first hypothesis, evidence that the Council perceives pressure from outside the EU for greater democracy, especially if measured over time, would prove confirmatory. On the other hand, a lack of this kind of pressure from the press, interest groups, and/or EU citizens themselves would falsify this hypothesis. As the Council is likely to take the general public's preferences more seriously than the media's preferences, for example, consistent and/or increasing support for greater EU democracy from citizens would constitute the most apposite type of evidence.

While it is common for the press intermittently to highlight the EU's ongoing "democratic deficit," indeed, a more ideal type of evidence can be found from Eurobarometer, the EU's internal polling organization. Although early Eurobarometer polls have only been taking place since 1989, from its inception forward there is evidence stemming from its biannual polling of EU citizens to the effect that the public has remained consistently in favor of greater democracy in the EU as a whole. This consistent pressure is felt most keenly by the Council, where the lion's share of political power in the EU resides. As supported by interviews of Council officials, it manifests itself in a greater overall inclination of the Council and its Member States to cede greater power to the Parliament—the only directly elected bastion among the Three—either via greater formal legislative powers or greater powers in the informal sphere.[14] Recall that the theoretical framework in Chapter 2 casts the constraint on the Council to infuse the EU with greater democracy as one of the argument's ultimate causes as to why informal accords get created, that is, a necessary if not sufficient causal condition.

According to the data, EU citizens have polled consistently in favor of a more democratic EU. Indeed, the trend line in this polling data suggests that, while a substantial percentage of all EU citizens have continued to express dissatisfaction in the degree of EU democracy, this number has decreased—slightly and consistently—over time. This would appear to suggest that public opinion has reacted somewhat favorably to increased power for the Parliament and a more transparent EU.

In 1989, 52% of the EU citizenry expressed themselves to be displeased with the degree of EU democracy; in 1994, 47% of EU citizens expressed such sentiment; in 1999, 37% did so; and in 2003, 38% of citizens across the EU declared themselves displeased with the state of democracy represented in the EU's supranational organizations.[15] Thus, it appears that while dissatisfaction with EU democracy has remained, expressed by at least roughly 40% of citizens for at least a decade and a half, the level of dissatisfaction has marginally decreased over time in sync with the greater sharing of power among the Three. Satisfaction has indeed risen over time, as Member States have parceled out a progressive allotment of power to Parliament—notwithstanding the sizable percentage of citizens apparently still in support of greater power sharing. There is speculation that the percentage

[14] EU official, interview by the author, Council of Ministers, Brussels, May 4, 2003.

[15] These statistics stem from the yearly reports of Eurobarometer polling, easily accessed via http://europa.eu.int/comm/public_opinion/archives/eb_arch_en.htm. At this Commission site you can access the biannual opinion surveys by clicking on their numbers: 59 and 60 for 2003; 51 and 52 for 1999; 41 and 42 for 1994; and 31 and 32 for 1989. The Eurobarometer surveys have been conducted since 1973; however, only in 1989 did the pollsters begin asking citizens about their views of democracy in the EU. Respondents in Eurobarometer polls indicate that they are "very satisfied," "fairly satisfied," "not very satisfied," or "not at all satisfied" with the level of democracy in the EU; the numbers here have come from combining the percentage figures for the latter two response categories. Also, not every year in-between the years reported asked this type of question about EU democracy.

of dissatisfaction was even greater in the years prior to 1989; however, no definitive EU-wide data has been collected to demonstrate this.

Evidence also comes in the form of interviews of EU officials. A Council official in the legal service of the Council secretariat speaks of "the ongoing pressure to increase democracy and increase transparency not going away."[16] She described the pressure to augment democracy as "real, legitimate, continuing, perhaps increasing over time," further commenting that an ongoing sharing of greater power with the Parliament is "an unstoppable process" because "the Parliament is directly elected and has attractive legitimacy, a principle others in general sign up to." Somewhat surprisingly, however, this official ascribed this effective pressure not to average citizens but to elites—it is "an elite-driven process." According to her, there has been a "sea change" in the Council, going from "a refusal to give documents to the Parliament" to a "willingness to give documents and information" to it on a regular basis.

Consistent evidence of this type is almost surprising in light of how the Council, traditionally speaking, is very zealous in guarding its prerogatives vis-à-vis the other organizational actors—especially among officials in the Council legal service.[17] However, Council officials beyond 2000 seem to hold a different view. Another legal service team member believes "in the long run we are all doomed to cooperate."[18] According to him, "the Parliament is still growing" and things are "moving in the direction of the Parliament." As such, because the Parliament is the beneficiary of any changes to ameliorate the alleged democratic deficit, any pressure of this kind from citizens is like wind in the sails of its influence attempts: "it is constantly pushing for more." Informal accords in the view of this official also serve other useful purposes: to fill in gaps in the formal EU legislative process and to dampen costly discord among the Three.

Still another Council official in an important position in its secretariat concurs. In his view, there is "more and more visibly a gap in democracy" in the EU "and that's why the Parliament has got cards."[19] Accordingly, the Parliament holds the best cards in playing this game with the Council: "the Parliament is constantly playing the game and increasing its powers, and

---

[16] EU official, interview by the author, Council of Ministers, Brussels, January 22, 2002.

[17] My earlier interviews of the very same Council official, among others, in 1994 and 1998 provide ample evidence of this sea change; in these earlier interviews this official and her colleagues expressed an antipathy bordering on disdain for the Parliament. The situation has clearly evolved.

[18] EU official, interview by author, Council of Ministers, Brussels, January 22, 2002.

[19] EU official, interview by author, Council of Ministers, Brussels, January 22, 2002.

the Council is constantly stepping back." However, the Council does resist when the Parliament from time to time oversteps its bounds; in such instances, the Council's view is that the Parliament must be realistic and await the next Treaty revision, for "the Treaty is sacrosanct and one must stick to the rules." Still, he observes, the momentum is with the Parliament; indeed, "there are many instances of the Council changing its preferences because the Parliament or the Commission persuaded it to do so, to do something it otherwise would not have done." Thirty years ago he did not "even look at Parliament's opinions—they were expendable and didn't matter in any fundamental way." Now, according to him, the Council feels as much an executive as a legislature.

In interviews with a Council official in a different division of the secretariat, this official described the early years of the codecision procedure and how, even though the Council was advantaged by a lack of true coequal status until the 1997 Amsterdam Treaty, the Council on several occasions could have overridden the Parliament (which lacked a true veto power under the Maastricht Treaty, from 1992) but did not: "it just couldn't be done."[20] While technically it could have, playing constant hardball with the Parliament was not politically feasible. According to him, the Parliament is the driving force behind informal accords because it desires more from the Treaty, "so it pushes the interpretation limit"—"the Parliament simply is not content." He concurred that the Parliament has augmented its influence via informal accords, which in his view leads directly to increased policy goal attainment (which he suspects is ultimately the reason the Parliament doggedly pursues even incremental increases in its legislative powers, formal or informal).

In confirmation of one of the project's proximate causal factors—that issue linkage is often a catalyst for negotiating a given informal accord—he observed that there have been increased opportunities for the Parliament to "take other pieces of legislation hostage" and it has done so. Additionally, still more recently he had begun observing that the Parliament has started to demonstrate a certain kind of maturity, in the form of finding more occasions to pick and choose which among these opportunities is worth exploiting. Ironically, in this official's view, such a measured approach is very shrewd, for by not pressing so hard with its shoot-for-the-moon strategy, the Parliament makes it even more difficult for the Council to

---

[20] EU official, interview by author, Council of Ministers, Brussels, January 22, 2002.

not relent—"by acting in a way that makes it in the Council's interest to give in to the Parliament's demands."

Finally, in further confirmation of part of the overall argument of this book, that is, that, in the ultimate causal terms, the Council is constrained by the desire of the holder of the Council Presidency to achieve a successful six-month Presidency—he criticized ministers from the Presidency for so desiring a good reputation that "the last thing they wanted was trouble with the Parliament" for "politicians can't say no to politicians." However, not all Council officials are resigned to these dynamics, as a different official claims that the Council is actively looking for an opportunity to take the Parliament to the ECJ to try to abrogate part of the Parliament–Commission bilateral accord called the Framework Agreement (2000) that it alleges violates the Treaty.[21] In his view, there is no need for informal accords, and–even if there were—they are to the advantage of the Council because the Council "can pick its negotiating partners;" moreover, "the Parliament has no ability to be monolithic."

Finally, with regard to evidence for the argument's claim that a key restraint on the Parliament has relaxed over time, namely that of the Parliament's traditional political ineptitude and lack of strategic political acumen—both scholarship and interviews concur with this claim. As discussed at length in Chapter 2, from its inception in the days of the European Coal and Steal Community (which metamorphosed into the EEC via the 1957 Treaty of Rome) the Parliament was a fairly inept organizational actor, replete with feckless appointed MEPs and generally lacking in both legitimacy and even a vision for playing the full traditional role of parliamentary bodies.

This all changed with the advent of direct elections for the MEPs in 1979, and since then evidence points directly to a relaxation of this traditional constraint on the Parliament's efficacy. In addition to concurrence by EU officials throughout the Three (see below), the insightful tome by three prominent practitioners from the Parliament itself details a handful of indicators of this endogenous change in the strategic interaction of the Three.[22] Ironically, while the percentage of the MEPs who previously held political and/or ministerial office has edged down since 1979 to the present, the perceived quality of the average MEP—in terms of sheer individual political skills—has gone up.

---

[21] EU official, interview by author, Council of Ministers, Brussels, January 22, 2002.
[22] Corbett et al. (2000b: 150–73).

A more salient indicator, however, is the rise in acumen of the Parliament's civil servants, as opposed to the elected MEPs themselves. Once their bosses gained democratic legitimacy as of 1979, the civil servant officials began strategizing and honing their skills to gain greater influence for the Parliament in the interorganizational balance of power—all under the guise of the principle that the only directly elected organizational actor among the Three must be given a full range of powers to play a traditional parliamentary role of legislating and providing oversight. Of great importance has been the contrast between the traditionally heavy turnover of MEPs during each European election—consistently in the area of 50%—and the lack of similar dynamics among the unelected officials; the coterie of Parliament's civil servants by contrast has experienced very little turnover in comparison.

With more formal powers allocated to the Parliament over time—and consequently greater responsibility—the technocratic officials have taken advantage of the incentives and opportunities to sharpen their skills and pass these along to MEPs. One salient example is how the Parliament's officials traveled to the United States on several occasions to do research into US Senate confirmation hearings of appointed executive officials; this fact-finding mission proved instrumental in the preparation for (and implementation of) the 1995 Commission investiture accord, namely how the Parliament cajoled the Commission President and individual commissioner designates. It has been the civil servants who devised and shaped the strategy of using the Parliament's Rules of Procedure strategically as a political instrument, despite the Treaty intent for this device to pertain to internal workings of the Parliament only.

Other indicators of this attenuated constraint on the Parliament include trends in the organization of the political groups of MEPs in the Parliament. Political groups are part ideological and part catch-all groupings of MEPs according to their national political parties; the number of political groups over the life of the Parliament has ranged roughly between three and ten, with the Socialist group and the European People's Party (the center left and center right groups, respectively) always being the largest. In an indication of the importance of the Parliament's increased attention to a political agenda over time, in terms of group membership the Parliament has become less fragmented over time via the European People's Party (EPP) and the Socialist group becoming larger and more dominant with time: prior to 1989 these two groups comprised merely 54% of MEPs, whereas ever since their membership (as the number of MEPs has also increased considerable, due to EU enlargement) has ranged between 63% and 69%

of all MEPs in Parliament (with the 2004 European elections this figure rose to 63.9%).[23]

Some of the interview-based evidence, with concurrence from numerous officials among the Three, involves some telling quotations.[24] "The Parliament has been increasingly responsible and strategic—it has earned its credentials."[25] As one council official put it, "The Council has failed miserably in the area of public relations; the Parliament has been brilliant."[26] According to this official this deficiency goes beyond merely being outmaneuvered by the Parliament on the democratic deficit issue—it is structural. Because the Presidency is the focal point for public relations, not the overall Council per se, the public relations task becomes muddied by a slew of individual Member States doing their own public relations work (often putting themselves ahead of the Member States as a collectivity). Clearly the Parliament has augmented its acumen.

This chapter began to unearth what amounts to a deep well of evidence in support of my argument and the predictions of my bargaining model. It not only delved thoroughly into the question of how informal accords have developed since their emergence in the 1960s—tracing their transformation from an innocuous beginning to a present-day use by the Parliament as a valuable weapon—but it furthermore began to lay out the empirical evidence of the book. Chapters 5–7 shift from the wide-angle lens employed above to zoom in on the informal accords themselves, bringing into sharp focus the particularities of their contents and wherever possible the dynamics surrounding their creation.

[23] EU official, interview by the author, European Parliament, Brussels, July 5, 2007.

[24] EU official, interview by the author, European Parliament, Brussels, May 5, 2003; EU official, interview by the author, Council of Ministers, Brussels, January 21, 2002; EU official, interview by the author, European Commission, Brussels, May 6, 2003.

[25] EU official, interview by author, Council of Ministers, Brussels, January 21, 2002.

[26] EU official, interview by author, Council of Ministers, Brussels, May 6, 2003.

5

Informal Accords and Non-Accords

Introduction

The Parliament's self-professed role as the EU's prime mover of informal interorganizational dynamics is on full display in this and Chapters 6 and 7. Lest one conclude from Chapter 4 that the Parliament somehow manages to always land on its feet despite its somewhat feeble status, recent empirical evidence from the EU's informal sphere highlights the Parliament's limitations. Throughout 2002 and 2003, the Parliament pushed for informal accords in the areas of comitology (concerning the Lamfalussy initiative) and "quality of legislation" (concerning the Commission's White Paper on governance), and in each instance the result proved fairly humbling—despite the Parliament being in possession of greater political power relative to any other point in its history. In light of such paradoxes, this chapter will document these two influence attempts and highlight the strategic interaction of the Three in the process.

This chapter furthers the presentation of the book's empirical evidence. Unlike Chapters 6 and 7, which will examine all the EU's successfully negotiated informal budgetary and political accords, respectively, this chapter will focus largely on failure. Why failure? In methodological terms, an exclusive focus on success, that is, extant informal accords, would represent a particular weakness, namely bypassing or overlooking all the failed or faltering attempts by one or more of the Three to negotiate new accords at various points in EU history. Indeed, it is immensely difficult to cleanse the book thoroughly of a sort of selection bias: there is simply little or no existing documentation of the so-called non-accords, and only a minuscule number of seasoned EU officials with a complete recollection of informal dynamics in the 1970s and 1980s still working in their positions today.

Nonetheless, this chapter shall attempt to compensate for minimal selection bias by examining the evidence surrounding the two most recent instances of the Commission and Parliament failing to cajole the Council into negotiating new informal accords (along the way of highlighting the Commission's waning influence, this chapter will digress briefly to assess the importance of an informal institution related to the codecision procedure). With copious documentation of all post-2000 informal dynamics at hand—and the pertinent EU officials among the Three available and fully capable of recalling empirical details—these two salient but failed influence attempts manage to avoid the numerous obstacles that have bogged down and inhibited investigators of informal interorganizational dynamics during the EU's three previous decades.

In doing so these non-accords serve to instantiate the Three's strategic interaction. While the accords in Chapters 6 and 7 are described and analyzed as to their potential contribution to integration, it is difficult to evince the bargaining dynamics surrounding their negotiation and, ultimately, their creation. Instead, examination of the accords is primarily subjected to content analysis and an elucidation of their contribution to the ongoing remaking of the institutional structure in which the Three interact to make EU policy. However, in this chapter an attempt will be made to fill this lamentable gap, that is, to illuminate not only the substantive details about non-accords and their importance, but also the context and political competition culminating in a result (irrespective of whether or not the influence attempt succeeded).

The influence attempt by the Parliament involving the Council's so-called Lamfalussy initiative—in the area of financial services—was unsuccessful. This non-accord was tied up in long-standing disputes among the Three over the Commission's shared powers of policy implementation—also known as comitology—over which the Council and Parliament have long sought to gain influence. In light of comitology's fairly arcane nature, prior to elucidating the Parliament's failed attempt to use the EU's recent financial services legislation debate to gain inroads into comitology, it is necessary to review its ins and outs. Likewise, prior to expounding on the Parliament's failed attempt to appropriate its preferred powers in the quality of legislation accord, it will be necessary to delineate the Commission's influence attempt in the form of its White Paper on governance—which the Parliament tried to utilize for its own purposes with only partial success.

Comitology

Once a piece of EU legislation passes successfully through the EU's policy-making process and becomes a part of EU secondary law, the EU executive actor must pick up matters at this juncture and implement the legislation (thereafter an executive actor must monitor what was implemented). In performing this classic executive governance function, the Commission acts in accordance with an array of specialized committees of implementation; hence, the derivation of the comitology nomenclature. Powers over policy implementation in the EU have long been fought over among the Three, and technically speaking the Commission shares this executive function with the Council (while the Parliament continues to bang at the door, demanding to be allowed in after being left out in the cold).[1]

Comitology emerged from EU attempts during the 1960s and 1970s to develop a system for delegating implementing powers to the Commission, although from the very start the Council's Member States have refused to hand over the reins. Indeed, the Commission is only empowered to act in conjunction with one of several specialized committees comprising Member State officials. Generally speaking, except in the case of a purely advisory type of committee, such committees are capable of blocking a given Commission implementation decision—either by qualified majority vote (QMV) or a blocking minority—therein referring a given matter back to the Council for a decision.[2]

The so-called comitology system has always been fairly muddled and confusing, but in the run-up to the 1992 Program, that is, the implementation of an array of single market measures—provisions in the SEA clarified the situation, and a subsequent formal July 1987 Decision by the Council laid out the comitology procedures in specific detail. This action cleared up

---

[1] As the literature review in Chapter 1 indicated, quite a lot of work on comitology has been performed by scholars. Most of these studies examine the degree to which the Commission has discretion in the policy implementation process—for example, formal models of the different comitology procedures seeking to determine the degree of discretion—and whether comitology involves deliberation or mere execution. See also Dogan (1997), Ciavarini Azzi (2000), Hailbach (2000), and Schusterschitz and Kotz (2007).

[2] Depending on the rules of a given democratic political system, in some cases a majority vote—of, say, 51% of votes cast—may not constitute a winning vote; if the rules allow for a blocking minority—of, say, 40%—then anything less than 61% of votes cast in favor of a proposal will constitute a losing vote. In the European Union, this state of affairs is referred to as qualified majority voting among Member States in the Council, whereby their votes are weighted according to population size, and for years a majority of 62 out of 87 votes was required for legislation to be passed—26 votes was a blocking minority, that is, 30% of the votes cast. Since the Nice Treaty came into force in 2005, a QMV of 71% has consituted 169 out of 237 votes by Member States in the Council.

general misconceptions, providing specification of how each instance of policy implementation should be handled. The procedural rules comprising this document continue to act as the bulwark of today's comitology framework (the procedures were further streamlined, with fairly minimal substantive change, in a second formal Council Decision in June 1999 and then a third in June 2006 which involved greater changes).[3]

According to the system, a given piece of policy legislation must specify which of the comitology procedures is to be applied: that of an Advisory Committee, a Management Committee, or a Regulatory Committee. An Advisory Committee can merely advise the Commission regarding its policy implementation: The Commission provides the committee of Council officials with a draft proposal; the committee then offers an opinion on it (if necessary by simple majority); the Commission may decide to observe or reject the opinion. A Management Committee can block the Commission via a qualified majority vote: The Commission provides the committee of Council officials with a draft proposal; the committee then deliberates and may suspend the draft by a qualified majority, in which case the Council proper has three months in which to replace the draft with its own implementing decision (also by qualified majority).

A Regulatory Committee must, by qualified majority, provide its approval for any Commission decision to be enacted (Regulatory Committee procedures allow for a blocking minority): The Commission provides the committee of Council officials with a draft proposal; unless the draft is supported by a qualified majority of the committee, the Council proper may decide by qualified majority within three months either to support or oppose the draft (it can veto the measure by a qualified majority or substitute its own by unanimous vote); if the latter, the Commission must resubmit the draft, submit an amended draft, or submit a legislative proposal; if within three months the Council does not oppose it (by either method), the proposal can be adopted by the Commission.

The Commission and Parliament did not support the 1987 Decision-based comitology procedures. Regarding the Commission, it has long favored amending Article 202 to allow for coequal implementing powers for the Council and Parliament; it has also called for a clearer delineation of executive powers overall. More recently, these views were expressed in the Commission's 2001 White Paper on European Governance.

---

[3] See Chapter 7 for greater detail on the comitology reforms in the 2006 Council Decision, which is a *de facto* informal accord negotiated between the Parliament and the Council.

As for the Parliament, in a series of legislative reports, open debates, and private discussions, the MEPs were highly critical of three aspects of comitology in particular: first, that the Parliament did not have a right to exercise control over the Commission's implementing measures and "call them back" like the Council did; second, that a blocked measure was called back to the Council and not the Parliament; and finally that, under Regulatory Committee procedures, the Council could continue to block decisions even in the absence of another measure proposed as an alternative. The Parliament, along with the Commission, also made its view known that the entire comitology framework was minimally transparent and highly obfuscating.

Subsequent to the 1993 Amsterdam Treaty and the advent of codecision—namely the allocation of essentially equal powers with the Council in specific legislative areas—resistance from the Parliament grew more intense. With regard to any EU legislation passed under the codecision procedure during the 1990s, the Parliament held that any of the Commission's policy implementing powers should be overseen not only by the Council but also itself (effectively, a joint delegation of the Commission's executive role). Beyond simply being given an equally prominent role, the Parliament pressured for a role in the creation of the comitology procedures themselves—chief among them being callback powers equivalent to those of the Council.

For its part, the Council responded that Article 202 of the Treaty remained the sole guiding legislative instrument for determining the comitology procedural framework. The Council's interests militated in favor of its retaining control, and all things being equal, the interorganizational balance of power allowed it the luxury of maintaining the status quo indefinitely. Nonetheless, even in the absence of any situational bargaining power for the Parliament on the comitology issue—the intermittent possession of which is often the key for successful negotiation of an informal accord—the Council eventually capitulated, at least in part: it agreed to alter the comitology framework somewhat in accordance with the Parliament's desires. Having granted the Parliament coequal powers in the legislative codecision procedure, in principle it was difficult for the Council to justify not giving in at least somewhat on the implementation side of the policy-making process.

Bargaining power for weaker actors like the Parliament and Commission stems from the proximate causes of preference intensity, time horizons, and issue linkage in EU interactions—the second-order constraints from my model. The Parliament's influence attempt in this instance lacked any shifts in these constraints that would have benefited it; as such, it had to accept the Council's terms and acquiesce to the Council's desire to dictate the terms of what was at best a tacit agreement that only moved partially toward the Parliament's preferences and not in the form or manner it preferred.[4]

Instead of an informal accord, the Council chose a unilateral instrument to change the rules—namely another formal decision. Under the auspices of Article 202, the Council altered the comitology framework via its June 28, 1999 Decision. Although the Parliament desired some form of bilateral agreement, from its perspective the new status quo amounted to a slight improvement, albeit not in regard to its principal demand for callback authority; instead of the full power to object to the substance of the Commission implementing a measure and block it, the Parliament could now merely register that—in its view—a given implementing measure exceeded the scope of powers delegated to the Commission.

Nonetheless, the Parliament could not but view three other changes as modest movements in its direction: a generally more coherent set of comitology procedures; a less powerful Council ability to block implementing measures (when it could not agree on an alternative), now by qualified majority voting; and greater overall transparency due to increased information granted to the Parliament (in the form of committee membership, draft measures, agendas, and minutes). Indeed, the Parliament officially expressed its reaction to the new comitology framework in a February 17, 2000 parliamentary resolution. In it the Parliament acknowledged its partial approval yet underlined, in a typical shoot-for-the-moon fashion, its unmet demands.

What explains this minimal success, short of an informal accord replete with Council commitments to the Parliament but nonetheless a slight move toward its preferences? Here lies evidence of two first-order constraint changes: pressure on the Council to democratize the EU further and increased political acumen on the part of the Parliament. Without the proximate causal triggers in place and the expected gains for the Parliament however, causal force was only exercised by these two ultimate causes— with more minimal gains for the Parliament. It only made inroads insofar as reiterating to the Council that it was only logical based on the Treaty's language for it to possess full-fledged codecision powers: over policy legislation but also over policy implementation. This made a mild impact on the

---

[4] EU official, interview by the author, European Parliament, Brussels, May 5, 2003.

Council's thinking and ultimately its behavior. With the need occasionally to find ways to augment EU democracy—defined in terms of sharing power with directly elected MEPs—the Council saw this as an opportunity to win democratic kudos without giving up too much.[5]

Thus, over the better part of a decade or more—both prior to the 1987 Decision and since the 1999 Decision—the Three have engaged in considerable conflict over not only the interpretation of legislative procedures themselves, but still also the specific apportioning of power—the weaker actors questioning, for instance, whether various circumstances allow for exceptions, as well as whether the procedures even possess the requisite legitimacy (and if not, whether they should be altered). At various points the discord has been particularly intense, with the Commission and, in particular, the Parliament fiercely resisting the Council's attempt to achieve dominance in the policy implementation sphere.

The Lamfalussy non-accord: failure (and partial success)

In the early 2000s, the EU's informal sphere received months of uncustomary attention, in the media and across national and supranational political spheres. Throughout the 1990s, as the Single Market was completed and EMU culminated in a common currency, some important economic areas outside the so-called real economy remained unintegrated: financial services, stock markets, and any concomitant financial regulation in the EU. This was due largely to the finance industry's political–economic sensitivity, as well as the inability of the Member States, let alone the Three, to come to some form of serious consensus as to whether financial services constituted merely a difficult issue—or also a special issue that required unique political procedures. While momentum grew across Europe in favor of supranational action on this issue, only late in the policy-making process (in the later months of 2000) did any potential activity in the informal sphere become apparent.

In unorthodox policy-making fashion, the Council appointed Baron Alexandre Lamfalussy to chair a Committee of Wise Men—the EU counterpart to a US Blue Ribbon Commission—charged with the task of formulating a report proposing how to legislate a single securities market and its debut EU regulation. Lamfalussy's resulting February 2001 Financial

---

[5] EU official, interview by the author, Council of Ministers, Brussels, May 7, 2003; EU official, interview by the author, European Parliament, Brussels, May 5, 2003.

Services Action Plan (FSAP) did indeed call for this unique policy area to be treated differently from the treaty-based policy-making process—not on the legislative side of the process (for it clearly would be handled by the codecision procedure), but on the implementing side. Lamfalussy's central recommendation was for comprehensive consultation (e.g., of the financial industry); in addition, the report called for speeding up the legislative timetable.

Specifically, the report recommended first that the EU adopt an ad hoc policy framework based on framework legislation to be handled by the codecision procedure. On the implementation side, Lamfalussy proposed that, unlike the typical comitology manner of delegating implementing powers to the Commission to be overseen by the standard committee types, oversight of policy implementation would be performed by two high-profile specialist committees: the European Securities Committee and the European Securities Regulators Committee. The Parliament was to be excluded from the oversight; yet, in the EU atmosphere at this stage, political pressure was growing for the various actors to agree on a significant—and permanent—derogation from the status quo comitology framework (based on the 1999 Decision).

Contributing to additional political drama, at first there was disagreement within the Council itself: certain Member State governments were fairly disgruntled about comitology. As it happened, they were fearful of delegating new and substantial implementing powers to the Commission for financial services under the preexisting comitology framework. The Council had already persuaded the Commission to propose legislation with specialist oversight committees, and Lamfalussy had proposed special implementing powers for the Commission, but based on the 1999 Council Decision on comitology the Commission could no longer be stymied as easily by oversight committees—specialist or otherwise.

With the political atmosphere framed to its advantage, the Council pressed the Commission for concessions—that is, some sort of indefinite derogation from the current comitology framework. A consensus in the Council was finally reached when, at the March 2001 Stockholm European Council meeting, the Commission struck a deal with it. The Council insisted on an unmitigated callback power in the financial services policy area for itself, and the Commission agreed in a bilateral informal accord to do just that; in this accord the Commission undertook that it "would not act against the prevailing view within the Council." Thus, at this stage the Council had effectively offered the Commission special implementing powers in return for new specialist oversight committees and a permanent derogation from the comitology framework. This left only the Parliament with remaining discontent.

The Parliament viewed these developments with one part trepidation and one part enthusiasm. On one hand, resorting to special oversight committees on an indefinite basis in this issue area would fly in the face of three important entities: the Parliament's preferences, the Treaty's comitology committee prescription for this policy area, and the general spirit of the codecision procedure. On the other hand, the Parliament was holding substantial situational power in its hands—due to financial services being on the legislative track of codecision (the policy-making procedural context in which the negotiations were taking place). Thus, the Parliament's veto power in this policy area enabled it to put considerable pressure on the Council to agree to its preferences for this ad hoc proposal. The Parliament wanted a new informal accord that would further, and finally, amend the comitology framework to give the Parliament coequal implementing powers with the Council, including a callback power akin to the Council's.

At this stage it appeared that the Parliament would be able to bargain successfully for a new informal accord—one that would come very close to, if not actually achieve, its long-standing desire for parity in comitology. It indeed appeared, for a while at least, that the prevailing political winds were blowing in its direction, with veto power at hand. However, the Parliament was facing a highly unusual political setting, one that involved not only its organizational counterparts among the Three, but also "society at large"—that is, the media and public opinion. Not the average arcane EU policy battle, media outlets and a sizable segment of elite public opinion were actively monitoring the legislative developments.

This was evidenced by the Council's unorthodox handling of what otherwise might have been a standard experience of the codecision procedure, namely serving up one of the "wise men of Europe" in Baron Lamfalussy to raise the stature of the financial services legislation. Being a highly regarded public official, and charged with a high-profile policy task at Europe's supranational level, Lamfalussy's involvement attracted a considerable degree of media coverage. Moreover, it helped the Council to gain an advantage by "setting the agenda"—namely by framing the policy context with the notion that financial services was a special policy area involving banks and high finance and the like, thereby necessitating a special policy procedure befitting the special circumstances.

Once this frame was established in the court of public opinion and assumed almost as fact by the media, it became highly difficult for the Parliament to contemplate dispensing with some or all of the Lamfalussy report's recommendations—if any were to run contrary to the Parliament's wishes. Effectively, the heightened circumstances made the Council situationally more powerful. This represented a considerable paradox, for the associated political drama ended up almost canceling out what otherwise appeared initially like a situation in which the Parliament would actually be situationally more powerful—due the intense preferences of the Council to nail down financial services policy in rapid fashion.[6] The Parliament partially failed as a result. As for its partial success, this was due to the modicum of bargaining power it held onto despite the swing in public opinion in favor the Council; the Parliament also had a partial ally in the Commission, amounting to a kind of issue linkage dynamic. Certainly the Commission and Parliament were at odds in many ways, but they were in accord in other ways. Thus, the causal influence of this linkage only extended so far.[7]

What had ensued from the March 2001 Stockholm Council was an eleven-month power struggle between the Parliament and the Commission. In order to obtain support from the Parliament for the FSAP report, the Parliament first needed some concessions from the Commission. The Parliament was similar to the Council in its reluctance to delegate such substantial powers, unless it obtained the ability to call back individual Commission measures if dissatisfied on either scope or substance grounds. Sticking to its principal aim, the Parliament insisted on equal treatment with the Council. Toward this end, negotiations eventually got under way, culminating in a new informal accord—although not the one the Parliament was aiming for at the outset of this entire episode.

Instead, the Parliament had to settle for something less than a trilateral endgame comitology accord or its coveted callback power. In February 2002, Commission President Romano Prodi sealed the accord by reading its text out loud on the floor of the Parliament's plenary session. The Commission made two primary commitments to the Parliament for financial services legislation: to extend the Parliament's standard one-month review period of draft-implementing measures to three months, and to "take utmost account" of any Parliament position on either the substance of a measure or a view that the Commission had exceeded the powers delegated to it.

The latter was not quite the ironclad callback power long sought by the Parliament, but it set a precedent that the Parliament had a role not

---

[6] EU official, interview by the author, European Parliament, Brussels, May 5, 2003.
[7] EU official, interview by the author, European Commission, Brussels, May 6, 2003.

only in regard to the scope of implementing measures (as already laid out in the 1999 Decision), but also their substance. This interpretation was confirmed by additional statements by Internal Market Commissioner Fritz Bolkenstein in the subsequent parliamentary debate that the Commission would go out of its way to assure that the Parliament benefits from equal treatment with the Council and further that the Council and Parliament should have an equal role in controlling the way the Commission carries out this executive role. Attempting to make the most of what it viewed as a bittersweet result, it incorporated a "sunset clause" in the legislation stipulating that this ad hoc delegation of implementing powers would cease after four years unless explicitly renewed by both the Council and Parliament, thereby allotting itself a guarantee that, if it were not satisfied by things in practice, it could fail to renew the legislation.

Yet, the Commission maintained that it would not support Parliament's "sunset clause" amendment to the legislation—claiming it would be unacceptable not only to the Commission but also to the financial markets, which, in order to operate effectively, require stable rules for the foreseeable future. Taking this position is indicative of how the Commission must incessantly attend to multiple constituencies: citizens, business, interest groups, the media, *and* its interorganizational counterparts. Despite spurning the Parliament on this point, the Commission has nonetheless sought to persuade the Council to agree to Parliament's demand for parity in comitology. While it effectively did the Council's bidding regarding the FSAP—in return for substantial implementation powers, that is—the Commission has long been a philosophical supporter of the notion that it, the executive actor, must be accountable to the Parliament, the legislative actor (technically the Council's other half of the EU's legislative branch).

In this guise the Commission in December 2002 proposed an amendment to the 1999 Council Decision: to revise the comitology framework for all legislation falling under the codecision procedure auspices. Specifically, it proposed two phases of oversight: (*a*) the Commission would submit a draft measure to an oversight committee; and if the committee were to oppose the measure, the Commission would be granted more time to find a compromise; (*b*) the Commission would submit the measure to both Council and Parliament, with either being allowed to oppose the measure within two months (by qualified majority and majority, respectively)—in which case the Commission would either proceed to adopt the implementing measure, perhaps amended in light of other preferences among the Three, or proceed to submit a proposal for new legislation. In addition to these "executive" and "control" type phases, there would also be an "urgency procedure" to allow, under certain exigencies, for a draft measure to enter into force on a provisional basis (prior to oversight actions). Moreover, the management committee type would cease to exist.

According to this proposal, beyond its status quo ability merely to object that a draft measure exceeds the powers delegated to the Commission, the Parliament would receive the ability to alter any draft measure's substance. Thus, in large part the Parliament viewed the proposal favorably. It did so not only from the general standpoint of parity of oversight power with the Council for all codecision-based legislation, but also from the specific point of making an important distinction—between mere administrative–procedural measures on the one hand (on which the oversight committee would be advisory and any callback ability of Council or Parliament non-existent) and more general substantive implementing measures on the other (which would be subject to this new comitology procedure).

While the Commission's proposal was pleasing to the Parliament in multiple respects, it took issue with several elements. First, the Parliament wanted a commitment that the new bilateral informal accord regarding financial services legislation would be applicable for all codecision-based legislation, thereby allowing the Parliament for example to have up to three months to register its views during the committee phase. Second, for practical reasons the Parliament found the proposal lacking provision for the Commission simply to withdraw a draft measure in the case of an objection by either the Council or Parliament; similarly, so as to maintain legal certainty, under the urgency procedure it insisted that a given implementing measure be maintained (pending its review) when an objection elicits a full legislative procedure.[8]

Most importantly, the Parliament wanted the Commission to be obliged fully to take account of objections raised by the Council and Parliament, rather than "possibly" take account of them (as the current text read). In its proposal the Commission was clearly bargaining for greater comitology power for itself, which the Parliament did not wholly object to—except for in this instance. Yet, while there appeared to be a sizable swath of common ground between the Parliament and the Commission, the Council evinced no proclivity for agreeing to these terms—let alone sitting down to bargain with its counterparts. There were hopes that these issues would be taken up in Member State negotiations for the Lisbon Treaty, but

---

[8] EU official, interview by the author, European Parliament, Brussels, May 5, 2003.

individual Member State governments did not come to the aid of the weaker supranational actors.

Thus, despite such maneuverings, overall the Parliament failed to secure its primary aim for a reallocation of powers in the comitology framework, and the final treaty does not include comitology reform. For in spite of the Parliament's partial gain in the area of financial services and securities market legislation, it will not apply to the implementation and oversight of other EU legislation. Thus, despite possessing a full-fledged veto power under codecision—the legislative procedure made use of for the initial policy-making in financial services—the Parliament got outmaneuvered by the Council and effectively sandbagged by public opinion and the media. Despite a significant concession from the Commission in its commitment to persuade the Council to give the Parliament parity in comitology, in this particular informal influence attempt the Parliament quite simply failed.

The White Paper on governance

In light of the Parliament and Commission's failure to achieve comitology reform—be it through a new informal accord or a formal Council Decision—both actors have held out hope that they might chip away at comitology in the context of a different proposed informal accord. Although the negotiations over a new constitution for the EU—under the auspices of the IGC deemed the European Convention—were taking center stage in Europe by mid-2002, prior to their emergence the most salient issue at Europe's supranational level was a noteworthy influence attempt by the Commission. Unable to eke out much comitology progress in previous forums, the Parliament and obviously the Commission turned their attention to the Commission's White Paper on European Governance.

A "white paper" in European parlance involves a high-profile proposal for policy change of some sort (a "green paper" by contrast is a discussion document). Proposed initially by Commission President Romano Prodi in February 2000, the White Paper represents the Commission's ostensible attempt to jumpstart an overhaul of the governance of the EU—that is, improve the EU policy-making process. By all accounts, considerable improvement was necessary, from bridging the gap between Brussels and the proverbial man in the street to upgrading policy-making implementation. However, although the Commission is unquestionably committed to solving problems and increasing effectiveness for the common good of the EU and its citizens, it has its own interests to pursue.

At the top of the list was the need for the Commission to make up lost ground, namely regain the policy-making power that had either eroded or been transferred to the Council or Parliament. The second item on the list was a Commission imperative to restore its organizational morale; and third was the arguable need to augment its own effectiveness as a political actor. While other rationale were certainly also involved, this trio served as all the motivation needed for the Commission to undergo a major influence attempt aimed at staking a new legitimate claim to its political authority and organizational independence. The vehicle for this influence attempt—under the aegis of improving EU policy-making—was its White Paper on governance.

What led to this tripartite motivation for the Commission? First, updating of the legislative procedure known as codecision transferred a portion of political power from the Commission to the rest of the Three (the procedure was crucially altered by the 1999 Amsterdam Treaty). Codecision, as introduced in the Maastricht Treaty in 1993, allowed for the Parliament during the procedure's first phase to amend the Council's "common" position on a Commission-proposed piece of draft legislation (in the first phase the Parliament could only communicate its desired amendments in the form of a non-compelling opinion); if the Council did not accept all of the Parliament's amendments, a third so-called conciliation phase was convened. If after six weeks no compromise could be negotiated in the conciliation phase, the Council could revert to its common position and the Parliament could veto it—formally rescinding the proposed policy legislation and thereby concluding the legislative procedure.

Alas, as of the Amsterdam Treaty, the present day codecision procedure offers the potential for the Council and Parliament to conclude the procedure—that is, establish a law—during the procedure's first phase, thereby leapfrogging the second and third phases (with profound implications for the Commission). This became possible whenever the Council is able to muster a qualified majority of Member States in favor of the Parliament's amendments to the *de facto* modified Commission proposal; such amendments, although in mere non-compelling "opinion" form during the first phase of the procedure, can nonetheless function as the basis for a hitherto precluded negotiation with the Council. As such, the Parliament can interact directly with the Council, for it is no longer required to rely on the Commission to support its proposed amendments (the procedure's second phase). If the Council and Parliament are able to strike a final deal on the legislative proposal during the first phase, the customary ensuing steps in the procedure can be skipped, thereby cutting out the Commission.

Indeed, the Council has been rather zealous in pursuit of securing a piece of legislation in the first phase of the codecision procedure.

> After realizing that it would not be able to handle the workload of potential conciliation in all these new areas, as defined by the Amsterdam Treaty, the Council, in particular, pressed for a multiplication of informal meetings with members of the EP [the Parliament] . . . to develop "early agreements" and to conclude the decision-making process on the first reading. Given that there are legislative tasks subject to deadlines and given the limited resources . . . the Council is keen to seek early agreements so that the cumbersome and time-consuming conciliation procedure [the third phase] can be avoided. This is reinforced by the fact that the Presidency of the Council has strong motives to come to early agreements, because such agreements allow the Presidency to set the agenda within its presidential term.[9]

Recall from the main argument that one of the primary changes in constraints on the Council involves pressure on it from the Presidency of the Council to secure frequent passage of EU legislation—not only in order to be better able to set the agenda during its six-month term but also to win plaudits and gain the reputation of a "successful" Presidency term.

As a result, Council pressure has stimulated a sizable spike in informal "trilogue" meetings during the first phase of the procedure, in which they previously did not occur. Trilogues are informal negotiating meetings among two or more of the Three—not stipulated by formal institutions in legislative procedures—that operate in accordance with a norm of reaching consensus among the actors. Trilogues had their inception circa 1988 as an attempt by the Three to deal with discord in their triangular relations; it soon became routine for the Presidents of the Three to meet for a trilogue on a monthly basis, normally on Wednesday during the Parliament's one-week plenary session. Having gained currency with usage, as of codecision's arrival in 1993 the Three began relying on trilogues among various officials of the Three to lower the transaction costs of the third phase of codecision, the conciliation phase (having fewer than 15 officials in the meeting, compared to up to over 100 during formal conciliation meetings), has proved preferable to all actors.

---

[9] Furrell and Héritier (2004, 3).

Since the 1999 alteration of codecision, and to the detriment of the Commission, trilogues have mushroomed far earlier in the process—particularly during codecision's first phase. Such a proliferation of interaction in the EU's informal sphere has positioned the Parliament to be considerably less dependent on the Commission, the rule for which amounts to an informal accord. This impact is partly measurable via the increased use of the codecision procedure. Codecision applied to a mere thirteen articles of the Treaty through Maastricht, but after being amended by Amsterdam it applied to thirty-seven articles fully; with the advent of Nice, forty articles had codecision applied to them. As a result, the vast majority of EU legislation—not involving agriculture, trade, fiscal harmonization, EMU, and justice and home affairs—involves the legislative procedure where the Parliament is particularly well placed by informal interorganizational dynamics. Moreover, trilogues are now taking place at such a dizzying pace—with sometimes fifty or more legislative proposals going through the codecision pipeline simultaneously—that it has become highly arduous for officials in the Three even to keep track of them, such is their increasing decentralization. With respect to the proliferation of both codecision and the use of informal accord-based trilogues, this is a sizable change.

What one seasoned EU observer has deemed a "cultural change" in relations among the Three—thereby engendering a "genuinely triangular relationship" with the Parliament taken seriously by the Council—has clearly come at a significant cost to the Commission.[10] Whereas all legislative proposals used to culminate in either the second or third phases of codecision—with the Commission fully involved and its decisions affecting the proposals content—the Commission is now cut out of nearly 25% of occasions of the procedure's use, for a growing percentage of proposals are being wrapped up during the first phase.[11] Thus, in lieu of any discord between the Council and Parliament, the Commission is increasingly finding itself shunted to the side.

Along with examining how the Commission is becoming increasingly sidelined in the manner noted above, thereby motivating it to seek to regain lost policy-making power, it is worthwhile briefly to explore a salient

---

[10] Nugent (2003, 358–9).

[11] Since 1999 this figure has not hovered below 20% for any sustained period; moreover, over the early months of 2004 it spiked above 30% (as of May). However, it remains possible that such a rate will not be sustained in the short term, as a sizable effort was made by the Three to complete an array of legislations by the end of the Parliament's plenary session and prior to the enlargement date of May 1, 2004—that is, accession of the ten new Member States of the European Union. These empirics come from two sources: EU official, e-mail correspondence, European Parliament, May 2, 2004, European Parliament, May 2, 2004, and Shackleton (2001, 5).

tangent—namely the degree to which the Commission's waning influence is accounted for by the creation of new informal institutions. As predicted in Chapter 2, often the main policy-making actors cannot make new formal institutions work—or work efficiently, as demanded by the legislative process—therein motivating them to seek alternative mechanisms to solve such problems. As such, the Three have increasingly sought recourse in the creation of new informal institutions, frequently bundled together in informal accords. As intimated above, the Parliament and the Council began to look to the EU's informal sphere to meet their interests—which meant beginning to bypass the Commission.

The routine of convening trilogues is recognizable as stemming from a series of informal institutional rules that stipulate their occurrence—at various times, in various places, and among various arrays of officials representing the Three. Each of these institutions was a product of informal interorganizational dynamics, the most salient of which—at least until ratification of Amsterdam—has been the institution stipulating a trilogue among the Three in-between the second and third phases of codecision. The Treaty stipulates nothing between phases, so the Three agreed in late 1995, during the Spanish Presidency, to create a trilogue to fill this gap and facilitate more successful negotiations in the conciliation phase of the procedure. Hence, the rules structuring the outcome of increased, regular informal interaction under the guise of trilogues stem from informal accords.

> This institutional innovation has been of great importance in helping to reduce uncertainty and to channel conflict. It has served to generate a variety of procedural norms and shared beliefs about how the parties should behave which can be described as 'rules of engagement.' By the end of the Maastricht era they had become so self-evident that no one contested them and all agreed that such meetings were an essential means of reaching a successful conclusion in conciliation.[12]

The ratchet effect, based on self-enforcement, has not been the only cement keeping this institutional building block in place; in addition, not unlike other related creations, the Council found this one-rule accord almost as desirable as the Parliament.

> These unwritten rules have together served to make trilogues an extremely successful instrument: it has become almost impossible to imagine the procedure without them. However, they are not just an instrument to be

---

[12] Shackleton (2000, 334).

> applied when appropriate. They have affected the way in which each side views the other and fashioned common attitudes which have contributed to the resolution of differences. In this sense, the growth of a shared culture between the delegations of the two institutions [Council and Parliament] helps to explain in general terms why the Parliament has had the influence it has had on the conciliation procedure.[13]

Yet, clearly the Parliament has benefited disproportionately, for its impact on final EU legislation has been measurably augmented as a result of advantages accruing from recent informal institutions. "Both in quantitative and qualitative terms, there is strong evidence that the Parliament has made a significant difference to the shape of Community legislation, a difference that goes well beyond what could have been achieved" exclusively as a result of operating within the parameters of formal treaty-based institutions.[14]

As a testament to the increased cooperation stemming from this initial codecision-related activity in the EU's informal sphere, the Three went further by negotiating the 1999 Codecision informal accord (thereby sweeping up several unwritten informal rules and giving them greater weight in the context of an informal accord). The 1999 accord stipulates several trilogues during the codecision procedure: during the first reading, during the second reading, and during the third phase of the procedure, that is, "the procedure within the procedure" known as conciliation. In fact, the accord stipulates that just about anything necessary to achieving a timely agreement among the Three should be pursued, for example, additional trilogues if necessary: "The institutions [i.e. the Three] shall cooperate in good faith with a view to reconciling their positions as far as possible so that wherever possible acts can be adopted at first reading."[15]

The ongoing utility of the various rules of this accord constitutes a classic example of informal institutions being interposed among formal institutions and equally adhered to by the actors, as if there are no distinctions between them in practice. The Commission was a signatory to this accord, indicating that at first it did not feel threatened by this development; for it also favors greater efficacy, *ceteris paribus*. However, although the

---

[13] Shackleton (2000, 336).

[14] Shackleton (2000, 327–8). Evidence cited here indicates that 74% of the Parliament's desired amendments to legislative proposals under codecision were either fully or partially accepted by the Council between 1993 and 1999—with this critical informal institution in place for the vast majority of this period—compared to an acceptance rate of only 24% from 1988 to 1993 under codecision's predecessor, the cooperation procedure.

[15] "Joint Declaration of 4 May 1999 on Practical Arrangements for the New Co-decision Procedure," *Official Journal*, C Series, 148, 28. 5. 1999, p.1.

Commission is "in the room" with its counterparts, its participation in numerous instances has become trivial as the Council and Parliament have used such occasions to negotiate directly with each other.

Before returning to the subject of the Commission's waning influence it is important to pause and note this empirical confirmation of the overall theoretical argument of this project, namely that both institutionalization and integration are in evidence via developments in the EU's informal sphere—that is, informal interorganizational dynamics. In this instance, the changes in the institutional rules of the game go beyond reinforcing the status quo power allocation among the Three. In terms of the most salient outcome of the Codecision accord, the resulting changes engendered a measurable increase not only in the Parliament's general power-based influence but also in its influence on policy legislation.

Overall, as a result of this informal accord, the Commission lost power; the Council gained relative to the Commission and lost relative to the Parliament; and the Parliament gained relative to both its counterparts. The Commission lost the agenda-setting power it had up until the informal reaction to the formal Amsterdam change and the power to reject the Parliament's amendments; with the Commission more sidelined, the Council gained a greater ability to achieve its policy preferences and a reduction in transaction costs; likewise, the Parliament achieved not only these two gains but also greater influence over the Council—both in explicit legislative terms and in terms of an overall increased prestige as part of a cultural change whose most significant upshot is the Council needing to reckon with the enhanced authority of the Parliament.

Contrary to Intergovernmentalist theory, this change was not an intended consequence of the formal codecision change in the Treaty; and even if deemed part and parcel of an unintended consequence, the variance of the outcome cannot be fully explained without taking the new informal institutional rules into account. And not just any institutions, rather, institutions pursued and bargained for by a weaker actor: the Parliament. Indeed, predicted neither by Neofunctionalism nor by HI theory but consistent with my bargaining theory's prediction of change, this informal accord provides clear evidence of the creation of consequential informal institutions that serve to reallocate policy-making power among the Three. As this constitutes the operationalization of the integration outcome, at least in this area of the EU, the organizational actors have become more accountable to each other *and* more able to compel each other to do what the other would have previously resisted.

Second, in addition to losing power in the context of codecision legislating, another reason behind the Commission's White Paper-based influence attempt is the fact that it has been suffering from a bout of low organizational morale stemming from l'affaire Santer, at the end of the 1990s: the resignation of the Santer Commission, which included former Commission President Jacques Santer himself. In March 1999, the Santer College of Commissioners (the cabinet of top appointed Commission officials under the President) was pressured by the Parliament into resigning, *en masse*, fully nine months ahead of the scheduled end to its term of office. Due to evidence of considerable financial mismanagement and corruption by at least one Commissioner—and Santer's insufficient attempts to address these problems—the Parliament was on the verge of voting formally to dismiss the Commission when Santer and his colleagues resigned.

Unable to recover in the ensuing years, the Commission felt feeble and feckless. Officials in the Commission spent years counting the costs involved in its waning influence, due especially to being cut out of the codecision loop and the Santer episode. Still worse from its perspective, since then it has been perceived as politically weak by its counterparts among the Three. Thus, even in lieu of losing direct ground due to changes in the codecision procedure the Commission would likely have still felt the need to regain lost ground.

Third, while the Commission has retained its sole power of policy-making initiative—the Council and Parliament can only request proposals from it—it has been progressively eclipsed by the Parliament in particular, though also by the Council, in both the formal and informal spheres of the EU. In the informal sphere the Commission has lost some authority to the Parliament as a result of a series of bilateral informal accords between the two actors (see Chapter 7). In the formal sphere the Parliament has gained numerous new powers while the Commission's powers have remained largely stagnant, for with each successive amending treaty the ongoing Parliamentarization of the EU continues apace. The Commission has often been a political ally of the Parliament's vis-à-vis the Council, for philosophically it has long been committed to the democratic principle of parliamentary accountability. However, despite acting in accordance with this principle for years—with the result of ceding ground to the Parliament in bilateral informal accords for example—toward the turn of the century the Commission began to grow weary of the Parliament's ascendance.[16]

---

[16] EU official, interview by the author, European Commission, Brussels, May 5, 2003.

Beyond any doubt, the final catalyst for an effort at regrouping by the Commission was the lack of response to its complaints to the Council and Parliament about their bypassing it 25% of the time in the area of codecision legislation. The White Paper was thus conceived to help the Commission reconstitute its unique status or role in the EU—and especially to regain lost political ground at the same time—all under a patina of making the EU more transparent, efficient, and effective under the rubric of "better lawmaking." It is under this guise that the Commission launched its most significant influence attempt in the EU's informal sphere to date.

The quality of legislation accord: success and failure

The White Paper itself called on its counterparts among the Three to negotiate a new informal accord, ostensibly to commit the Three to a series of ways in which the EU can legislate more effectively (i.e., more efficiently, transparently, and simply). Primarily the Commission's influence attempt was aimed at eliciting commitments in writing from its counterparts that would give explicit credence to the Commission's traditional role as both "conscience of the Community" and the EU's sole legislative initiator— which is alluded to in the EU parlance of "the Community method" (i.e., the traditional manner of EU policy-making whereby much emphasis is placed on the legislative initiation by the Commission and its incessant involvement at all stages of the various legislative procedures). Never quite clear, however, was which sort of specific measures, that is, commitments from the others, the Commission was looking to achieve in the desired informal accord.

This lack of strategic specificity opened up an opportunity for the Parliament. True to form, from very early on the Parliament became quite keen to heed the Commission's call and do a deal on a new accord; however, the Parliament had other ideas than helping the Commission achieve its political agenda, either its explicit attempts to improve EU policy-making or the implicit attempts to regain its stature and influence. Indeed, the Parliament viewed the Commission's informal influence attempt as an opportunity to augment the Parliament's own influence. Although several specific agenda items for these actors have continued to overlap, for example, wresting power away from the Council in the area of comitology, the Parliament was determined over the course of the negotiations during 2001–2 to bring both the Council and the Commission further to heel.

As for the Council, it was the least keen of the Three. With less to gain and more to lose, the Council's negotiation pace was plodding at best, for it was content to keep things in slow gear. True enough, the Council saw some plausible improvement potential to various proposals in the White Paper, particularly a number of basic commonsense suggestions for enhancing the quality of EU policy-making. Yet, the Council was also aware of the agendas of its rivals and therefore wary; moreover, the Member States were far more focused on the European Convention and the formal negotiations among governments to agree to a new draft treaty that would for the first time designate the EU Treaty as a full-fledged constitution of the EU. Negotiations in the formal sphere over a constitution thus provided the Council with a ready justification for dragging its feet on both comitology and the negotiations over a "better policy-making" informal accord.

To kick-start negotiations, the Commission formulated a draft accord in July of 2002—which followed months of informal discussions at different levels among different officials of the Three, stretching back into 2001 (all of which was subsequent to the activities and discussions that went into the July release of the White Paper). Just prior to drawing up its draft the Commission committed itself to a series of changes, all under the aegis of "better policy-making": for example, "better involvement," "wider consultation," "greater number of policy instruments," "more focused institutions," "greater transparency," "better regulation," "better implementation." By positioning itself once more as the "driving force" behind EU policy-making, the Commission aimed to augment its degraded influence among the Three.

In its draft the Commission, by design, did not seek to go into excessive detail at the outset; its intention was largely to set the agenda, ensure that its priorities would become a part of a final accord in some form, and elicit responses from the Parliament and Council. As such, the very first provision/article of its draft made reference to "common principles" and "co-responsibility of the institutions." In addition, while other articles set out general commitments concerning the aims elucidated in the preceding paragraph—with draft articles focusing primarily on legislative coordination/simplification/quality and transparency—in terms of moving into new policy territory the thrust of the Commission's forward thinking came in the form of the articles calling for a small-scale revolution in the way EU regulation is carried out.

The two novel aspects of this new approach to regulation comprise "self-regulation" and "co-regulation." The former involves non-EU nongovernmental policy actors—firms, interest groups, labor unions, NGOs, and so on—working together to adopt common guidelines at the supranational level of Europe (with the Commission suggesting itself as the overseer of such efforts, to ensure conformity with EU law and ensure any formal legislative action is taken—if necessary—in the absence of necessary self-regulation). By contrast, co-regulation involves a more definitive role for the Commission in such activities of nongovernmental policy actors, namely introducing EU legislation in direct conjunction with and on behalf of these actors.

Overall the two suggested modes of regulation involve a number of similarities, with the primary distinction being the formulating of informal, voluntary agreements (similar to the EU's informal accords) in self-regulation versus the formulating of formal legislative proposals in co-regulation. Together these regulatory innovations pick up on the buzz generated in EU circles over the past few years concerning the "open method of coordination," that is, the general involvement of non-EU actors in the regulatory sphere of the EU. Self-regulation and co-regulation can be viewed as putting the flesh on the bones of the "open method." Interestingly, however, quite unlike the status quo in comitology, the Commission has called for itself to be the primary and perhaps sole actor among the Three to play a coordinating role in these newfound regulatory instruments; indeed, to the degree the Commission wins consensus on its novel ideas about regulation, it will be less fettered than it is at present under comitology. Herein lay the thrust of the Commission's influence attempt to reassert itself in general political terms, and more specifically to regain policy-making territory lost to its organizational counterparts.

Not surprisingly the Parliament, in addition to pursuing an agenda of its own, in response to the Commission's draft sought to offer support to the latter's notions regarding regulation, albeit with full accountability to itself. While pressuring the Commission to be very precise and accountable about its choice of what type of regulation to engage in—and reviving its concerns about comitology in the context of standard EU regulation—the Parliament brought its own set of aims to the negotiating table. In order to enhance its own policy-making influence vis-à-vis its counterparts, the Parliament sought articles in three areas it deemed "safeguards," "transparency," and "innovations."

Under the safeguards category the Parliament sought communication/ justification of the Commission's legislative instrument (i.e., procedure), prior to the status quo occurrence of this action in the context of the Commission's formal submission of a legislative proposal; moreover, the Parliament called for the Commission to issue an alternative proposal—with a different legislative procedure selected—if either it or the Council were to object to the original proposal. In perhaps its most ambitious influence attempt, the Parliament further sought a "callback" mechanism to be included in any proposal in which a procedure other than the typical legislative procedure enshrined in the Treaty is proposed; as envisaged, a callback would be a sort of veto power allowing the Parliament to force the Commission to change procedures—for example, selecting the codecision procedure instead of the consultation procedure for a proposed law on EU-wide taxation schemes. Finally, regarding co-regulation and self-regulation, the Parliament demanded being fully consulted and given monitoring abilities once the Commission reaches a draft agreement with non-EU policy actors.

In the area of transparency, the Parliament called for all discussions among the Three in the stage prior to a formal legislative proposal from the Commission—referred to as the "pre-consultation phase"—to have the results of the discussions recorded and made public. The Parliament also called on the Council to conduct all its internal legislative deliberations in public—which, given how long the Parliament has been demanding this, more or less amounts to "pie in the sky"—as well as to provide full justifications to the Parliament for all the results of these deliberations. Finally, regarding "impact assessments"—a new mechanism called for by the Commission in the White Paper aimed at following up legislation with a formal assessment of efficacy—the Parliament insisted these be issued in a standard, consistent format and also made public.

And in terms of the "innovations" area of its preferences for the accord, the Parliament sought provisions for multiple changes: for the Three to jointly agree multi-annual legislative programs (i.e., the skeletal nature of expected and/or planned legislation in the coming years); for the Council to agree with it on deadlines for the first and the second readings of all legislative proposals; for the Council to work with it to set deadlines for earlier transposition of EU legislation into national law; and, aside from a few additional but minor points, for the Council to agree to a new bargain on comitology in the context of the accord, primarily including a callback mechanism for it (along with complete transparency for all comitology procedures).

As for the Council, perhaps for the very reason the Parliament calls on it for transparency of internal legislative deliberations, there are almost no publicly accessible documents that indicate its preferences for the "better lawmaking" accord proposal aside from the conclusions of the European Council (biannual meeting of the EU heads of government) in Seville, June 22, 2002. A single paragraph in the eight-page document under the heading of "Better Lawmaking" is devoted to negotiations for the accord:

> The European Council welcomed the communications from the Commission on better lawmaking and, in particular, the Action Plan for simplifying and improving the regulatory environment. It invites the three institutions concerned (Parliament, Council and Commission) to adopt an interinstitutional agreement before the end of 2002, on the basis of proceedings in the High-Level Technical Group, in order to improved the quality of Community legislation and conditions, including timeframes, for its transposition into national law.[17]

The Council found it useful to look for some improvements in the legislative process, as long as it did not have to give up any authority to achieve them. And, in a confirmation of the book's argument involving a key first-order constraint, the Council—feeling constrained by the pressure on it to augment the EU's democratic credentials—found in the buzz about the idea of a better lawmaking informal accord an almost irresistible and fairly pain free opportunity to be a "good partner" in interorganizational terms and, more importantly, take some small steps toward greater democracy in the Union.[18]

However, the Council smelled a rat in the keenness of the Parliament and Commission for a deal, believing it odd to include regulation and impact assessment under the "better lawmaking" rubric and asking the Parliament what "better lawmaking" means (but not receiving a definitive answer).[19] From interviews of EU officials it is nonetheless clear that the Council was largely distracted by its intense focus on the European Convention and the formal negotiations of the Treaty revision that it led to. Beyond this, the Council was generally interested in being a "good partner" to its counterparts when it came to the fairly innocuous elements of the White Paper—who could argue with an aim of better legislative efficiency? In sync, it sought to appear cooperative yet avoid giving up any power or authority to either the Commission or the Parliament.[20]

Despite how keen the Commission and Parliament were for the finalization of a new accord, negotiations languished throughout the latter half of 2002 and well into the first half of 2003. Preparations for negotiations took

---

[17] Presidency Conclusions, Seville European Council, June 21–2, 2002, p. 3

[18] EU official, interview by the author, Council of Ministers, May 7, 2003; EU official, interview by the author, Council of Ministers, May 7, 2003.

[19] EU official, interview by the author, Council of Ministers, May 6, 2003.

[20] EU official, interview by the author, European Commission, Brussels, May 6, 2003; EU official, interview by the author, European Parliament, Brussels, May 7, 2003.

place among the Three in the first half of 2002, but then aside from contacts and preliminary discussions among the Three in mid-2002—including the agreement for the Commission to present a draft document, the issuing of the draft by the Commission (in late July), and the Parliament's responses to the draft accord (during August)—very little negotiating took place late that year, let alone the achievement of momentum toward a conclusion.

While informal accords "work, and we all agree on this, you cannot understand or do policy-making without them," the Council set up a special ad hoc internal group to come up with a strategy for responding to what momentum there was behind a better lawmaking accord, labeled the Mendelcan Group.[21] It needed a high-level Coreper mandate in order to negotiate with the others, but the Member State ambassadors decided comitology—among other things—was not on the table. With the Council dragging its feet and in any case otherwise occupied, the lack of any negotiating and/or momentum led numerous EU officials to become highly cynical about and skeptical of whether an accord would ever be realized; indeed, many began to predict failure.[22] Indeed, this was so much the case that the conventional wisdom among officials across the Three came down to this expectation. In early 2003, prevailing circumstances were highly inauspicious for a new informal accord regarding "better lawmaking."

Yet, in evidence of one of the main arguments of this book, pressure on the occupier of the Council Presidency for success began to build during the spring of 2003. Greece held the Presidency reins during the first six months of that year, and steadily it became clear that the Greeks were more amenable to a better lawmaking accord than either the rest of the Member States or the Council secretariat. A fair degree of skepticism remained, but by late spring the Presidency began some new rounds of negotiation with the Council's counterparts. Kicking in with the increased constraint on the Council for a successful Presidency was the second-order constraint of intensity of actor preferences. When this first-order constraint tightened, *ipso facto* the Council's preferences became fairly intense—thereby temporarily weakening it vis-à-vis its counterparts and generating propitious conditions for a new accord.

---

[21] EU official, interview by the author, European Council, Brussels, May 7, 2003.

[22] EU official, correspondence with the author, European Parliament, October 12, 2002; EU official, correspondence with the author, European Parliament, December 6, 2002; EU official, correspondence with the author, European Commission, Brussels, March 19, 2003; EU official, interview by the author, Council of Ministers, May 6, 2003.

The Commission and Parliament had remained interested in a deal throughout, as the torpor was Council-based (for its part, the Commission felt the Parliament had been threatening its right-of-initiative). Intriguingly, however, as midyear loomed, Greek officials in Brussels and the Greek foreign office under its Foreign Minister began to look around for ways in which to burnish its reputation at the Council's helm; indeed, their gaze fell on the seemingly moribund non-accord born of the White Paper. Notwithstanding the headline grabbing developments in the European Convention, the Greeks steered negotiations to a tripartite draft accord on June 3, and before the month was out (and their Presidency elapsed) in the eleventh hour they brokered a new informal accord. Actually, things proceeded rapidly on the heels of the draft accord with the final agreement taking place the next day on June 4. The text of the new accord ended up being printed in the *Official Journal* on December 31, 2003.

In support of the argument, in sync with an intensification of preferences in late 2002 the Council was constrained enough by the Presidency occupier's desire for being perceived by its peers as a "successful Member State." In this case, strategic interaction among the Three culminated in an accord against the odds and in the face of considerable internal EU skepticism, as Greece surprised everyone when it resuscitated the languishing draft accord. In addition to other efforts to shepherd formal EU legislation through final procedural gates into law, indicative of how Greece spared no effort to burnish its leadership credentials, the Presidency culminated in achievements both in the formal *and* informal spheres.[23] Thus, as predicted the Council's options narrowed as its constraints strengthened, thereby creating a temporarily weakened Council whose evolving preferences crossed over enough with the Commission and Parliament that the Three could find sufficient common ground to tie up the negotiations.

The result was a classic compromise, with each of the actors giving a little without taking a lot. Thus, the result can be characterized as partly a success—a deal was reached with a few novel institutional rules getting created—and partly a failure—as neither the Commission, as progenitor, or the Parliament, as eventual co-prime mover, were able to achieve their most sought after rule-based changes: it was not an accord that shook up the status quo (formal and informal) to any substantial degree. Thus, the

---

[23] EU official, correspondence with the author, European Commission, June 10, 2003; EU official, correspondence with the author, European Parliament, July 2, 2003; EU official, correspondence with the author, European Commission, Brussels, July 2, 2003; EU official, correspondence with the author, European Parliament, September 8, 2003.

result merits the appellation of part success/part failure, for although the accord got created its rule-based contents range from the redundant to the perfunctory, with few exceptions—namely, in the area of regulation. Yet, within these exceptions some novel rules that put this accord in the running for a Category III designation can be found (see Chapter 4).[24]

Naturally, the marquee element of the accord, so to speak, is the series of "common commitments and objectives" it contains "to improve the quality of lawmaking." However, few of such vague pronouncements like "the three institutions agree to ensure that general coordination of their legislative activity is improved"—or "the three institutions…will ensure that legislation is of good quality, namely that it is clear, simple, and effective"—actually serve to alter the ability of the less powerful to either hold the more powerful more accountable or compel the more powerful to do what they otherwise would not. In other words, few current policy-making powers of the Three were altered.

Much of the accord is odd in the extent to which its provisions cover old territory in interorganizational relations, particularly repeating—sometimes with slight word changes—rules from previous informal accords, in particular the two bipartite accords between the Commission and Parliament (the 1995 Code of Conduct and 2000 Framework Agreement accords). An apposite example is the often seen and heard commitment by the Commission to "take account of requests made by the European Parliament or the Council…for the submission of legislative proposals"—as opposed to the Parliament's preference for the power to compel the Commission to initiate a proposal when the former requests such and on its terms.

Yet, there are some salient novelties to the newly created informal rules worth noting. As mentioned above, the better lawmaking accord creates a new regulatory apparatus—a series of related rules that create, define, and constitute the new regulatory procedures of self-regulation and co-regulation, the so-called alternative methods of regulation. With the Commission situated as the regulatory agent of the Council's Member State principals, these rules lie at the heart of the Commission's core influence attempt; to the extent they are put into practice the Commission has achieved something noteworthy and highly likely—if proven successful over time—to find their way into the Treaty-based formal sphere of the EU in the not so distant future.

---

[24] EU official, correspondence with the author, European Parliament, May 2, 2004; EU official, correspondence with the author, European Parliament, June 6, 2003.

In essence the Commission is charged with being the regulatory "point person" in this new regulatory environment distinct from comitology in that EU regulation will now for the first time involve non-EU actors like firms and interest groups. Not surprisingly, much like the Council's Member States rely on the Commission to negotiate external trade agreements, it is well placed to do what would be highly inefficient for Member State governments themselves to attempt. Moreover, the outcome is considerably close to the traditional Community method (which the Commission has sought to reinvigorate after a decade of sagging morale and its having become increasingly eclipsed by Council and Parliament à la codecision).

Self-regulation in particular will involve the creation of new policy rules of an informal, voluntary nature—the whole idea being to institute a more bottom-up, flexible way for regulated entities in the EU (i.e., non-EU actors) to solve practical, quotidian problems that may arise. Under self-regulation the non-EU actors will essentially create their own informal rules with the Commission present to facilitate only. Whereas co-regulation leads to what will be the EU's first informal "legislative act," whereby the non-EU actors and the Commission create a set of rules—first in the form on a "draft agreement"—that are then vetted by the Council and Parliament, but without any of the traditional, elaborate formal Treaty-based procedures like consultation and codecision.

However, beyond being allowed to "suggest" amendments, "object" to an agreement's entering into force, and "request" the Commission to submit a formal legislative proposal instead, the EU's legislative authority (Council and Parliament) has little power—at least at the outset before the application of the rules gets worked out in practice and creates routine expectations for the Three. This will be critical, for the Parliament interprets these three words as giving it a callback mechanism for co-regulation. If it works out like this in practice, then the Parliament (and Council) will have made some important gains along with the Commission. Thus, additional informal rules will have to be created to determine how compelling the legislative authority's suggestions, objections, and request will actually be.

Regarding the Council and Parliament, the Council gains to the extent that the accord's rules actually lead to increased legislative efficiency and intra-EU democracy among the Three—as well as the extent to which it did not capitulate to the demands for greater comitology power for the Parliament and Commission (on comitology it only committed to a future overhaul of the status quo). The Parliament gained in several ways: it became more intimately involved with new efforts of the Three to create multi-annual legislative programs; it grew more satisfied with several provisions for increased transparency in the EU; and it was satisfied with the new legislative "impact assessments" that the Commission will be performing for proposed EU legislation—moreover, for legislation on the codecision track, it and the Council will have a compelling power to get the Commission to produce an impact assessment prior to the adoption of amendments.

Overall, if one leaves aside the redundancies from past informal accords, it is the Parliament that receives the lion's share of commitments from its counterparts, forty-two in all (the Commission and Council receive twenty-eight and twenty-seven, respectively). Yet, although there are a substantial number of new rules that allow the less powerful to hold the more powerful more accountable, almost all of them specifically stop short of redistributing political power; there are also redundancies, that is, old rules bundled together with new ones. As such, overall the gains and losses are fairly even for the Three—none is a big winner or big loser, and each came away both pleased and disappointed.

The Commission was the most successful (due to the new regulatory mechanisms and an ethos more akin to the traditional Community method), with the Parliament somewhat less so (due to a trove of commitments to be consulted and kept informed by both other actors), but the Council a close third (due to its staving off comitology changes and sharing in most of the Parliament's gains). One Commission official refers to the accord as "politically the most ambitious interinstitutional agreement that has ever existed . . . a tactical success."[25] The Council gave way by allowing itself to be more accountable to the Parliament; the Commission gave way on allowing itself to be more accountable to both others; and the Parliament gave way in terms of not getting its preferences for comitology powers, multiple callbacks, legislative deadlines, and control over the Commissions sole power of legislative proposing.

---

[25] EU official, interview by the author, European Commission, Brussels, July 4, 2007.

6

Informal Accords and Budgetary Politics

Introduction

In order to better gauge the effect of informal interorganizational dynamics, this chapter will examine informal accords in the budgetary sphere (accords in all other policy areas will be analyzed in Chapter 7). This policy area is particularly important, as informal interorganizational dynamics effectively originated in the budgetary sphere, in large part because of exigencies stemming from political discord between the two arms of the EU's budgetary authority—the Council and the Parliament. Notably, a significant segment of the rules that govern the EU's annual budgetary procedure stem not from the Treaty and Article 272, but from a series of informal accords stretching back to 1975. Indeed, the formal Treaty provisions that pertain to budgetary policy-making have gone unchanged for three decades; the EU budget procedure, however, has changed substantially—entirely informally.

This leads to a second important reason why the budgetary sphere is particularly significant in informal terms, namely the greater credence given to informal rules by the Three. Quite paradoxically, the Three do not always give priority to the rules that have the force of primary law; in fact, on occasion these actors give less credence to formal rules and more to the informal rules ensconced in informal accords. Some of the most salient examples of this phenomenon occur in the budgetary sphere, where informal rules somewhat frequently and directly contradict their formal counterparts; in other words, one set of rules tells the Three to do X with regard to issue Z, whereas the other tells them to do Y on issue Z. Remarkably, in every single case the Three behave more in accordance with the informal rules—they situationally act as if they are not bound by the provisions of primary law! Indeed, the Three effectively ignore formal rules in each instance of informal rules directly contradictly them, despite the formal legitimacy lacking in the latter.

A third important reason was because the organizational actors viewed it as a semi-isolated policy sphere conducive to experimenting with informal accords. Given the self-contained nature of the budgetary sphere in the mid-1970s, the Three were able to experiment with different ways of organizing their relations without "stepping on the toes" of Member State governments under anti-EU pressure, as they clearly would in such places as the agricultural sphere.[1] In addition to featuring the forerunners of the post-Maastricht batch of informal accords, such accords in the budgetary sphere have had more of an impact on EU interorganizational relations than their counterparts in any other policy area.

The section to follow will review some of the more pertinent history of EU budgetary policy-making; this background material will help set the stage for the ensuing discussion of informal budgetary accords. The second section will examine the 2006 budgetary accord, offering an up-to-date highlighting of dynamics in the budgetary area of the EU's informal sphere. The third section will elucidate the 1975 and 1982 informal budgetary accords, while the fourth will analyze those from 1988 and 1993. The final section of this chapter will examine the 1999 budgetary accord, placing particular emphasis on the most consequential new informal rules it comprises.

Background

Daniel Strasser has characterized the evolution of the budgetary sphere of EU policy-making as a forty-year history of "struggle for budgetary power" between the Parliament and the Council.[2] The 1975, 1982, 1988, 1993, 1999, and 2006 informal accords served to resolve, at least partially, interorganizational disputes in the budgetary sphere that were not adequately addressed in or staved off by the amending treaties. Discord between the Parliament and the Council, concerning the need to agree a yearly EU budget, continued despite the dramatic procedural changes effected by the 1970 Luxembourg Treaty and 1975 Brussels Treaty.

The Luxembourg Treaty was intended to amend specific budgetary provisions in the original EEC treaties. In granting the EU a degree of financial

---

[1] EU official, interview by the author, European Commission, Brussels, July 25, 1994.
[2] Strasser (1992: 23).

independence for the first time in the form of "own resources," this Treaty benefited the Parliament by raising the threshold for the Council to carry out its own will.[3] The Treaty granted the Parliament the ability to propose "modifications" to sections of the draft budget involving "compulsory" expenditure (the Council could reject with a qualified majority) and "amendments" to the section involving "noncompulsory" expenditure (on the second reading the Parliament could adopt them with a three-fifths majority within the "maximum rate of increase"),[4] and granted the President of the Parliament the power to declare the budget finally adopted.[5] These formal changes stemmed from a formal bargain, namely an amending treaty negotiated by the Member States.

The host of new budgetary powers gained from the Brussels Treaty five years later gave the Parliament a broader and stronger base from which to seek additional policy-making powers. The Brussels Treaty granted the Parliament its four main budgetary powers: the exclusive right to grant discharge of the budget to the Commission; the power to reject the final proposed budget; the ability to distribute the approved expenditure levels among various sectors of the budget; and the right to increase noncompulsory expenditure irrespective of Council opinion up to half the maximum rate of increase.[6] The host of new budgetary powers the Parliament gained from the Brussels Treaty gave it a broader and stronger base from which to pursue even greater policy-making authority. Nonetheless, the Parliament was not satisfied. Particularly after direct elections in 1979, it would begin to use informal accords as a device for prying more policy-making powers from the Council and Commission.[7]

---

[3] "Own resources" now consists of four kinds of revenue: customs duties, agricultural levies on EU imports, a proportion of national value added tax (VAT) receipts, and Member State contributions based on a small percentage of GNP (the last of these elements was added in 1988).

[4] The "maximum rate of increase" is a ceiling on the amount the Parliament has the authority to increase beyond the amount adopted by the Council for a given item of expenditure; it is calculated yearly by the Commission on a statistical basis taking factoring in several standard economic indicators; the Parliament is allowed to increase expenditure up to half the maximum rate in certain situations.

[5] The distinction between *compulsory* and *noncompulsory expenditure* was created by the Council to retain control over certain politically sensitive areas of the Community budget. By the Council's definition, compulsory consists of unavoidable expenditure to which third parties have a legal claim, whereas noncompulsory consists of avoidable expenditure over which the Community exercises considerable discretion. In practice the Common Agricultural Policy (CAP), refunds to Member States, and any spending related to international agreements are considered compulsory, whereas basically all other expenditure is noncompulsory.

[6] Strasser (1992: 29).

[7] EU official, interview by the author, European Commission, Brussels, July 25, 1994.

As the formal budgetary procedure stood in 1975, notwithstanding the changes introduced by the first budgetary informal accord in March of that year, there was a certain balance between the Council and the Parliament—particularly in terms of noncompulsory expenditure—although the procedure was clearly tilted toward the Council in pure power terms.

> This budget procedure thus had the trappings of a bicameral system for the adoption of the budget, with two readings in each body and the final say in some areas for one branch, provided it had the necessary majority to overrule the other, and in other areas for the other branch. Joint agreement was necessary for major increases.[8]

However, a variety of limitations from the Parliament's perspective subsequently motivated it to form aggrandizing power preferences. Among these were the Parliament's limited ability to increase the budget (due to the calculation of the maximum rate of increase), the small size of the budget (less than 2% of combined Member State government spending), and particularly the meager nature of the Parliament's powers regarding compulsory expenditure as compared to its noncompulsory powers (the latter comprised merely 17% of the EU budget in the mid-1970s).[9]

Nonetheless, in possession of final determination across competing budget lines (in terms of noncompulsory expenditure) and the ability to overrule the Council with a three-fifths majority, the Parliament proved to be a robust budgetary legislator that frequently and seriously clashed with its co-budgetary legislator.

Yet, a competitive political posture on the part of the Parliament did not become a reality until the advent of the direct elections of MEPs in 1979, which was the catalyst for a political transformation of the Parliament both internally and externally. Despite the significance of the 1975 informal accord—as described below—the Parliament did not begin to compete with the Council politically in pursuit of its own policy preferences until the eve of direct elections, when in late 1978 it sought spending levels that were at odds with the Council and used the full extent of its formal powers to achieve a policy victory in the form of the 1979 budget (namely a near doubling of the incipient Regional Fund).[10]

The next year featured an altogether more assertive actor, as the Parliament brimmed with a host of new and elected MEPs and a palpable infusion of democratic legitimacy. Herein lay a substantial shift in one of the

---

[8] Corbett (1998: 95).

[9] EU official, interview by the author, European Parliament, Brussels, August 1, 1996.

[10] Strasser (1992: 32).

two primary constraints on the Parliament, that is, its traditional lack of competitive political skills and political efficacy. Despite possessing a modicum of formal policy-making powers—the most prolific of which were budgetary—over the course of the 1960s and 1970s the Parliament neither acted like nor conceived of itself as a normal parliamentary body. With few powers in comparison to its national counterparts and comprised only of appointed MEPs who tended to be either less talented than MPs or near the end of long political careers, without a full-fledged parliamentary identity the Parliament's vision and behavior were consistent with that of a fairly apolitical collective actor. Indeed, it was not until mid-1987 when it even became officially known as the European Parliament, having been previously labeled the Parliamentary Assembly in the Treaty of Rome (and the Common Assembly in the EEC's forerunner, the European Coal and Steel Community).

Only with the inception of a directly elected membership in sight did the Parliament begin to develop more fully as an explicit political actor, including developing a vision for its role more in sync with traditional national parliaments, divergent power and policy preferences from the Commission and Council, and a concomitant competitive bent toward clashing with these counterparts.[11] Thus, direct elections amounted to an exogenous political shock of sorts, impelling the Parliament to seek to develop its rudimentary political skills—such as the strategy for seeking to exploit the potential of informal accords for obtaining additional powers beyond those prescribed in the Treaty.

Yet, although the Member States were responsible for granting the Parliament its long-standing goal of directly elected MEPs, after capitulating to the pressure to democratize the EU more fully, the Council energetically defended its power prerogatives and nonetheless sought to, so to speak, "put the Parliament in its place." After a considerable assertion on the part of the Parliament in preparation of the 1980 EU budget—it rejected the budget with a massive majority for the first time in the autumn of 1979— the Council played political hardball by delaying its formal response to the Commission's new preliminary draft budget in early 1980. This had the effect of starving the Parliament just when its demand for resources had spiked due to the numerous facets of its expansion, forcing the Parliament to make do with fewer financial resources than it needed for multiple months.

---

[11] EU official, interview by the author, European Parliament, Brussels, July 29, 1996.

Satisfied that it had taught the Parliament something of a lesson, the Council reached agreement with the Parliament to adopt the budget finally in July 1980. Yet, the Council ended up compromising to a degree by allowing greater spending levels than it initially preferred, not only for agriculture prices but also for the Regional Fund. The Parliament thereby achieved a portion of its divergent preferences, but nothing close to the full extent envisaged, which would have involved a substantial overhaul of the EU's budgetary procedure. The fecklessness constraint of the model in Chapter 2 was further relaxed by this series of events, as it served to galvanize the Parliament's preferences and political strategies. "There is little doubt that this episode helped convince many of the need for fundamental reform in the Community system, as it appeared that Parliament, even in the one area where it already had significant powers, would in practice have little scope to use them."[12] Part of its newfound strategizing involved exploiting the opportunities perceived to be in the informal sphere of the EU.

Informal accords tend to be created in the wake of amending treaties, which extend or create new formal rules entailing the EU's policy-making procedures. The same scenario operates in the budgetary sphere. Moreover, treaty amendments are frequently the source of new interorganizational conflict. In the case of the Luxembourg Treaty, the treaty article dealing with "own resources" engendered a dispute between the Council and the Parliament over the control of EU finances, which necessarily involved the Commission (from which all budgetary policy proposals must emanate). Informal accords have often functioned as a means of dealing with nearly incessant budgetary discord among the Three, particularly the Council and the Parliament. In terms of informal interorganizational dynamics, the 1975 informal accord was not only the first of its kind in the budgetary sphere but also the first of this particular type of informal accord in EU history.

The 2006 informal accord

The EU has grown accustomed to reexamining the entire budgetary policy-making process each time a new financial perspective needs to be agreed; however, any necessary adjustments tend not to be made in the EU's formal

---

[12] Corbett (1998: 95).

sphere but in its informal sphere, in the body of an informal accord. The Lisbon Treaty is the first to update this policy-making process at the formal level, which would involve a substantial sweeping up of all the informal institutions created over the years—most recently in the 2006 budgetary accord. The regular pattern of finalizing a new budgetary informal accord every five years or so is designed to lay out the financial perspective, roughly a six-year reference framework used to enforce interorganizational budgetary discipline. The framework may be revised in response to any initially unforeseen circumstances, with regard to the ceiling of own resources. The accord calculates the margin available under this ceiling, that is, the maximum rate of increase. However, the 2006 accord created a series of new informal institutions that set out additional changes.

In late 2003, six Member States requested that the next financial framework not exceed 1% Gross National Income per capita, which amounted to a difference in €130 million from the Commission's proposal. During the course of the negotiations the gap grew to about €210 billion, thereby making an agreement more elusive. In the view of the Commission and Parliament, this allegedly 1% increase was actually a substantial budget cut, an overall 23% cut not counting agricultural subsidies. This would have prevented a series of initiatives being planned by both of them. Actual regular negotiations kicked in under the 2005 Luxembourg Presidency, but the Council itself did not come to collective Member State agreement until the end of 2005: several Member States got their contributions reduced in the process.

The Parliament primarily sought a substantial degree of flexibility over the course of the perspective. Four trilogues took place between January and April of 2006, with the major bump in the road occurring in February when the Parliament had strong objections to a revised Commission draft text. Over the next two months a variety of giving and taking led finally to agreement among the Three. The accord was thus agreed by the Three in April of that year and generally sets out to accomplish several agreed on tasks: ensure budgetary discipline over all spending, ensure sound financial management, and improve functioning of the budgetary procedure (part formal rules, part informal). The accord's three sections involve laying out the financial framework for 2007–13, improving collaboration of the Three in the budgetary procedure, and instituting sound management provisions. Thus, the bulk of the accord is taken up with breaking down EU spending by category and setting the annual ceilings in each.

The primary novel elements to this accord entail the following: more flexibility in the management of the financial framework (not only the flexibility instrument and the emergency aid outside the framework but also the so-called legislative flexibility that gives more control to the joint budgetary authority); the introduction of a completely new Part III which has opened the door to an important revision of the financial regulation and to a more active role of the European Investment Bank to complement EU budget financing; the creation of new procedures for the monitoring of CFSP, which keep the Parliament involved by ensuring "democratic scrutiny"; inclusion of the Parliament in a 2009 midterm wide-ranging review of the framework by the Commission; quality of implementation improvements requested by the Parliament; and the creation of new agencies.

"This IIA is a further step of the recognition of the EP as an equal partner with the Council. The budgetary procedure has evolved from a sharing of competences (compulsory and noncompulsory) to a more balanced codecision procedure. The achievement of this process will be consecrated in the modifications that will be introduced by the new treaty, if adopted and ratified."[13] This appears to be an accurate assessment, as the Parliament made a series of gains that have placed it in on still more equal terms with the Council. Commission gains were slight, involving some spending priorities; and Council gains were mild in similar fashion. The new commitments in the accord almost without fail benefited the Parliament, new informal institutions that augment its influence over the budgetary process. This accord stands out more so for the achievement of the Parliament's policy preferences; its power preferences were largely achieved, but they were mild in comparison to its policy aims. Most informal accords involve the creation of new rules related more to interorganization power than outcomes related to different policy priorities among the Three. Issue linkage was the primary catalyst for a final deal, for the Parliament successfully e.g. linked its demands, for example, involving CFSP financing to its ongoing cooperation in several specific areas of the budgetary process. Hence, a shift in this second-order constraint proved instrumental for finalization of the bargain at the heart of the 2006 accord.

The earliest informal accords that occurred in the budgetary sphere stretch all the way back to the 1970s. The remainder of this chapter loops back to introduce and analyze each economic informal accord in chronological order.

---

[13] EU official, correspondence with the author, European Parliament, September 18, 2007.

156

The 1975 and 1982 informal accords

At some stage in the aftermath of the Luxembourg Treaty, the Council realized that the Parliament could potentially exploit its newly minted formal budgetary powers perhaps to preclude the implementation of certain policy legislation that is budgetary in nature. Thus, on the Council's initiative it sought some form of agreement with the Parliament that would reduce the risk posed by this scenario. The fairly weak and politically constrained Parliament of the day was only too pleased to cooperate in this regard. These efforts led to the following informal accord.

In March 1975, the *Joint Declaration of the European Parliament, the Council, and the Commission* established the original conciliation procedure.[14] Because of the substance of the changes involved and new rules created, it is now considered an informal accord—the first *procedural type* informal accord in EU history. The newly amended budgetary procedure applied to "acts of general application which have appreciable financial implications, and of which the adoption is not required by virtue of acts already in existence" as well as Financial Regulations themselves.[15] As prescribed by the accord, when the Commission submits a proposal it must state whether the act in question falls within the scope of the procedure. Both the Parliament and the Council can request the procedure. If the Council objects to the Parliament's opinion and the request meets the above criteria, it then becomes the task of a conciliation committee—involving representatives of the Parliament and Council with the Commission as an active participant—to seek a compromise and reconciliation of views. When the positions of the two organizational actors become sufficiently close, the Parliament may offer a new opinion, after which "the Council shall take definitive action."[16] This procedure must normally be completed within three months of the initial request.

With regard to its effect on interorganizational relations, the changes initiated by the 1975 Joint Declaration clearly involved more than marginal adjustments or slight variations of existing procedures. Its principal contribution was the creation of a new mechanism designed to facilitate decision-making harmony. After 1975 the Council's practice of making important budgetary decisions in private meetings was reduced, and, as a consequence, a more genuine dialogue between it and the Parliament began to

---

[14] *Official Journal* of the European Communities, C Series, 89, 4.22.1975.
[15] *Official Journal* of the European Communities, C Series, 89, 4.22.1975, p.1.
[16] *Official Journal* of the European Communities, C Series, 89, 4.22.1975, p.1.

develop. According to Strasser, although "there is no precisely defined procedure to ensure that conciliation will lead to agreement…the new procedure substantially alters the climate of relations among the Community's institutions [organizational actors] and gives the Parliament an additional means of action in the form of a certain degree of participation in legislative power."[17]

The results from the Parliament's perspective, however, were mixed. Although the new informal rules appeared fairly consequential on paper, in practice some believed that the *de facto* reality was that the only new element achieved was a supplemental opportunity for MEPs to press their views on the Council often in vain. The Parliament's conciliation team had little bargaining power over the Council other than to threaten not to vote in favor of specific items in the ensuing budgetary procedure, which lacked credibility unless the Parliament was totally opposed to the proposal.[18] In this view, the Council had little incentive to capitulate to the Parliament in conciliation, for in effect its bridges were already burned to the extent that any concessions could well upend the entire effort by forcing Member States to try to find a new compromise within the Council. As it happened, the Parliament saw the new informal procedure used a mere five times prior to direct elections. Nonetheless, in terms of precedents, as a testament to its lasting importance the conciliation procedure was expanded in later informal accords and formalized as part of the new codecision procedure introduced in the Maastricht Treaty.

The Parliament did not achieve the power to force the Council's hand, per se, but it did achieve the ability to force the Council to engage in negotiations in which it could further press its position directly with Council officials—this would be exploited more frequently in the wake of 1979 (an average of five per year by 1982).[19] In this manner, legislative relations between the two organizational actors departed slightly from the terms of the Treaty, as the Parliament clearly garnered a limited, *de facto* power from an informal accord between it and the other two organizational actors. Although the Parliament's relative gain involved something more substantial than routine institutionalization, it did not engender a significant shift in the organizational balance of power—that is, integration. A more plausible conclusion is that the 1975 accord gave rise to a political outcome somewhere in between the two, namely an alteration of the budgetary

---

[17] Strasser (1992: 38).
[18] Corbett (1998: 117).
[19] Corbett (1998: 117).

framework which left the Parliament in a slightly better position while not definitively curbing the Council's position.

As stressed by Strasser, the informal accord did at least prove propitious in regard to increasing direct contacts between the Council and the Parliament, thereby facilitating the beginning of a normalization of relations between the two actors. Prior to the enactment of the accord-based conciliation procedure, most contact between the two was indirect via the Commission. With the advent of conciliation, Council officials (including Member State cabinet ministers) were confronted with MEPs directly. From the discipline of psychology we know that it is difficult for more powerful individuals, or actors, to resist every single request or influence attempt on the part of a weaker actor if the shadow of the future is long, that is, there is a mutual expectation of future interaction. Indeed, this proved to be the case. All told, the conciliation procedure and the new informal rules from this accord set the stage for future integrative developments in the informal sphere.

In 1977, the Council issued a Declaration in which it noted the Commission's difficulties in authorizing the expenditure of budget items that lacked a legal base. The Council agreed that expenditure could not be made until after the legal base of all budget lines had been adopted. Furthermore, the Council expressed an understanding that consultation with the Parliament might be required to this end. In the early 1980s the two actors edged toward consensus on this issue, and in 1982 they brokered an informal accord, again under the label of "Joint Declaration."

Over the history of budget-related antagonism between the Parliament and the Council, with the Commission normally entering the fray on the side of the Parliament, the Parliament has drawn several conclusions regarding its strategy beyond direct elections in 1979.[20] First, for reasons related to the arbitrary distinction between compulsory and noncompulsory expenditure, the Parliament has always had a vested interest in pressing for increases in the overall level of EU spending. As the Parliament came to wield more power vis-à-vis noncompulsory expenditure, increasing the levels of such spending has always been in its direct interests. Moreover, increasing levels of other types of spending, for example, for one of the other organizational actors, have had the effect of offsetting what until the 1990s had seemed like an inexorable rise in compulsory expenditure, particularly the financing of the CAP.

---

[20] EU official, interview by the author, European Parliament, Brussels, July 25, 1994.

A second conclusion involved the need to limit the rapid rise of compulsory expenditure, which necessitated placing CAP reform on the Parliament's agenda. The purpose was to free expenditure for other EU policies, particularly those on the Parliament's list of priorities. A third conclusion follows directly from the first two, namely, that Parliament must pursue whatever means necessary to break down what it views as an arbitrary distinction between compulsory and noncompulsory expenditure. For this reason the Parliament has engaged in a series of assaults on the Council's definition of each type of spending in hopes of shifting the balance of classification toward noncompulsory spending.

During preparation of the 1981 budget in late 1980, the Parliament again clashed with the Council in its ongoing efforts of poking and prodding the Council in an attempt to gain new policy-making leverage over it. The Parliament attempted to stymie agricultural spending once more and in its first reading opted for a sizable 254 million ecu of compulsory expenditure to be transferred to an ad hoc reserve and a full 70 million ecu to be reduced in agriculture spending (as well as a 2% cut across the board).[21] In addition it inveighed in favor of an immense 834 million ecu for a variety of noncompulsory spending items.[22] In the event, the Council agreed to 183 million of the latter and could not sustain an attempt to derail the 2% cut. However, on its second reading the Parliament outmaneuvered the Council by remaining within the limits stipulated by the maximum rate calculations by adding 266 million ecu to the "supplementary budget" for 1980, which would be carried over into 1981.[23]

The execution of the budgetary procedure in late 1981 was equally fraught.[24] In its first reading for the 1982 budget the Parliament reappropriated 366 million ecu to various noncompulsory budget lines (e.g., social policy spending and regional aid) and reduced agricultural spending by 300 million ecu—the budget line for Monetary Compensatory Amounts (MCAs).[25] The Council actually took a considerable amount of these proposed changes on board, opting to accept the vast majority of proposed MCAs reductions and half of the suggested noncompulsory expenditure increases. But the Parliament chose to pick a fight, and did so by restoring

---

[21] Corbett (1998: 118).

[22] The ecu (European currency unit) was the currency of the European Union—albeit not in paper/coin form—prior to the advent of the Euro currency in 1999.

[23] Corbett (1998: 118).

[24] The substance of this section draws liberally from Strasser (1992, chapters 1 and 2).

[25] MCAs are funds set aside for maintaining stability in agricultural prices by offsetting currency realignment-induced price shifts.

204 million ecu from its first reading amendments which the Council clearly desired to reject—for in accordance with its compulsory and noncompulsory classifications the Parliament's amendments were surmounting the maximum rate of increase. The Parliament knew this, but was attempting to exercise some influence pressure via making the point that if the spending pendulum were to swing more in favor of noncompulsory spending then its proposals would indeed be within the maximum rate. Under a Belgian Presidency at the time, the Council opted to take the Parliament to the ECJ while at the same time sounding a conciliatory note by offering to hold talks over the compulsory/noncompulsory breakdown. These negotiations bore the fruit of an informal accord (after which the Council dropped its court case), which involved the first occasion on which the Council acknowledged that it could not unilaterally dictate the breakdown of expenditure classification.

The 1982 *Joint Declaration by the European Parliament, the Council, and the Commission on various measures to improve the budgetary procedure* was generally designed to provide for more harmonious cooperation between the Three.[26] It consisted of four primary elements: issuing a definition of compulsory expenditure, introducing a system for classifying the legal base of new EU legislation, instituting a series of measures for greater collaboration in the context of the budgetary procedure, and clarifying a number of items with regard to speeding up the budgetary process. The most important of these was the second element, which was designed to settle the continued controversy over the legal base. The specific provision read as follows: "The implementation of appropriations entered for significant new Community action shall require a basic regulation."[27] The Joint Declaration accord, concluded by the Presidents of the Three, was an innovation in the EU. The Presidents were able to adopt an attitude of collaboration instead of confrontation, particularly between the Council President and the President of the Parliament.[28]

The Council expected the definition of compulsory expenditure to stave off the Parliament's criticism of the distinction between compulsory and noncompulsory. The Parliament expected to benefit from being named a "full partner" in the process of classifying the legal base of new budget items and the fixing of new maximum rates of increase. In practice, however, the accord lapsed as the Council did not involve the Parliament as

---

[26] *Official Journal* of the European Communities, C series, 194, 7.28.1982.
[27] *Official Journal* of the European Communities, C series, 194, 7.28.1982, p.1.
[28] Strasser (1992: 178).

fully as the wording of the document called for, and the Parliament continued to harangue about the definition of "compulsory." Moreover, the Council took advantage of the ambiguous wording of the accord by deeming much of what the Parliament considered "significant" or "new" legislation to be "insignificant" or "old," thereby preventing Parliament's involvement in classifying the expenditure type. And, regarding the length of time taken up by the budgetary procedure, the organizational actors frequently failed to establish legislative frameworks in time to meet the targets identified in the accord.

There were, however, two exceptions to the accord's failure to live up to their expectations. One of these involves the continued applicability of the accord's basic mechanism for classifying the legal base of new Community acts (compulsory or noncompulsory), as well as those whose legal base is changed. It provides an example of an informal bargain made between the organizational actors for the purpose of filling in an obvious gap in the Treaty. The Three negotiated this particular aspect in order to facilitate adoption of the budget in spite of the Treaty's ambiguous and complicated procedure for doing so.

The other exception is actually an extension of the first. It involves the specific instrument for solving disagreements over budgetary classification. If either the Parliament or the Council does not accept the Commission's suggested classification, then the Three must convene a trilogue (to reiterate, a meeting between the Presidents of the Three designed to resolve major disputes). This informal practice proved rather auspicious, even from the Council's point of view, and since its inception in the mid-1980s it has been used to deal with a wide variety of interorganizational disputes, budgetary and nonbudgetary. Trilogues have in fact become such a routine occurrence that a monthly trilogue now takes place in Strasbourg—over a Wednesday lunch between the three Presidents when the Parliament is in plenary session.[29]

In the budget sphere this practice has benefited the Parliament in that it has become an interlocutor in discussions that would otherwise probably have taken place without it. Yet, although the accord specifically stipulates that new budget items shall be classified "by agreement between the two [organizational actors]," differences in opinion in trilogue discussions have often resulted in stalemates. Typically, as the Council was the more powerful organizational actor, these stalemates were in the end resolved largely in

---

[29] EU official, interview with the author, European Parliament, Brussels, January 13, 1995.

the Council's favor. Thus, although the Parliament procured a *de facto* power—to convene a trilogue if its choice of classification was not being pursued—the power is relatively modest in that it does not allow the Parliament to compel the other organizational actors to do anything.

One might argue that the 1982 accord resulted in a further increase in the Parliament's powers in that it opened the door for the Parliament to initiate new policies by means of adopting appropriate items in the budget.[30] But this line of argument does not hold because the 1975 Brussels Treaty had already granted the Parliament the power to initiate new items of noncompulsory expenditure. The 1982 accord merely provided an important clarification that opened the door for the Parliament to exercise its power unhindered by the Council. The dynamics of the 1982 informal accord, therefore, were limited to ongoing institutionalization of interorganizational relations in the budgetary process.

However, as demonstrated above, the Parliament clearly gained from the accord. This was shown by the Council's aborted 1984 attempt to alter the language of the accord to state that new Community acts would only become "significant" after two years and only if their cost exceeded a certain amount. The Council had apparently decided that its gamble had not paid off, presumably because it found itself compromising more often than it would have preferred.

Patterns continued in the procedure leading to the 1983 budget, in which the Parliament once again reduced CAP spending and increased various noncompulsory spending items 600 million ecu in total. For its part the Council fully rejected the proposed CAP reductions but accepted over half of the Parliaments noncompulsory increases. Nonetheless, in its second reading the Parliament further pushed the envelope by resorting to an argument about why a reinstatement of 138 million ecu would not break the maximum rate ceiling. Minutiae aside, as the dispute was by any standard rather arcane, the Council vigorously protested the Parliament's maneuver related to establishing the true size of the noncompulsory portion of the budget. Yet, in the end it capitulated by not following through on its threat to take the dispute to the ECJ—perhaps because it was more occupied with the Parliament's concurrent rejection of a supplementary budget involving the infamous Thatcher UK refund.

In preparation of the 1984 budget it had become clear that the maximum rate of increase would not be an issue, for a second formally mandated

---

[30] Corbett et al. (2000b: 229).

budgetary ceiling would be reached first—namely that of the ceiling of own resources (i.e., the EC budgetary resources in total). True to form, however, the Parliament pressured for the Member States to take action to increase own resources by calling for 546 million ecu in additional spending in its first reading, which was substantially beyond the legal ceiling. At the simultaneous Athens Council, Member States allowed a sizable 377 million to go forward but could not reach agreement on the own resources issue, so the Parliament upped the ante by freezing half of the UK's budget rebate and 5% of CAP spending. Yet, despite the fact that a large faction of MEPs pressed for a rejection of the whole budget, the Parliament contented itself in the end by reinstating another 132 million. Indeed, it emerged the winner of the skirmish, as the Council proved content that the budget had not been rejected and went on to focus on hammering out a compromise among the Member States for increasing the EU's own resources (i.e., its funding revenue/budget).

But the Council remained dissatisfied by its semi-capitulation, believing the Parliament had exceeded its formal powers once more. Thus, in 1984 it issued a resolution: *Council Conclusions over Cooperation with the Commission and the Assembly on Matters of Budgetary Discipline.*[31] In this declaration the Council made three pronouncements/commitments. First, it called on the Commission and the Parliament to examine possible means of interorganizational cooperation necessary to effect greater budgetary discipline among the Three. Second, the Council invited a delegation from the Parliament to convene with it directly before the meeting in which it fixes the yearly financial framework. And third, the Council instructed the President-in-Office to inform the Parliament of the results of this meeting either in written form or verbally in plenary session, laying particular emphasis on the agreed measures of budgetary discipline and cooperating with the other organizational actors on these measures.

The 1988 informal accord

Fragility and discord in the budgetary sphere remained problematic throughout the mid-1980s, despite progress in the informal sphere. Although Member States eventually agreed to an augmentation of own resources in late 1984, it was not scheduled to take effect until mid to late

---

[31] Council Conclusions, European Council, Brussels, March 19–20, 1984.

1986, thus presenting the preparation of the 1985 budget with a similar own resources exhaustion dilemma—the only difference being there was now a precedent in place from the previous year's procedure involving Member States topping off own resources in order to fund the budget in full.

Sensitive to this and the Parliament's presumed assumption that the Member States would simply cover whatever deficit emerged from the standard budget procedure, the Council attempted to stave off similar dynamics by submitting a draft budget for only ten months instead of the customary twelve. Its gambit involved a new strategy of putting the final two months in brackets (on its second reading after the Parliament did away with this in its first reading) and claiming that the amounts within them could only be spent upon revenue being made formally available through own resources. Wholly opposed to what it viewed as a gimmick, the Parliament for the second time in its history formally rejected the budget—by an overwhelming vote of 321 to 3. Issues were not resolved in a finally agreed budget until more than six months later, when in June 1995 the Council finally put together a budgetary top off that included taking on board the full funding levels for regional aid and food aid sought by the Parliament.

The 1986 budget-making procedure led directly to a case before the ECJ. The Parliament was pitted against both the Council and the Commission due to neither actor taking into account that both arrears that were coming due and the costs associated with the newly enlarged EC, which now included Spain and Portugal for the first time. The Commission did not calculate a maximum rate that incorporated these exigencies, and the Council submitted a draft budget that did not diverge too sharply from the rate determined by the Commission. The Parliament responded by, in its view, fixing the problem by raising the Council's 31.8 billion ecu to 34.06 billion, to which the Council responded with 32.7 billion—which amounted to a 20.5% maximum rate of increase.

Still without agreement on the legal calculation of the maximum rate, the Parliament plowed ahead by formally adopting a 33.3 billion budget. Immediately the Council took the Parliament to the ECJ, and the latter decided in its favor declaring that the Parliament's action was illegal in lieu of a legally completed budgetary procedure (including an agreed maximum rate)—as indeed the Council's first and second reading amounts were by inference. The ECJ judgment sent the actors back into negotiations, which eventually—again a full seven months late—led to a July 1986 agreement on a budget amount even beyond what the Parliament originally sought: 35.2 billion ecu at a maximum rate of 39.18%. Discord with the Parliament was proving costly to the Council.

Despite the new own resources ceiling in late 1986, projections for the 1987 budget once more took the European Union to the very limit of own resource's revenue ceiling. In order to stay beneath the own resources ceiling, the Council was determined to preserve agricultural spending levels and reduce noncompulsory areas, for example, research funding and development aid. Naturally, the Parliament viewed this as a naked attempt to prop up agricultural subsidies by assailing noncompulsory programs; it reacted by reinstating research and development funding and taking similar amounts from milk production and agricultural stock reduction efforts. The Council was opposed on both counts, and the Parliament demonstrated its pique by knowingly approving a budget in excess on the maximum rate in its second reading (the ECJ had been eminently clear about this only the year before). The Parliament ended up able to use this as a bargaining chip, as ensuing negotiations with the Parliament led to a final agreement that not only sustained some of the cuts in agriculture but, also formally increased the maximum rate from what the Commission originally calculated—from 8.1% to 8.149% (interestingly, the Council attempted to save face by claiming that the rate remained the same as only the first decimal point "counted").

Preparations for the 1988 budget took place in a context of crisis, with the European Union quite literally in severe financial straits and the Council for the first time unable to meet its formal October 5 deadline for presenting a draft EC budget at its first reading of the budgetary procedure. The European Council summit in Copenhagen in December 1987 failed to reach a conclusion on the Commission's proposals, which entailed some prescriptions for heading off the EU's financial collapse by increasing own resources, Member State top offs, and strenuous EC budgetary discipline. The traditional mainstays of own resources—agricultural levies and customs duties—were being depleted on a yearly basis, and the VAT consumption tax was kept static at 1.0% until even its formal increase to 1.4% in 1986 proved inadequate. Belt tightening on the budgetary side proved arduous as the Council refused to curtail compulsory expenditure and the Parliament refused to curtail noncompulsory expenditure.

Budgetary preparations at this juncture took place in a funding environment transformed not only by crisis but also by the Commission's Delors package (rapidly accepted by the Council), a more sanguine development that mandated *inter alia* a doubling of regional aid by 1993 as part of the so-called 1992 Program's financial package for completing the Single Market. This clearly necessitated some sort of major compromise with the Parliament—directly increasing its bargaining power—for in theory the

Parliament was not obliged to abide by the Commission–Council agreement at all and could quite easily have reallocated this significant increase in revenue as it wished. At the Parliament's behest, the Council agreed to negotiate a new informal accord that would govern budgetary procedure outcomes and yearly budgets through to 1993.

Prior to the culmination of these informal negotiations, at the Brussels Council summit in June 1988 the Council issued a formal Decision in which it set a new guideline for CAP spending that limited growth in the main subsidy budget line—namely that agricultural spending could not exceed 74% of the annual growth rate of EU GNP; this was a binding stipulation with the force of law. Moreover, on the revenue side the Council mandated that henceforth the EU's own resources revenue would be linked explicitly to the EU's GNP instead of the more arbitrarily selected own resources ceiling predecessor. The Council determined that the overall ceiling on own resources would be set at 1.2% of EU GNP for payments and 1.3% for commitments up to 1992.

> The importance of the agreement on increased resources reached at Brussels should not be underestimated. At a time of significant efforts to limit national budgets, it represented a commitment to allow the Community budget to expand over five years by as much as 14% in payments and 16.5% in commitments and this in real terms, at 1988 prices. In addition, the 1988 starting-point of 43.8 billion ecus was a high one, more than 7.5 billion ecus above the budget of the previous year, an absolute increase unparalleled in the history of the Community.[32]

The Council had placed the EU's revenue on firm ground, but it was the result of informal negotiations with the Parliament that arrived at similarly firm ground on the budgetary side.

The *Interinstitutional Agreement on Budgetary Discipline and Improvement of the Budgetary Procedure* of 1988 grew out of a series of Council decisions surrounding the Brussels Summit.[33] The accord introduced the EU's first "financial perspective," whereby budgetary appropriations for each year of a fixed period (in this case from 1988 to 1992) are largely established in advance. It was based on the principle of mutual authorization of financial perspectives according to category of expenditure, which entailed prior acceptance by both arms of the budgetary authority (Council and Parliament) of annual maximum rates of increase for noncompulsory

---

[32] Shackleton (1990: 14).

[33] "Council Decision of 24 June 1988 Concerning Budgetary Discipline," *Official Journal* of the European Communities, L Series, 185, 7, 15. 1988.

expenditure within each category (over a five-year period).[34] The accord committed budgetary appropriations by category for all foreseeable EU expenditure through 1992, including the initiation of new policies.

Considered to be the prototypical IIA, it "radically changed the nature of the budgetary process in a number of fundamental ways."[35] As discussed in Chapter 2, bargaining in the EU's informal sphere involves competition not only over power allocation but also over policy aims. First, as already alluded to, the heads of state and government agreed to a new framework for EU financing, which not only provided the European Union with a substantial increase in revenue but also imposed restraints on the expansion of various types of expenditure, most notably in the area of agriculture. Second, the accord was the first to consider budgetary provisions beyond a single year's duration. Third, the accord stipulated a doubling of the structural (i.e., regional) funds by 1992, thereby achieving something akin to a separate agreement between the Council and Parliament to substantially upgrade the maximum rate, in advance of the budgetary procedures convened.[36] In basic terms, the fundamental bargain underpinning the accord involved an exchange of a larger budget for budgetary discipline.[37]

Both organizational actors took a sizable gamble in concluding this accord, for neither knew with certainty what they were likely to benefit or suffer from. The Council and the Parliament both made substantial concessions in the 1988 IIA. The Council made two primary concessions. The first involved committing itself to five predetermined yearly increases in the maximum rate of increase, which otherwise might not have been as high. The second, and more substantial, involved agreeing to constraints on the rate of increase for compulsory expenditure. Effectively, the Parliament achieved a *de facto* veto over increased spending on agriculture. Prior to the 1988 accord, the Council had always adhered to its strategy of preventing the Parliament from ever gaining legislative access to CAP financing; hence, the breaking of a twenty-six year old taboo constituted a rather significant concession to the Parliament.

The Parliament also made two primary concessions. The first corresponded to one of the Council's, for it was impossible to calculate with

---

precision what the maximum rate would be in several years time; the Parliament likewise committed itself to respecting previously established maximum rates of increase for five years. As a consequence, its actions had the potential of forgoing the fullest use of its treaty-based powers vis-à-vis noncompulsory expenditure. Because the IIA established expenditure patterns by category, the Parliament's second concession involved relinquishing its ability to transfer noncompulsory funds from category to category as it wished. Both organizational actors made a concession in the form of accepting expenditure ceilings in advance of each budgetary procedure, thereby limiting the yearly procedure to allocating only a small fraction of the financial perspective.

Both organizational actors also made substantial gains. The Council's primary gain involved garnering the so-called budgetary peace, which would have constituted a gain in previous years as well, but in the wake of the SEA the Council had placed a premium on its achievement. In its view budgetary stability was a necessary precondition for the culmination of the 1992 Program and the corresponding creation of the Single Market. Budgetary peace was essentially secured by the Parliament's agreeing to suspend not only its power to transfer expenditure from item to item in the noncompulsory area of the budget but also its power to increase expenditure each year up to half the maximum rate of increase. The Council's other important gain involved creating a clear expectation of future increases in expenditure. The financial perspectives have given Member State governments a clearer idea of how much they can expect to pay out and to receive over a multiyear period, thereby making it easier for them to plan public spending.

The limits on compulsory expenditure, that is, the CAP, and the ultimate doubling of the structural funds represented significant gains for the Parliament.[38] Limits on agricultural spending made slightly more funding available for noncompulsory expenditure, which had the effect of augmenting the Parliament's legislative role at the same time as releasing some funding for its own priorities. The increase in spending on the structural funds and research was also a clear gain, for in addition to fulfilling one of its long-standing policy aims the Parliament was able to exert more democratic control over EU expenditure as in this case it was defined as noncompulsory. Moreover, the gain of steady increases in noncompulsory expenditure

---

[38] It is important to note that certain Member States in the Council were also pressuring for similar policy outcomes, for example, Italy, Spain, Portugal, and Ireland.

was preordained and guaranteed. This eventuality represented a radical departure from the previous status quo, which in the mid-1980s precluded significant growth in noncompulsory expenditure at the same time that its compulsory counterpart constantly exceeded the established guidelines.

Also of importance, the doubling of the structural funds effectively created a new type of EU expenditure that some EU practitioners have referred to as "compulsory non-compulsory," a sort of hybrid of the two previously extant types. Although the newly augmented structural spending was technically still noncompulsory, as a result of the new IIA it was no longer subject to the formal budgetary rules laid out in the Treaty. Indeed, the guaranteed annual increase of 1.3 billion ecu was both a legal ceiling to be adhered to and a political target to be obtained, the latter element rendering it somewhat akin to compulsory expenditure strictures.[39] The implication of the informal commitment was that this amount would both be budgeted and spent. Interestingly, none of the new informal rules directly contradicted the Treaty's formal provision that the Parliament retained the ability to reallocate any technically noncompulsory expenditure in the budget (whereas they contradicted and shunted into abeyance a host of other formal rules from Article 272—old Article 203). Thus, the Parliament retained its power to transfer funds earmarked for structural/regional spending to other policy areas; nonetheless, the Parliament stuck to the allocation set out in the informal accord.

Shackleton has taken the view that the resulting budgetary procedure comprised a marked degree of autonomy from national interference and explicitly recognized principles established outside the national sphere to guide relations between the EU as a whole and its constituent parts:

> Such a movement is one which has generally been resisted in the Council and been at the root of many of the conflicts which have pitted it against the EP over the years. Traditionally, for example, the Parliament argued that entry in the budget constituted a sufficient legal base fore the implementation of appropriations. The Council, for its part, took the view that the budget procedure was subordinate to the legislative process where it enjoyed the last word. A temporary truce was agreed in 1982 with the signing of a Joint Declaration which stated that "the implementation of appropriations entered for significant new Community action shall require a basic regulation." However, this still left plenty of room for argument as to what

---

[39] Shackleton (1990: 20).

actions are neither significant nor new and thus permit implementation without a legal base agreed in Council.[40]

What qualified as "new" and/or "significant" was arguable, and the Parliament's post-1979 political shrewdness would continue to compel it to seek to exploit such potential "wiggle room."

Indeed, in the years running up to 1993 there were several budgetary modifications made at the Parliament's behest. In 1990, the Parliament successfully prevailed upon the Council to include in that year's budget an additional 500 million ecu for aid to Eastern European states—which necessitated a specific revision of the financial perspective. Upon the accession of the former GDR to the European Union in 1991, the Parliament succeeded in its aim of extending EC budgetary assistance beyond the monies already allocated to regional aid budget lines. That same year it also won a financial perspective revision to accomplish the following: enlarge the East European aid program, create a new financial instrument for environmental policy, and provide aid to Gulf states affected by the Gulf war.

> Altogether, apart from technical adjustments to cater for movements in GNP and prices and conditions of implementation, Parliament obtained revisions of the financial perspectives between 1990 and 1992, totaling some 6,641 million ecu—all to non-agricultural policy areas (and mostly external policy). The Inter-Institutional Agreement was not a straitjacket.[41]

These instances appear to indicate that the Parliament had not fully sacrificed its maneuverability as some predicted at the outset of the 1988 IIA.

As indicated in previous chapters, while at times it would seem plausible that the Parliament often pursues increased power for power's sake, in the budgetary sphere it is at least somewhat clear that the Parliament has sought additional policy-making powers in order to pursue its divergent policy aims, differing that is from the Council's policy preferences. Already presented in this section is a raft of evidence not only that the policy aims of these two organizational actors often clash, but also that the Council quite clearly has not preferred a variety of new rules contained in informal accords which redistribute either increased influence or policy-making power to the Parliament. Some additional cumulative evidence will help support this critical proposition:

---

[40] Shackleton (1990: 68).
[41] Corbett (1998: 105–6).

> Thus, the sums over which Parliament had the final say were a growing proportion of a growing budget. In absolute terms, they rose from 2.3 million ecu in 1979 to 25.6 million ecu in 1992—a 1121 per cent increase in nominal terms and a 440 per cent increase after allowing for inflation. In terms of policies, the most notable development is that of the structural funds. The regional development fund was a mere 400 million ecu in 1977. By 1992 some 8559 million ecu were spent on it. On the social fund, 173 million ecu were spent in 1977, compared to 4303 million ecu in 1992. Yet it is especially on some of the smaller items that Parliament was able to use its powers to a greater proportional effect, helping to develop a wide range of new Community policies.[42]

Of considerable significance is the fact that the broad scope of these policy outcomes did not stem from a confluence of mutual preferences on the part of both the Parliament and the Council; on the contrary, a large percentage were engendered over Council opposition at the behest of the Parliament— not only on the basis of its formal treaty-based powers but also as a result of informal interorganizational dynamics.

Where the Parliament was able to increase its budgetary bargaining power enough—via divergent preference intensities, divergent time horizons, and issue linkage—from 1975 to 1993 it induced the Council to negotiate three informal accords with it (others were negotiated in different policy areas during the same period; see Chapter 7). The newly created informal rules contained in such accords did offer the Council specific gains—the most salient of which was budgetary policy-making peace; yet, gains for the Council like this one often did not come at the expense of Parliament. Whereas a substantial number of the newly created informal rules provided the Parliament with gains that the Council had previously resisted, most notably those which transferred influence (greater ability to hold another accountable) and power (the ability to compel another to do what it otherwise would not do) to the Parliament. These outcomes defy the predictions of Intergovernmentalist theory and realist theoretical takes on the European Union.

Such Parliamentary gains occasionally came at the expense of the Commission, and on occasion at the expense of both the Council and the Commission. For example, one of the most consequential instances of the Parliament managing informally to usurp policy-making power from its organizational counterparts occurred during this period, also in the budgetary sphere. This involved the creation not of an informal accord,

---

[42] Corbett (1998: 108–9).

but of an informal precept instead (recall that an informal precept constitutes an informal institution created by a single actor, whereas informal accords are bundles of informal institutions, or rules, created by two or more actors). This influence attempt of the Parliament's is a salient example of its not always successful ability to arrogate additional authority to itself, despite the opposition of other actors.

Circa the early 1980s, the Parliament eked out a power not formally granted to it by the Treaty. Over the course of numerous iterations of budgetary policy-making, the Parliament sought after the ability to create new items or lines in the EU budget—a power, according to the Article 272 of the Treaty, solely possessed by the Commission (the Treaty gives the Parliament only the power to amend the draft budget drawn up by the Commission and previously amended in the Council's first reading). Nonetheless, the Parliament's shoot-for-the-moon strategy of constantly attempting to create new budget lines each year paid off in the form of an informal precept that henceforth has allowed it to do precisely what it intended.

When the Parliament began unilaterally creating new budget lines in its first reading, the Council vigorously opposed this—on the grounds that the Parliament was precluded from doing so by the Treaty unless a legal basis already existed as a consequence of previous EU legislation. But after the Council would remove these items in its second reading, almost invariably the Parliament would reinstate them in its own second reading—and adopt them (based on former Article 205 that required the Commission to execute the budget, the Parliament's inference having been that the inclusion of a line in the budget was a sufficient legal basis in and of itself). The Council effectively lost this dispute when the Commission began treating newly creating budgetary lines by the Parliament as full-fledged budget lines and executing them, so long as they abided by other formal provisions such as remaining beneath the maximum rate.

It would appear that while the Council opposed this "squatting" approach, the Commission acquiesced to the Parliament's influence attempt, calculating that it and the overall EU would gain from this outcome. Whether this proved to be the case is arguable, but it chose to be a handmaiden to the Parliament in this instance where it could presumably have ignored the budget lines the Parliament created. The Commission did not however support every single attempt by the Parliament, preferring to spurn certain new budget line allocations that it considered too large or ill advised in its role as "conscience of the Community"; however, it actually did acquiesce on most occasions of the Parliament's impertinence.

Finally, the Council and Parliament reached something of a compromise on the issue under the guise of the 1982 informal budgetary accord discussed earlier. The two parties to that bargain agreed that new legislation would be required for "significant" new budgetary lines for EU action. Under such a condition the Commission was directed to put forward a new budgetary proposal in the form of a draft regulation by the end of January, after which the Parliament and Council would attempt to adopt the regulation by mutual agreement before the end of May. In the event of their failure to do so, the Commission would propose transfers to other budget lines in order to maintain appropriations consistency. Intriguingly, as already alluded to, the ambiguity of the word "significant" proved not altogether satisfactory, but practice soon made clear that the Parliament's adoption of an item in the budget was sufficient in and of itself. Indeed, the Parliament appears to have made use of this informal precept every year since.

The 1993 informal accord

So successful and mutually acceptable was the 1988 prototype that in 1993 the Council and Parliament signed the second *Interinstitutional Agreement on Budgetary Discipline and Improvement of the Budgetary Procedure.*[43] It set out a financial perspective for the years 1993–9 and in many ways mirrored its predecessor. The gains and concessions of the 1988 IIA were by and large replicated in the 1993 IIA, an indication that both sides had concluded that the concessions made were worth the gains received; the risks evidently proved worth taking. There were, however, several additional changes, for example, a gain for the Parliament involving a recategorization of several compulsory expenditure items as noncompulsory expenditure (including the long coveted Council concession that international agreements with financial components would henceforth no longer be deemed compulsory).[44]

Gains and losses for the actors in question can come in either of two areas in this type of informal accord. The budgetary IIAs have two primary components: the financial perspective (which sets out the budgetary ceiling amounts for each category of expenditure over multiple years) and the

---

[43] "Interinstitutional Agreement of 29 October 1993," *Official Journal* of the European Communities, C Series, 331, 7. 12. 1993.

[44] Some in the Parliament wonder whether such concessions may, upon reflection, cause the Council to be less disposed to giving way in the future: EU official, interview by the author, European Parliament, Brussels, January 13, 1995.

budgetary procedure (which sets out the rules by which the Three go about negotiating and determining the actual yearly EU budget, within the perspective's ceilings). In the latter area the Parliament obtained a new power in the form of what the accord deems a "two-pronged inter-organizational collaboration mechanism": a trilogue meeting to kick-start the yearly budget procedure as well as a conciliation procedure to secure agreement between the two arms of the budgetary authority (note: according to the IIA's rules, this procedure was applicable only to compulsory expenditure).

To reiterate, a trilogue is more than just a mundane meeting; rather, it is mandated, providing the weaker organizational actors with an ineluctable opportunity to make their preferences known to the Council at the outset of the process by which they determine the yearly budget (which in the Parliament's case matters, for its views must be taken quite seriously given its power of final budgetary discharge). A "conciliation," on the other hand, is an actual mandated negotiation between the Council and the Parliament, with the Commission in an observer role. This procedure can be invoked by either organizational actor, with an example, as stated by the IIA, being an invoking by the Parliament when the Council intends to depart from the preliminary draft budget. According to rules of the IIA, they are obligated to reach an agreement of some sort. Hence, the updated conciliation procedure in the 1993 IIA augments the Parliament's legislative power by not only stipulating a framing meeting in the form of a trilogue but also granting it the capability of compelling the Council to enter into negotiations with it—negotiations that are mandated to culminate in agreement.

In addition, the Parliament achieved several specific policy aims in terms of the 1993 financial perspective. First, concerning its objective of expanding the overall budget, the 1988 and 1993 accords involved the largest average yearly increases in the EU budget since 1975. It is impossible to determine whether the yearly maximum rate increases provided for in the accords would have amounted to more or less than Parliament otherwise might have been able to achieve. However, given its record between 1975 and 1988, as evidenced by the relatively small yearly increases, it would appear one can safely conclude that proportionally similar rates of increase would not likely have occurred. The primary trade-off involving the relinquishing of the Parliament's power to reject yearly budgets is in evidence here.

Second, concerning the Parliament's twin objectives of decreasing the compulsory expenditure and increasing the noncompulsory expenditure proportions of the overall EU budget, the IIAs have played a prominent role in achieving this objective. The percentage of compulsory expenditure as a proportion of overall expenditure decreased steadily from 1988, when the first financial perspective was initiated.[45] In fact, this is linked to the reform of CAP, which was undertaken outside the budgetary framework.

Third, concerning the Parliament's objective of reducing the scope of compulsory expenditure, that is, the number of policies deemed compulsory by the Council, the 1988 IIA marked the first occasion on which the Council accepted some form of constraint on compulsory expenditure. The Parliament had increasingly been putting the Council on the defensive up to 1988 with repeated denunciations of the arbitrary nature of the Council's compulsory–noncompulsory distinction and the lack of a sound principle on which to base the distinction, but nothing of substance had been achieved. Thus, the consensual approach of brokering informal accords has proved far more effective than Parliament's previous unilateral and essentially adversarial attempts to increase noncompulsory expenditure.[46]

In light of how the Parliament is essentially the most active source of impetus behind the concluding of informal accords—a product of its having more to gain than either the Council or the Commission—it is appropriate to analyze the extent to which the Parliament has achieved its strategic objectives via informal accords, in terms of both its legislative power objectives and its policy objectives. Having secured three of its major strategic objectives, did the Parliament effectively relinquish its most prolific budgetary tools in the process thereby negating its gain?

One might argue that the power to reject the overall budget has constituted the Parliament's most prolific power, which was suspended for the remainder of the accord's financial perspective. There can be little doubt that this was a significant *prima facie* gain for the Council. However, the Parliament's ruminations in the wake of its three budget rejections between 1979 and 1984 have called this proposition into question. Given the Parliament has not invoked this power for over twenty years, it would appear that budget rejection had lost its appeal to the Parliament and was therefore valued less than it previously had been. The Parliament also agreed to suspend its powers to distribute approved noncompulsory

---

[45] This was not the case for absolute amounts, but this is not a legitimate measure of this policy objective.

[46] Westlake (1994*b*: 127).

expenditure levels among various items of the budget and to increase overall noncompulsory expenditure up to half the maximum rate of increase. Has the Parliament done itself more harm than good by relinquishing these two powers?

The counter argument to this contention is that the Parliament has *de facto* retained its ability to increase noncompulsory expenditure in that both budgetary IIAs have provided for substantial increases in this area of the budget, more than likely in excess of what the Parliament would otherwise have been able to achieve. The power to transfer expenditure between noncompulsory budget items, however—including the ability to fund newly created items—remains fully in abeyance. Hence, the Parliament has temporarily suspended much of its ability to take advantage of the reclassification of budgetary items, that is, when the Council changes a budget item's classification from compulsory expenditure to noncompulsory expenditure.

It must also be pointed out that the financial perspectives' increases were essentially decided by the Heads of Government in the 1988 Brussels Council and the 1992 Edinburgh Council meetings. Thus, the Parliament's gains appear to have been largely due to decisions made prior to the conclusion of the negotiations over both IIAs. As discussed below, the Council's position and aims have been crucially important for interorganizational relations. Yet, in order for the Council to achieve policy-making harmony in the budgetary sphere and deliver benefits for national budgetary planning to the Member States, it had to make a series of concessions to the Parliament. Thus, what may appear *prima facie* as a unilateral series of decisions by the Council in fact represented more of a bargained quid pro quo.

Like the Joint Declaration of 1975, the 1988, and 1993 informal accords have not only further legitimized the Parliament's existing budgetary powers but also transferred a modest degree of legislative authority/power to the Parliament. This has been accomplished largely by how they have served not only to transfer new powers to the Parliament but particularly to expand the size and scope of the noncompulsory expenditure section of the budget—the only budget section to which the Parliament's treaty-based budgetary powers apply. For example, the 1975 accord granted the Parliament a specific new power, namely the ability to compel the Council to enter into a conciliation procedure with it. The Council has also gained, especially with regard to limiting certain tendencies of the Parliament and achieving much sought after stability in this policy area.

> There is no question that the European Council meeting held in Brussels in February 1988 marked the end of a long period of bitter argument about the financing of the EC and generated a widespread feeling that the Community had been dramatically reinvigorated.[47]

The overall result has altered the relationship between the Parliament and the Council, and, as a consequence, the Parliament has gained increased influence in the budgetary process—well beyond what the formal Treaty provisions alone afford it.

In light of the considerable credence given by the Three to the 1988 and 1993 IIAs, the next logical step at that stage appeared to be either to negotiate a similar accord in sync with these or fully formalize the informal aspects of the yearly budgetary procedure by incorporating them in the next amending treaty (which would be the Amsterdam Treaty).[48] Though the subsequent IGC did take up this topic and give it extensive consideration, the Council saw fit to continue to utilize the informal sphere, preferring, as it happened, to seek not to scuttle what it and the Parliament had successfully built and implemented. Although the Parliament did press hard for the Member States to incorporate financial perspectives in the pre-Amsterdam IGC, its participation was limited to having two representatives on the Reflection Group (the preparatory group for the 1996 IGC).

The 1999 informal accord

Under the aegis of Agenda 2000—the EU's legislative package aimed at streamlining EU policies and preparing for post-2000 enlargement—and also under its attendant financial perspective (2000–6), the Council, the Commission, and the Parliament forged the EU's third corresponding IIA, designed largely as a complement to the perspective and substantially in keeping with its 1988 and 1993 forerunners. Indeed, in the Commission's view, the 1999 IIA is very much the core of Agenda 2000 (the Commission's legislative plans for the outset of the twenty-first century).[49]

The first part of the IIA comprises the financial perspective and its implementing details, setting out specific expenditure amounts, and making detailed budgetary appropriations in each heading and subheading of the

---

[47] Shackleton (1990: 1).

[48] EU officials, European Parliament, joint interview by the author, European Parliament, Brussels, January 13, 1995.

[49] "Interinstitutional Agreement of 6 May 1999," *Official Journal* of the European Communities, C series, 172, 18.6.1999.

EU budgetary framework for the remaining years of the perspective. In terms of function, these appropriations serve as budgetary ceilings for the seven main areas of EU spending, with a heading for each area. Not only do the appropriation figures change, but the Three agreed to alter several other components—as well as introduce some additional ones.

The 1999 IIA comprises multiple components: First, it increases budgetary appropriations in each of the seven budgetary headings, at modestly varying rates of increase. Second, it creates and/or formalizes several mechanisms which allow adjustment, or so-called flexibility, in the financial perspective (provisions for ceilings revisions, new reserves, and a "flexibility instrument" designed to allow the organizational actors to increase a specific year's budget due to unforeseen circumstances: all serving as the EU's mechanisms for exceeding a given budgetary heading in the financial perspective). Third, with the aim of improving the functioning of the annual budgetary procedure, the 1999 IIA stipulates a series of procedural rules which amount to a significant overhaul of the procedure—including some rule changes that engender a further shift in the balance of policy-making power among the organizational actors.

The procedural rule changes relate to interorganizational cooperation and specifically address several points of contention between the Council and Parliament, including provisions regarding distribution of fisheries spending, incorporation of financial provisions in legislative acts, the question of legal bases, classification of expenditure, etc. However, the most important rule changes are subsumed under an overhaul of the conciliation procedure. First, the conciliation procedure is extended to incorporate *all* expenditure—compulsory and noncompulsory (previously it covered only noncompulsory spending). Indeed, the IIA specifies not only a strict definition of the distinction between the two expenditure types but also classifies each heading and subheading as specifically one or the other.

Second, the accord injects some clarity into a previously gray area involving which types of codecision-based legislative acts are allowed to include financial provisions and which are not, which is taking place against a backdrop of the Parliament having consistently pressed for the inclusion of a financial component in general policy legislation (as its powers are most pronounced in the budgetary sphere). In accordance with the 1999 IIA, now only multi-annual program type legislation can contain financial provisions, that is, allocation of expenditure over multiple years and for the duration of the program; financial provisions in other acts can only serve as illustrations. Third, the accord spells out four specific spending categories that are exempt from the general requirement that all acts of legislation must have a legal base.

Fourth, in addressing the unresolved nature of how the second pillar's CFSP expenditure is handled in the budgetary process, the IIA stipulates that the Three shall utilize the conciliation procedure in order to secure agreement on the amount to be charged to the EU budget each year. While the Parliament thus gains inroads into the second pillar activities of the European Union via partially determining not only the overall amount of CFSP spending but also the distribution of this amount among the different CFSP policy subheadings, it will not have any role in earmarking expenditures for specific CFSP policy actions.

Finally, and most importantly, the 1999 budgetary IIA comprises a substantial overhaul of the EU's yearly budget-making process, which is officially referred to as "the conciliation procedure" and appears in the document under the heading: "Interinstitutional Collaboration in the Budgetary Sector." The new rules depart significantly from their 1993 IIA-based forerunners; in fact, this IIA subsumes not only that accord but also the following previously agreed budgetary informal accords: the 1982 Joint Declaration, the 1996 Declaration, the 1996 Joint Declaration, the 1997 accord, and the 1998 accord.[50]

The 1993 IIA stipulated merely two trilogues and a lone conciliation meeting, or conciliation, whereas its 1999 counterpart designates three additional trilogues and one additional conciliation. As the entire procedure now stands, the four trilogues take place before the establishment of the preliminary draft budget by the Commission; before the establishment of the draft budget by the Council; before the first reading by the Parliament; and after the first reading by the Parliament. As for the two conciliations, the first occurs after the second trilogue, and the second transpires after the fourth trilogue, ahead of the Council's second reading. These new rules amount to an upgrading of the Parliament's policy-making role in the yearly budgetary process: it now sits in deliberations with the Council on twice as many occasions as it did previously. The Parliament's ability to achieve its policy preferences is clearly enhanced by these changes.

It would thus appear that the new conciliation procedure rules involve specific transfers from the Council to the Parliament: transfers of influence

---

[50] Respectively, the *Official Journal* of the European Communities, C 194 28.7.1982, C 102 04.04.1996, C 20 20.01.1997, C 286 22.09.1997, and C 344 12.22.1998.

as a consequence of the increased trilogues and transfers of power as a consequence of the additional conciliation. As previously discussed, the more one political actor interacts with another actor of different preferences and less power, the more difficult it becomes for the politically superior actor to refuse to accede to at least a modicum of the inferior actor's preferences. This tendency is all the more pronounced the more iterative contact between the actors is and the more opportunities there are for weaker actors to retaliate against stronger actors. It is particularly pronounced in this EU context, for the Council continues to be increasingly buffeted by pressures to democratize the European Union (typically interpreted as allowing for greater prowess on the part of the Parliament). Indeed, my argument identifies this increased pressure over time as an important independent variable—involving a change in one of my model's constraints—which helps substantially to account for changes in the dependent variable.

The arguable transfer of power that is detectable in the new conciliation procedural rules slightly adjusts the original conciliation and introduces a second at an important juncture. There used to be merely a single conciliation, in an early stage in the budgetary process, just prior to the point at which the Council establishes its draft budget. The new IIA places the first of two conciliations on the actual date that the Council does this. In addition, it places another on the day before the Council performs its second reading, with a specific allowance for a continuation of discussions or negotiations after the second reading—the critical penultimate stage of the process ahead of the Parliament's second reading. Moreover, both the trilogues and the conciliations—part of the overall conciliation procedure—now apply also to noncompulsory expenditure.

The altered nature of these conciliations in the budgetary sphere augments the Parliament's organizational status with the Council, particularly because a conciliation meeting mandates arrival at an agreement of some sort—and also because of the Parliament's ultimate treaty-based power to reject budgets. As emphasized earlier, the fact that the Parliament surrendered this specific power in the 1988 and 1993 IIAs and again in this one amounts to a rather significant departure from the formal Treaty text, especially in the sense that the Parliament is bound to this rule in the IIA context. However, although held in abeyance by the 1999 IIA, it still exercises influence over the budgetary proceedings. For if the Council were consistently to stymie the Parliament in these conciliations and not treat it as a equipotent actor, the Parliament would withdraw from the IIA, thereby nullifying the accord while simultaneously calling into question how bound it would be by the other thirty-plus informal accords. The Council clearly does not wish to risk such a scenario.

Overall, the Parliament is therefore in a more powerful position, being able to negotiate with the Council at a minimum of two junctures in the policy-making process as a coequal actor, rather than simply being able to accept or reject the entire budget at the end of the process—a less powerful position to be in. Clearly, conciliation is more integrative in the budgetary sphere than it is in any other policy sphere. The accord in the Commission's view "clearly established new rules and procedures" with the Parliament's aim being "not only to organize internal matters but to create law."[51]

Institutionalization or integration?

In the budgetary sphere, institutionalization does appear to be in evidence—in terms of measures to increase efficiency, to expedite the pace of the budgetary process, to share information, and to increase general collaboration between the Council and the Parliament. However, the type of concessions being made by the Council indicate that the effect of IIAs and other accords on the overall interorganizational balance extends beyond a mere entrenchment of the spirit of standing primary law, indeed, beyond a mere reinforcement of the status quo. Taken as a whole, the new rules created in the informal sphere do indeed augment the position of the Parliament vis-à-vis the Council. The Parliament has garnered not only a greater capacity to hold the Council accountable to it but also a modicum of powers to compel it to do what it otherwise would not. Yet, the number of new legislative powers the Parliament has accrued from the budgetary accords do not amount to a wholesale transfer of power from the Council. Thus, while interregnum integration is in evidence, it must be concluded that the aggregate effect is modest, albeit significant—at least in the budgetary sphere.

While the Parliament has not quite amassed a fully formidable array of legislative powers in the budgetary sphere via informal interorganizational dynamics, it has succeeded in securing several significant policy objectives. Though at times the Parliament pursues new legislative powers as an end in itself, its efforts ultimately constitute means toward the end of achieving

---

[51] EU official, interview by the author, European Commission, Brussels, July 4, 2007.

particular policy objectives. The three budgetary IIAs analyzed above have allowed the Parliament to secure several objectives of considerable worth. The objectives achieved—substantially expanding the overall EU budget, increasing the EU's structural (regional) funds, expanding the noncompulsory portion of the budget, and reducing the scope of compulsory expenditure—do not represent policy outcomes in the traditional sense, for example, an increase of x for budgetary item y in the year z. Rather, they comprise a policy package that will continue to condition interorganizational relations in the budgetary sphere for a considerable time to come. Critically, the Parliament obtained these objectives *outside* of the formal budgetary procedure—a phenomenon still undocumented and unexplained by the regional integration literature, despite the fact that variance of the integration outcome in Europe cannot be fully accounted for without it.

A fundamental alteration of interorganizational relations is particularly evidenced in how the 1988, 1993, and 1999 IIAs have effectively suspended Article 272 of the Treaty for the duration of the current financial perspective. In other words, a critical piece of primary European law is left unheeded and not abided by; instead, informal rules are taking direct precedence over formal rules, despite the far great traditional legitimacy of the latter. Each of the three multi-annual financial perspectives, to which these IIAs have been connected, set a large portion of the formal budgetary procedure in a broader context than laid down by the Treaty in this Article—that is, outside of the treaty-prescribed formal sphere. A key portion held in abeyance is Article 272's stipulation that the maximum rate must be calculated yearly; the accords' fixing of the maximum rate over a multi-annual period amounts to a direct abrogation of primary EU law. In fact, the only element that remains in use is Paragraph 9, which relates to the Commission's calculation of the maximum rate of increase. This provision has remained in use because Part I of the 1999 IIA stipulates that within the budgetary framework the Parliament and Council agree to accept the Commission's yearly calculation of the maximum rate, in accordance with the long-standing attendant provision in Article 272.

The only exception to this informal practice since 1988 occurred in 1992 when the Three had fully to revert to the traditional procedure because the 1988 IIA had expired; moreover, the 1993 EU budget had to be fixed before the organizational actors were able to reach final agreement on the 1993 IIA. Still, each successive budget to the present day has literally departed from the Treaty with the exception of Paragraph 9 of Article 272. Parliamentary officials refer to this practice as a "permanent derogation," which is only a partial exaggeration.[52] Without this informal abrogation of the Treaty, one of the more consequential bargains in the history of the European Union could not have been achieved, namely the Council's automatic approval of any higher spending rate increases in return for the Parliament's renouncing its prior margin of maneuver for altering rate increases and switching spending categories, as well as its power to reject the budget.

Thus, as a result of an informal accord agreed by the organizational actors, one of the most important provisions of the Treaty has successively been suspended in de facto indefinite terms, for the Three concur that when a current budgetary accord ends a new one will be negotiated to take its place. Clearly, informal accords in these instances—as well as in others elsewhere—*have taken precedence over formal law.*[53] Thus, "there is good reason to believe that the old-style Council–Parliament battles about increases in the maximum rate, with spectacular rejections and occasional spillovers into the Court, have given way to a more subtle (and probably more obscure) but ultimately more effective strategy of slow but constant advance [for the Parliament]."[54] In view of the success of this trio of budgetary IIAs, it is clear that the Parliament has adroitly utilized informal interorganizational dynamics in the budgetary sphere as a prolific political wedge.[55] Without them, there is little question that it would be in a considerably worse interorganizational position in terms of its ability to achieve its preferences, policy-based and otherwise.

In essence, the Parliament has managed noteworthy success in reframing the context in which specific policy outcomes are pursued. This means of augmenting its authority is more indirect than procuring a slew of new outright powers, though not altogether less significant. As evidenced by the EU's informal interorganizational dynamics, one of the more effective means of achieving one's political objectives, which the shift in the EU organizational balance is ultimately about, is to frame issues or scenarios to one's own advantage. This appears to be what the Parliament has achieved in the budgetary sphere: a recasting of the EU's budgetary framework to its advantage. As a result, in terms of achieving a greater percentage of its objectives, the Parliament occupies a relatively superior position to that

---

[52] EU officials, joint interview by the author, European Parliament, Brussels, January 13, 1995.

[53] EU officials, joint interview by the author, European Parliament, Brussels, January 13, 1995.

[54] Westlake (1994*b*: 126).

[55] EU officials, joint interview by the author, European Parliament, Brussels, January 13, 1995.

of the Council in the altered framework. One can therefore conclude that the balance between the two organizational actors has shifted discernibly toward the Parliament's advantage.

Hence, although the Parliament has gained only a handful of new legislative powers—to compel the Council to convene budgetary conciliations and to engage in budgetary trilogues in particular—it has significantly augmented its influence over the policy-making process in the budget sphere. By altering the milieu of budgetary policy-making the Parliament in addition has achieved four major policy goals in this area of EU policy-making. Typical of the impetus behind the EU's informal interorganizational dynamics, despite the necessity of making certain changes in the policy-making process, precisely because formally amending the Treaty proved too prohibitive the Three turned to the informal sphere. The best indication that they have done so successfully is the fact that the Three have shown themselves intent on maintaining the informal framework that has not only built on the *acquis* but altered it as well.[56]

As indicated in the first section of this chapter, organizational-based integration implies a shift in the power relations of the Three, that is, an increase or a decrease of an organizational actor's legislative power vis-à-vis the others. As indicated above, to suggest that a massive degree of integration has taken place would constitute an exaggeration of the effect of the budgetary accords. Short of a major transfer of power from the Council to the Parliament, a subtler dynamic is at work, one that shifts relations between the organizational actors more by altering the budgetary policy framework than by redistributing a vast array of new powers.

Because it does so to the advantage of the Parliament, as evidenced by a policy package outcome which fulfills more of the Parliament's objectives than the Council's, one can conclude that the amalgam of informal budgetary accords has beyond any reasonable doubt augmented the Parliament's influence vis-à-vis the Council.[57] Whereas informal interorganizational dynamics in the budgetary sphere have, for the most part, resulted neither in mere institutionalization nor full-fledged integration, they have in fact tilted the organizational balance notably more toward the Parliament—and away from its counterparts—than was previously the case.[58]

---

[56] EU official, interview by the author, European Commission, Brussels, January 12, 1995.

[57] It is of course possible that the Council's preferences have moved closer to the Parliament's, but there is no demonstrable evidence of this.

[58] A bevy of officials concur; EU officials, separate interviews by the author, European Parliament, European Commission, European Council, January 12, 1995; January 13, 1995; July 27, 1994; January 11, 1995.

7

Informal Accords and Legislative Politics

Introduction

Arguably the strongest indicator of the significance of accords negotiated by the Three is how often and to what extent the institutional rules they encompass—created and developed in the informal sphere—are effectively transferred to the formal sphere by way of incorporation in an amending treaty. The Maastricht, Amsterdam, Nice, and Lisbon treaties formalized a large number of these rules. All of them were created by informal accords that had been used extensively, prior to being formally "swept up" in an amending treaty.

Thus, in each case, an amending treaty effectively enshrined already existing practices, putting an official stamp on bargains previously negotiated, but altering nothing in practice. In other words, as procedural rules they did not change; they were merely given greater stature and a definitive legal base, being transformed from mere policy-making rules in legal limbo to full-fledged policy-making rules. Whereas their legitimacy came to be based on the Treaty, previously it was based on bargains ensconced in informal accords that usually appear as IIAs but have also taken the practical form either of unilateral Council declarations or rules from the Parliament's Rules of Procedure.

This chapter will examine all informal accords of a nonbudgetary nature which nonetheless have had a marked impact on interorganizational relations in the European Union—that is, the *standard*, *procedural*, and *substantive* types of accords (but few if any of the *basic* type). An attempt will be made to discuss them in terms of the formal procedure that either necessitated their creation or with which they are most closely associated by EU practitioners. In each case they will be analyzed briefly in relation to the overall argument, namely that the dynamics of informal

186

interorganizational agreements involve both institutionalization (a re-inforcement of the status quo organizational balance) *and* integration (a redistribution of policy-making power and influence). Informal accords have grown in number and significance over time, though not always in parallel to concomitant activity in the formal sphere.

First, however, a reference caveat is necessary. Most informal accords up until the late 1990s did not appear in published form, with the exception of those in the budgetary sphere (which were often, though not always, published in the EU's *Official Journal*). As mentioned previously, quite a number of them were either not written down at all, or appeared in unconventional places such as exchanges of letters among different officials working in the various organizational actors, especially the presidents of the Parliament, the Commission, or the Council. As such, the empirical material described and analyzed below stems either from interviews with EU officials or secondary sources. Concerning the latter, almost all the accords below that lack formal references can be found in Corbett et al. (2000).[1]

External economic relations

One of the earliest informal accords in the EU dates from 1964, when the Council undertook in a letter from its President-in-Office, Joseph Luns (the Dutch foreign minister at the time), to allow the Parliament to hold a discussion with the Council prior to the beginning of negotiations for Association Agreements and to keep the Parliament informed of developments throughout the negotiation.[2] The procedure that has evolved is initiated by the Parliament holding a debate on the subject (in which both the Council and Commission participate), after which the Commission reports to the relevant parliamentary committees over the duration of the negotiation. That negotiation is followed by an appearance of the Council President-in-Office before the same committees to brief the relevant committees in the Parliament, confidentially, on the results of the

---

[1] The reader can assume, if no reference appears for an informal accord mentioned in the following text, that sources for the analysis are found in chapters 11, 12, or 13 of Corbett et al. (2000b).

[2] Association agreements are formal treaties between the EU and non-EU nation-states based on Article 310. They tend to set out reciprocal rights and obligations of a general nature, largely concerning trade access, EU aid, political dialogue, etc. Some also pertain to aspiring EU Member States and indicate a prospective timetable for membership.

negotiation. The Parliament often receives confidential briefings on the substance and content of negotiation mandates and outcomes, and on occasion the other two also participate in a debate after agreement has been reached (or broken down).[3]

In a May 1973 memorandum to the Parliament, the Council agreed to take part in any debate the Parliament convenes either in plenary or committee prior to the negotiation of external trade agreements, as well as to brief the Parliament throughout the negotiations. Furthermore, in an October 1973 letter from President-in-Office Westerterp, the Council pledged itself to allow a modified version of the Luns procedure to be applied to trade agreements and also committed to supplement the confidential briefing of committees with a formal, public appearance in plenary after an agreement is signed but not before it is finalized.

The growing spate of international agreements led the Council to undertake in a 1977 letter to distinguish between two different types of external agreements and alter the Luns–Westerterp procedures in the process. For "important" agreements the Council committed to brief the relevant committees at a special meeting in Brussels instead of at a Strasbourg plenary session, before which the President-in-Office would submit a written *aide-memoire*. For all other international agreements the Council committed itself simply to inform the Parliament in writing about the initiation and conclusion of negotiations, unless the Parliament specifically requested to follow the other procedure within two weeks. As a part of the 1983 Stuttgart Solemn Declaration, the Council further committed to formally consult the Parliament on all "significant" international agreements prior to their conclusion, including accession treaties. The Luns–Westerterp procedures were also extended to cover all "important" agreements.

The SEA generated a discrepancy in the Parliament's powers regarding the EU's external agreements. Whereas the Parliament's assent was required for Association Agreements—which often only involved additional protocols or other minor adjustments—according to the Treaty the Parliament was merely consulted for trade and economic agreements. The Parliament reacted by pressing for the Council and Commission to invoke Article 310 (re: Association) whenever there was a question over classification of an external agreement. Hence, the Europe Agreements and the European Economic Area (EEA) agreement were classified as association agreements. In addition, the Parliament changed its Rules of Procedure to treat any

---

[3] This section draws extensively on Corbett et al. (2000b: 195–213).

188

"significant international agreement" (the only type that the Stuttgart Declaration had stipulated Parliament be consulted on) in accordance with the assent procedure (this simple legislative procedure simply offers the Parliament a veto on any Council decisions). In other words, it expected the Council not to proceed unless it gave its assent to do so.

The Council was amenable to this assertion on the part of the Parliament and altered in a highly symbolic way the relevant treaty provisions in the Maastricht Treaty in order to provide for the Parliament's assent for all "important agreements." An important agreement was defined as any that established a specific institutional framework, had important budgetary implications, or required the amendment of EU legislation related to the codecision procedure. For all other external agreements the Parliament has continued to be consulted, with the lone exception of the normal practice allowing the Council to assign deadlines for the rendering of Parliament's opinion.

All of these informal accords in the area of external relations have extended the Parliament's role in the approval of international agreements, much of which was based purely on the accords' informal institutions until being formally swept up by the Maastricht Treaty. Up until 1993, when Maastricht legally came into force, these informal accords served to extend the Parliament's limited oversight powers, thereby further legitimating its supervisory role. Furthermore, the Commission undertook in a February 1990 statement by President Delors to include MEPs on delegations negotiating international agreements as observers, which has provided the Parliament with increased information about the negotiations (and a modicum of increased influence).

Although its only formal power outside of the budgetary sphere remained its right to be consulted, the Parliament's position in the mid-1980s stood some distance from where it had started out in the late 1950s. Excluding the two informal accords in the budgetary sphere, prior to the SEA the Parliament was already the beneficiary of a wide range of informal accords, most of which took the form of unilateral undertakings by the Council and the Commission—these served to codify the informal bargains they had struck with the Parliament. The latter benefited considerably from being informed with greater regularity and in greater depth, as well as from coming into much more personal contact with officials from the other organizational actors, particularly the Council. The Parliament's influence was amplified as a result.[4]

If one takes account of the budgetary informal accords of 1975 and 1982, then clearly the Parliament had also gained increased authority via informal interorganizational dynamics by this stage. Outside the budgetary sphere, however, the effect of the aforementioned new institutional rules of conduct (ensconced in informal accords) did not extend a great deal beyond the institutionalization outcome. Additional rules for the consultation procedure were informally created, but the crux of the procedure remained unaltered. Even the Parliament's delay power, which it created of its own accord after 1980, did not significantly shift relations between them. Nonetheless, the new rules bequeathed by informal accords were not inert. In fact, most of those discussed thus far were procedural type accords and therefore of consequence, militating in favor of integration if not contributing wholly to such an outcome.

Commission–Parliament relations

The SEA and its concomitant deficiencies, the raft of envisaged legislation, the short- and long-term deadlines, the new legislative *navette* (the cooperation procedure), and a host of treaty gaps and ambiguities which threatened to undermine it if they were not rectified, together necessitated some sort of reinforcement of interorganizational relations and the establishment of new formal and informal institutional rules.[5] The efforts to rectify these deficiencies and meet the challenges presented by the SEA increased the need for interorganizational dialogue, which partly reflected the closer contact engendered by the cooperation procedure, but which also reflected an improvement of the structure of the SEA itself.

In the late 1980s, there was a common view among various officials in the Three that the cooperation procedure as laid out in old Article 149 was complicated, vague, and riddled with drafting anomalies.[6] Even the Council was dissatisfied and open to options for improving the status quo at the time. In a manner that would become more common thereafter, the Parliament viewed this set of circumstances as auspicious. At its behest, the Three

---

[4] Corbett et al. (2000b: 207).
[5] Westlake (1994*a*: 97).
[6] Westlake (1994*a*: 21).

created the Inter-Institutional Coordination Group, more commonly known as the Neunreither Group.[7]

The purpose of the Neunreither Group has been to maintain efficiency, iron out procedural problems as they develop, and solve the practical problems of making the organizational actors work together smoothly when new procedures are introduced to the policy-making process. The group meets on the Thursday preceding the Parliament's plenary session in Strasbourg and consists of representatives from the Commission, members of the secretariats of the Council, Economic and Social Committee secretariat members, officials from the current Council Presidency, and Parliamentary officials from the secretariat and Office of the President. Initially the understanding was that the group would deal exclusively with matters related to the SEA, but its members agreed to extend their remit to deal with items on the Parliament's plenary agenda and to establish priorities for future plenary agendas. The Neunreither Group became a technical talking shop for officials of the Three, the value of which was recognized across the Three.[8]

Regarding the problems with the cooperation procedure, one of the Neunreither Group's more important actions was to resolve the Treaty's failure to establish precisely at what point the Parliament's three-month period to take action on the Council's common position—that is, the Council's preliminary decision—during the second reading actually begins. The Group determined that the Parliament should be allowed to begin to take action the day on which it receives copies of the common position in all nine of the EU's working languages. The Group has also become responsible for monitoring follow-up to interorganizational agreements and was active preparing for and then sorting out the procedural minutiae resulting from the Maastricht Treaty. Other matters it has successfully dealt with include determining the nature of Commission reexaminations, providing structure to the Commission's formal responses to the Council's common positions, and creating a common coding system for all SEA and Maastricht proposals. Basically, each time the members of the Group agree to something in this setting they are creating new informal institutions.

On a more political level, the necessity of finding ways to work together despite their differences provided the impetus for the Commission and the

---

[7] The Group is named after its former chairman, Karl Heinz Neunreither, one of the Parliament's former Director Generals.

[8] EU official, interview by the author, European Commission, Brussels, January 24, 2002.

Parliament to arrive at a number of understandings and informal arrangements which culminated in the *Code of Conduct*, a 1990 informal accord. The Commission proposed the idea of negotiating an accord for the purpose of governing relations between them, particularly in the numerous areas of mutual dispute and contention. Although the Council is not a party to the accord, the accord's institutions relate directly to it in several instances, such as its habit of reconsulting the Parliament when original proposals are radically altered. These informal rules have enabled various formal procedures in the Treaty to operate more smoothly.

In the Code of Conduct, the Commission makes multiple commitments to the Parliament: to urge the Council to wait for the Parliament's opinion on all measures (even those outside the scope of the cooperation procedure); to explain its reasons for not incorporating any second reading parliamentary amendments it rejects at the next meeting of the relevant parliamentary committee; to forward any proposals it modifies to the Parliament and keep it fully abreast of the important aspects of Commission–Council discussions; to ensure the Council reconsults the Parliament when it substantially modifies a Commission proposal and to take the Council to the Court whenever it fails to do so; regarding international agreements, to take account of the Parliament's preference to select a legal base related to Article 310 (which gives the Parliament assent power) and to include MEPs as observers in EU delegations negotiating these agreements; and to increase informal discussions surrounding the Commission's decisions regarding the legal base of its proposals. These undertakings generally reflect the Parliament's desire to make the most of its allotted formal powers. The informal commitments on the Parliament's part mostly reflect Commission discontent with the sluggishness of the Parliament's legislative activity and its pledges to change its behavior.

In the parliamentary debate concerning the negotiation of the Code of Conduct, President Delors remarked: "The Commission...took what amounted to seven decisions which it believes will help to improve relations between Parliament and the Commission. And we know from the past that good relations between our institutions allow the Community to make progress....Which brings me, in conclusion, to the distinction between the day-to-day democratic deficit...and the institutional democratic deficit. On the day-to-day deficit, I trust that the Code of Conduct I have outlined will produce progress that is satisfactory all round. In any event, this House can always alert the Commission—or its President if you like—and arrange an evaluation meeting with the Enlarged Bureau."[9]

Agreement on putting into place the informal institutions that comprise the Code of Conduct was considered a significant improvement by both organizational actors. Mutual understanding between the Parliament and the Commission was considerably enhanced as a result of the more intensive interorganizational dialogue. Of the two, the Parliament was the greater beneficiary in that the Commission's commitments to it included a number of new procedural modifications, whereas every commitment made by the Parliament involved a pledge to improve the workings of current procedures, such as appointing its rapporteurs—the MEPs taking lead action on a given piece of proposed legislation—in a timely manner. In conjunction with the 1988 informal accord on budgetary discipline and the concurrent fixing of the financial perspectives, the Code of Conduct accord became an important element in fully completing implementation of the SEA, particularly with regard to the "1992 Program" to complete the single internal market.[10]

In the wake of the SEA's entry into force, the Parliament's dialogue with the Council expanded. Communication and meetings between either committee chairmen or rapporteurs and presidents-in-office increased, and committee chairman began occasionally to be invited to pertinent Council meetings. Links between parliamentary committee secretariats and their counterparts in the other organizational actors were also cultivated. Most significant, however, was the agreement of an informal institution involving routine appearances of the different Councils' Ministers-in-Office before pertinent parliamentary committees. The status quo now involves each appearing at least twice before a committee during each six-month Council Presidency. Upon the inception of the cooperation procedure in 1986, these encounters began to allow increased opportunities for the Parliament to press the Council to adopt any of its amendments still pending ahead of second reading. Today, the Commission also reports regularly to the parliamentary committees on Council decisions.

[9] European Parliamentary Debates OJ N 3–386 13.2.90 pp. 29–30. The Enlarged Bureau used to refer to a leadership team in the Parliament comprising its President, the Vice Presidents, and the MEPs leading its various political groups (i.e., its parties). However, this group has since split into the Conference of Presidents (the President of Parliament and the Political Group leaders) and the Bureau (the President, Vice Presidents, and the Questors—the MEPs elected to deal with internal administrative matters).

[10] Westlake (1994a: 63).

After the entry into force of the Maastricht Treaty in 1993, the Parliament decided to pursue the conclusion of a new Code of Conduct accord with the Commission in order to enhance its supervision and control over it. In late 1994, the Parliament communicated its intentions to the Commission, and in January 1995 it circulated a new draft Code of Conduct to the Commission. As of March the two concluded negotiations with a final draft which the Parliament formally approved in plenary in mid-March. The *1995 Code of Conduct* represents a major expansion of its 1990 predecessor. Whereas the 1990 agreement consisted of a single section, the 1995 update consists of ten different sections. It retains or expands all but one of the previous ten or so informal institutions, incorporates several other previously existing informal institutions, and adds over twenty new ones. Once more, the bulk of the accord comprises commitments of the Commission to the Parliament, some of them involving significant departures from the status quo.

Several changes are worth mentioning. In the first informal accord of its kind, the Commission pledged not only to remind the Council that it must reconsult the Parliament whenever it alters the legal bases of a proposal or departs substantially from the original proposal but also to inform the Parliament when it does so in either case. The Commission further pledged to forward drafts of its green and white papers to the Parliament and to inform it whenever it intends to withdraw legislative proposals. In one of the more important rule-inscribed bargains, the Commission committed to withdrawing any legislative proposals the Parliament rejects under the codecision procedure, which amounts to a new *de facto* power for the Parliament. The Commission further pledged to "take the utmost account of" the Parliament's requests under Article 192 (at the time, the Parliament's new indirect right of initiative), though it was short of the guarantee for which the Parliament was aiming. And in a departure from the Luns–Westerterp informal accord, the Commission undertook confidentially to inform the relevant parliamentary committee of its draft recommendations for negotiating instructions concerning international agreements—on top of keeping the relevant committee fully informed throughout the negotiations. Once more, the Parliament's commitments contained nothing new in terms of status quo departures.

The Parliament achieved quite a lot with the implementation of the second Code of Conduct, particularly in light of the assurances from the Commission to treat it "on an absolutely equal basis" in a phrase that appeared throughout the document. With reference to earlier drafts, the Parliament achieved most of its objectives. The only major objective it did not achieve was eliciting a Commission undertaking automatically to accept every parliamentary recommendation for a new legislative proposal. It did manage to secure its other major objectives regarding the legal bases and particularly regarding the commitment from the Commission to withdraw proposals that the Parliament rejects under codecision.

By not asking for too much or for any extreme commitments, according to officials in the Commission, the Parliament made it very difficult for the Commission to disregard its influence attempts. Commission officials viewed this at the time as a new parliamentary shrewdness—the Parliament placing more pressure on the Commission to acquiesce to its demands, ironically enough, by asking for less.[11] This behavior was quite unlike that of the actor throughout the 1980s and much of the 1990s, when the Parliament's zeal for increased power and influence seemed to permeate practically its every action (this "getting more through less" strategy in the 2000s began to make serious inroads into its traditional "shoot for the moon" strategy). In any case, from the second Code of Conduct's panoply of Commission undertakings, it has become clear that the Commission was rapidly becoming accountable to the Parliament.

Given the Parliament's newly acquired *de facto* power in particular, via the revamped Code of Conduct, the Parliament was able to augment its authority beyond a mere reinforcement of previously existing procedures. While some of the newly created rules were inert, others significantly altered the status quo. Thus, while further institutionalization occurred in the process, a shift in relations between the Parliament and the Commission was clearly evident as a result of this particular informal accord. This conclusion is all the more evidenced by other informal accords still to be discussed, such as the accord that presaged the Parliament's relatively new formal power under Article 214 regarding its vote of approval of the Commission. As shall be seen, the Code of Conduct has helped to engender a consequential shift in the organizational balance among the Three.

This is evidenced directly by two additional informal accords in the 2000s, both bilateral accords between the Parliament and Commission which essentially carry on from the Code of Conducts under the new rubric of Framework Agreements. A new norm developed at the outset of the 2000s, whereby the Commission is obliged to revise this series of bilateral accords each time a new Commission comes into office—hence the predictable follow-up revision of the 2000 Framework Agreement with the 2005 Framework Agreement.

---

[11] EU official, interview by the author, European Commission, Brussels, January 24, 2002.

The 2000 Framework Agreement represents a clear advance over its 1995 predecessor and is more binding regarding the commitments that are largely one way: from the Commission to the Parliament.[12] The accord introduces greater accountability to the Parliament when the Commission formulates its annual legislative program, which tends to presage what pieces of legislation the Commission will propose for the following year. Several rules commit the Commission not only to keep the Parliament well informed on a specifically timely basis but also take "utmost account" of the Parliament's own guidelines for the Commission's program. Moreover, the Commission uses the same language to allow the Parliament more accountability over any considerations it makes to alter the legal basis of any legislative proposal; if the Commission fails to take on board the Parliament's views about such, it must provide a written set of reasons in a specifically timely manner explaining why it did not accede to the Parliament's wishes.

In the accord the Commission further commits itself to inform the Parliament about all substantive discussions it has on a bilateral basis with the Council, another departure from the previous accord; specifically, the Commission commits to informing the Parliament of any alterations of its proposals that are dictated by Council preferences. It further undertakes to try to prevent the Council from reaching any common position before taking on board the Parliament's opinion, for any legislation outside of the scope of the codecision procedure. If the Commission has one of its proposals amended by the Council, it commits to reconsulting the Parliament in each instance. If the Parliament rejects a Commission proposal outside of codecision scope, the latter commits to withdraw its proposals except under extraordinary circumstances. This is a major commitment, and as with all of these new rules not called for by the Treaty.

The Parliament commits to a few things, which amount to less substantive commitments to the Commission: to meet deadlines regularly, appoint the chairpersons of its parliamentary reports in a timely manner, consider Commission priorities in developing its legislative program guidelines, and to bring some of its internal practices in line with the Commission legislative program.

The 2005 Framework picks up where its predecessor left off and involves two major new powers for the Parliament.[13] This accord was negotiated with the advent of the Barrosso Commission. The first and most important

[12] OJ C 121, 24.4.2001, p. 22.
[13] OJ C 117 E, 18.5.2009, p. 123.

gives the Parliament a veto power over the nominations of individual commissioners—the appointed heads of all the executive agencies of the Commission—in addition to the one it holds on the basis of an informal accord over the Presidential nominee of the Commission and the overall Commission college as a whole (as indicated above, the President has to gain a majority vote in Parliament to stay in office). Under the rubric of "political responsibility" the Commission commits to abiding by Parliament's votes on individual commissioner designates and if under extraordinary circumstances it wishes to proceed, the Commission President must come to the Parliament and explain this in a plenary session in person. Informally, even Commission officials view this as a *de facto* veto power, unable to envision such a scenario given the politics of the situation and what the Parliament would do in response. Moreover, President Barrosso himself made a verbal commitment to abiding by the Parliament's understanding of the new rule. "This is a kick in the crotch of Commission collegiality. Before only the whole Commission had to go [if it did not receive parliamentary approval]; now they can remove them one at a time [individual Commissioners]."[14]

The second new major commitment to the Parliament involves a Commission obligation to open up the veil of secrecy on who lobbies it. The so-called expert groups of lobbyists will now have their members reported on by the Commission to the Parliament, including specific information on which companies are involved. There is simply no precedent for such a rule in the EU. For its part the Parliament merely makes a new commitment to reorganize its plenary sessions to put more of the work requiring the presence of Commission officials into the same working day.

Overall this pair of accords tilts the balance of bilateral relations far more in favor of the Parliament, for fully four-fifths of the commitments involved favor the Parliament at the Commission's expense.[15] Together these accords "have a more binding character" to them, because they are specific and cover so much more than their predecessors. As such, the Commission's accountability to the Parliament increases measurably with each accord.[16] Particularly because of these two major capitulations to the Parliament, the Commission is now actively considering a strategy to fight back and may not agree to negotiate a new accord in 2010 in light of

[14] EU official, interview by the author, European Commission, Brussels, July 4, 2007.
[15] EU official, interview by the author, European Commission, Brussels, July 4, 2007 (interviews on this date were conducted with seven different Commission officials).
[16] EU official, interview by the author, European Commission, Brussels, July 4, 2007.

how much internal backlash has taken place in the years following finalization of the 2005 accord: the Commission "internally is starting to wonder seriously whether this will go on and on if a stop is not put to it."[17]

From the Commission's perspective, each time the Parliament aims for the stars in putting considerable pressure on it to do a deal: "It's cynical—ha, ha—but it's the reality."[18] Resistance has thus become "vital" to resist the trend of these two accords making Commission commitments to the Parliament far more detailed and binding at the same time. The primary causal catalyst for these accords involves the issue linkage second-order constraint, for the Parliament holds considerable leverage over the Commission and has consistently issued informal political sanctions whenever the Commission has tried to back off from one of these informal institutions—hence, the ratchet effect is alive and well in the EU.

Although the Treaty of Rome provided the Parliament with the power to dismiss the Commission—by firing the President and the appointed Commissioners—it prescribed no role for the Parliament in the appointment of the Commission.[19] However, by informal means the Parliament has cultivated a rather prominent role in this process, some of which has been formalized by being incorporated in the Maastricht Treaty. Treaty provisions now require the nominated Commission to be subjected to a parliamentary vote of approval prior to taking office. A negative vote by the Parliament would constitute a formal rejection of the President-designate and his or her would-be Commissioners, obligating Member States to nominate a new team. The formal rules that stipulate such procedure originated in an informal accord.

Prior to Maastricht, the Members States collectively appointed each Commission to a four-year term of office. According to the Treaty, the Commission President was supposed to be nominated for a two-year term by the members of the Commission. However, in yet another indication of the Treaty's malleable nature, in practice the Member States have always selected the Commission President and automatically reappointed that person to serve a total of four years with the rest of the Commissioners. After the Parliament became directly elected, it used its Rules of Procedure "to create" a plenary session debate and vote of confidence for incoming

---

[17] EU official, interview by the author, European Commission, Brussels, July 4, 2007.

[18] EU official, interview by the author, European Commission, Brussels, July 4, 2007.

[19] "The Commission" consists of the President of the Commission and the 20 appointed Members of the Commission—or Commissioners—each of whom heads one or more of the Community's 24 bureaucratic agencies, known as Directorates-General (or DGs), and is expected to uphold the general interest of the Community.

Commissions on the occasion of the presentation of their legislative work programs to the Parliament for the first time. This practice became routine procedure via its status as an informal institution, which the Council acknowledged in the Stuttgart Solemn Declaration (the 1983 informal accord).

The Parliament first applied this procedure to the Thorn Commission in 1981 and then to the Delors Commissions of 1985 and 1989. On the latter two occasions the Commission demonstrated its acceptance of the procedure by waiting for the Parliament's approval before being administered the oath of office by the ECJ. This was a symbolic gesture by the Commission, whose consent to the Parliament's predilection set an important precedent to the effect that the Commission would be unable to take office without the Parliament's vote of confidence; tacit acceptance of the practice constituted the existence of an informal institution (as confirmed by the Stuttgart Declaration). In the view of the Parliament, violation of this institutional rule would provide firm grounds for dismissing the Commission through a motion of censure.[20]

In the Stuttgart Declaration the Council also undertook to consult the Parliament's Enlarged Bureau over its choice for Commission President. Beginning in 1984 the Council President-in-Office has on each occasion consulted the Parliament in this manner, except in 1988 when this consultation took place with the President of the Parliament during his attendance of a Council meeting. In 1994 this consultation took place during a July meeting between Chancellor Kohl and the Parliament's Conference of Presidents (of political parties), which has replaced the Enlarged Bureau as the chief internal decision-making body of the Parliament.

Hence, the Maastricht provisions for altering appointment of the Commission formalized existing practices, sweeping up a number of informal institutions found in the Stuttgart Declaration and the Parliament's Rules of Procedure. The most significant of these—the Parliament's vote of confidence—thereby became enshrined in treaty form, which was further reinforced by treaty language stipulating that it must take place prior to the Commission taking office. The incorporation of this informal practice in the Treaty has consolidated the vote of confidence particularly by ensuring that the whole of the Parliament is consulted on the Commission President-designate instead of only a small section of it (the Conference of Presidents), thereby lending further legitimacy to the practice.

---

[20] EU official, interview by the author, European Parliament, Brussels, January 15, 1995.

Thus, the Parliament's vote of approval is now tantamount to a vote of confirmation. Furthermore, its role as overseer of the Commission has been enhanced still further now that the terms of both Parliament and Commission have been made to coincide, although obviously this treaty provision is not based on an informal accord. The relationship between the Parliament and the Commission has yet to achieve status akin to that of the lower house of parliament and the government of a national system, but the Maastricht provisions can be viewed as a sizable step in that direction.

The Commission headed by former Luxembourg Prime Minister Jacques Santer was the first to be appointed in accordance with the modified procedure. In typical fashion, via the post-Maastricht 1994 revision of its Rules of Procedure, the Parliament sought to expand its role in the appointment of the Commission still further by cajoling it to conform to additional proposed modifications of the appointment procedure. The Parliament's rules were altered to call for the Presidential nominee to present a statement in plenary that is followed by a full plenary debate of the individual's fitness for office culminating in a roll-call vote.[21] Although the Treaty is silent on the issue, in the event of a negative vote the Parliament's Rules call for the nominee to be withdrawn and a new nomination put forward.

Considering the circumstances of his compromise appointment, Santer had little choice but to participate. In light of how the whole of the EU was in a frenetic state given the British veto of the original President-designate, Belgian Prime Minister Jean Luc Dehaene, Santer literally had to campaign among MEPs on his own behalf in a wholly unprecendented fashion. By visiting the different political party groups in order to win their backing, he set a further precedent. Quite clearly, a vote of disapproval would have forced him to stand down, thereby necessitating a new choice by the Member State governments. After a bit of brinkmanship and a rather vituperative plenary question and answer session with Santer, the Parliament voted narrowly in favor of his appointment: the stakes were high.

In addition to this, the Parliament managed to coax the Commission into abiding by its Rules of Procedure by sending each individual commissioner-designate to "hearings" before the parliamentary committees corresponding to their Commission DG portfolios. The event was modeled on US Senate-style confirmation hearings, which the Parliament had actually sent its officials to research in the United States. The Parliament's original idea was to hold individual votes of approval for each commissioner-designate, but it feared a proposal on this basis would give the Commission grounds

---

[21] Rule 33, June 1994 Rules of Procedure, the European Parliament.

for refusing to participate. Instead the Parliament and Commission agreed that the appearances would involve simple question and answer sessions, and the MEPs were instructed by the Conference of Presidents to treat the unofficially appointed commissioners with "kid gloves" and were specifically told not to be abrasive in the sessions.[22] Cleverly, according to Commission officials, the Parliament planned closed-door committee sessions to follow, which were discharged to draft letters of recommendation to the President of Parliament.[23]

The "hearings" then took place, and most proceeded without difficulty. However, the Parliament found four particular commissioner-designates lacking. To the surprise of most observers, after he had received the various committee recommendation letters, President Haensch called a press conference and demanded the Commission take action, even hinting it should consider replacing some of them. This maneuver acted effectively as an indirect way of holding individual approval votes, and the Parliament succeeded in imposing it on the Commission. The Commission had wanted to hold the question and answer sessions earlier (before the 1994 winter holidays), but the Parliament refused on the grounds that enlargement proceedings interfered. Hence, the old Commission was forced to remain unofficially in office beyond its legal mandate—which expired on January 7, 1995— effectively rendering it a caretaker Commission. This occurrence was unprecedented; it demonstrated that the Parliament had even managed to gain control of the timing of the process.[24]

All of this took place prior to the Parliament's vote of approval for the Commission as a whole, which forced Santer to meet with President Haensch and other MEPs yet again. Had he not offered enough concessions to mollify the Parliament's concerns, including taking part of a portfolio away from one of the commissioner-designates, the Parliament might have voted the new Commission down (as indeed it appeared on the verge of doing). In the end the Parliament voted approvingly, though not by the typically wide margin that it had in the past. One can be certain that, according to the ratchet principle, the Parliament will seek to move still further beyond this scenario on the next propitious occasion. Certainly it will attempt to insert this informal procedure in future IGCs, but short of a treaty alteration it conceivably had several options in 1998: to actually hold individual votes in committee, to hold a preliminary vote on either

---

[22] EU official, interview by the author, European Parliament, Brussels, January 15, 1995.
[23] EU official, interview by the author, European Commission, Brussels, January 12, 1995.
[24] EU official, interview by the author, European Commission, Brussels, January 12, 1995.

all or some commissioner-designates, or convene longer, more involved hearings over a several-day period.

This episode provides a salient example of the Parliament's technique of creating an often elaborate informal procedure and bringing enough pressure to bear on the other organizational actors—in this case also exploiting the politics of the situation, i.e. severe preference intensitie—to win their acquiescence to its scheme. The treaty provisions constituted the thin edge of the blade, as it were, wielded by the Parliament in the form of an informal accord in which it managed to secure the participation of the other actors. The Parliament managed to parlay a specific power into something more substantial, putting itself in a decidedly better position. In this case the Commission became, by its own admission, more accountable to the Parliament than it previously had been.[25]

This was accomplished by parliamentary leveraging on the basis of a single treaty provision. With the Commission under direct pressure from the investiture vote, the Parliament managed to exploit the situation to its advantage. Thus, effectively it used the technique of brokering informal accords to create large portions of the appointment process. Through activity in the informal sphere, relations between the Commission and the Parliament were further altered beyond the shift brought about by Maastricht. In the words of one of the Parliament's most knowledgeable constitutionalists, former MEP Sir Christopher Prout: "It is no exaggeration to say that the extension of the term of office of the Commission from four to five years and the acquisition by Parliament of a veto over the appointment of the new Commission have transformed the constitutional balance of power between the Parliament and the Commission."[26]

Improving legislative procedures

Although informal accords in the EU have only recently begun to receive much attention, their history stretches back to the early 1960s when and there was a need to improve the *consultation procedure*. Most of these extant accords are not so much esoteric as quotidian in nature. As in national political systems, themselves fairly riddled with an assortment of unreported informal accords, informal accords in the EU have become part of the policy-making status quo to the point that none of the organizational

---

[25] EU official, interview by the author, European Commission, Brussels, January 15, 1995.
[26] European Parliamentary Debates, OJ, N 3–434 (September 14, 1993): 39–40.

actors in practice distinguish between which of their policy procedural practices have a distinct treaty base and which have nothing more than an informal base—in the cut and thrust of policy-making, rules are rules.

Among the early difficulties with the consultation procedure was the lack of clarity as to whether it was the Council or the Commission who was meant to consult the Parliament, ambiguity over the extent of the consultation of the Parliament, and questions involving whether or not the Parliament should be reconsulted if the text of which it was originally consulted is altered. As a result, in a series of informal accords throughout the 1960s and early 1970s the Council committed to more closely involving the Parliament with regard to most legislative and nonlegislative proposals.

In March 1960, the Council agreed to seek the Parliament's opinion on all matters of importance, whether the Treaty specified doing so or not. These became known as "voluntary consultations." In February 1964 it undertook to consult the Parliament on all legislative proposals, except those that were urgent, confidential, or of marginal importance. In November 1968, the Council agreed to seek the Parliament's opinion on most nonlegislative texts, including Council resolutions and Commission memoranda. And in May 1973 it undertook to consult the Parliament on all texts.[27] Effectively speaking, each of these constituted single-rule informal accords—requested by the Parliament and granted by the Council. They were rules to live by, and political sanctions were applied by the Parliament whenever the Council failed to live up to them—chiefly in the form of delaying providing its legislative "opinion" where the Treaty prescribed it.[28]

A number of informal accords were also created with intent to improve the quality of the consultation procedure, that is, increasing the extent of the consultation as opposed to increasing the number of legislation categories to which the consultation procedure applies. In a series of letters exchanged between the Council President-in-Office and the President of the Parliament—dated November 1969, March 1970, and July 1970—the Council committed itself to informing the Parliament of its reasons for departing from the Parliament's "opinion" whenever it did so over the course of adopting EU legislation.[29] At first the commitment was confined to legislation with financial implications but was eventually extended to basically all legislative proposals.

---

[27] Today the Council consults the Parliament on all texts aside from those of a temporary or purely technical nature.

[28] EU official, interview by the author, European Parliament, Brussels, January 22, 2002.

[29] The President-in-Office refers to the foreign minister of the Member State government currently occupying the Council Presidency.

The communiqué of the 1972 Paris Heads of Government Summit expressed a desire to strengthen the Parliament's powers of control, inviting the Council and Commission to put into effect a series of measures designed to reinforce those powers and to improve their relations with the Parliament. In the June 1973 *Communication from the Commission of the European Communities on Practical Measures to Strengthen the Powers of Control of the Parliament and to Improve Relations Between the Parliament and the Commission,*[30] the Commission reiterated a host of commitments previously made to the Parliament and introduced a few additional measures. The Commission expressed its approval of the Parliament's suggestions to increase opportunities for the Parliament to question the Commission and to hold specific parliamentary debates on issues of political substance between the Parliament and the other two organizational actors. The Commission agreed not only to communicate with the Parliament whether or not it agreed with the Parliament's political approaches during or after such debates, but also to participate in additional debates were the Parliament to indicate its desire. It also expressed approval of the Parliament's suggestions for holding hearings for the purpose of examining EU policies and their implementation.

The Commission committed itself to making its practice of expressing its views of all parliamentary amendments more systematic by conducting an overall review of all the Parliament's expressed opinions and views, after each plenary session, to ensure that any undertakings it made to the Parliament were put into effect. At the beginning of the following plenary session either the President or Vice President with responsibility for parliamentary affairs is to present a consolidated statement of any action taken on the basis of the Parliament's views. The Commission also undertook to press the Council to institute a regular procedure for a second reading in the Parliament whenever the Council departs markedly from the first reading of the text. It suggested that a Council representative should be present during any second readings to explain the reasons behind its actions. It further suggested that after the second reading the Council should allow the Parliament to present its views once more prior to the Council's final decision.

Also in response to the Paris Summit at that juncture, the Council made a series of commitments in October 1973 under the guise of an informal discussion document with the heading *Improvement of Relations Between the*

---

[30] The European Commission, Document (73) 999, 1973.

Council and the European Parliament. These included pledges to reply to all oral as well as written questions, to consult the Parliament within one week of receiving Commission proposals, not to examine a Commission proposal until it has received the Parliament's opinion (except in cases of urgency and unreasonable delay), to better inform the Parliament about any action taken in response to its opinions, and to hold general quarterly meetings between the presidents of both organizations. In addition, both the Commission and the Council agreed the same year to reconsult the Parliament whenever significant changes are made to texts on which it has already delivered its opinion.[31]

Although no explicit powers were gained as a result of any of these informal institutions and accords, the Parliament clearly benefited from their creation and promulgation. The Parliament's novel inclusion in nearly every sphere of activity allowed MEPs henceforth to take part in important legislative discussions, have their views heard, and apply greater pressure. Although this hardly seems significant in today's terms, at that stage it was of enormous significance from the Parliament's perspective, as among other things the Council had altogether bypassed both the Parliament and the Commission in its adoption of the first EU budget. The informal agreement to consult, and reconsult if necessary, the Parliament in a timely manner on virtually all EU texts not only contributed to the Parliament's inchoate legitimacy but also represented a series of clear departures from the Treaty. These new informal rules would not be fully exploited until after direct elections in 1979, but they provided a foundation on which the elected Parliament would build. Obviously, the Parliament continued to lack any means of formally blocking Council actions or imposing its will on either of the other organizational actors, but links formed at this stage allowed future Parliaments to go further.

More recently, the Council has made additional commitments to the Parliament with regard to consultation. In a 1981 Resolution, the Council undertook to inform the Parliament of its reasons for discounting parliamentary opinion, via the President-in-Office either verbally in plenary session or in writing (in the cases of financial considerations always in plenary). In the 1983, Stuttgart solemn declaration the Council pledged that, in addition to its providing the Parliament with an annual report, the President-in-Office would issue a report during each six-month Presidency. A 1990 exchange of letters between the President of the Parliament and the

---

[31] EU official, interview by the author, Council of Ministers, Brussels, May 5, 2003.

President-in-Office of the Immigration Council established an informal accord whereby the latter meets with the responsible parliamentary committee, with the Commission represented, once every six months to discuss issues connected to immigration and the free movement of persons. And in a separate 1990 exchange of letters, the Commission undertook to keep the Parliament regularly and discreetly informed of its work concerning multilateral surveillance, that is, tracking Member States' attainment of the convergence criteria during Stage One of EMU.[32]

An important aspect of the changes that affected the consultation procedure involved an actor not among the Three, namely the ECJ. With the advent of direct elections in 1979, the Parliament's legitimacy grew considerably relative to its prior existence as a body of appointed officials. As a result, the Parliament's accountability shifted from the governments that had appointed its members to the European electorate to which MEPs have since appealed for election every five years. This development proved to be rather important to the ECJ when it ruled in the 1980 Isoglucose case that the Council had violated the Treaty by failing to wait for the Parliament's opinion prior to making its decision.[33]

The Isoglucose ruling set a precedent dictating that the Council could not proceed to adopt any EU legislation under the consultation procedure without the Parliament's formally expressed opinion. The extant consultation procedure does not involve any consequential policy-making power for the Parliament. Indeed, the Parliament merely offers its opinion on a piece of Commission-proposed legislation, any piece of which the Commission may or may not choose to include in its modified proposal (in the form of amendments); the Council then has the choice whether to adopt the proposal into law as is (via QMV), reject it (via blocking minority), or amend it prior to adopting it (via unanimity). Prior to this case before the ECJ, the Council would intermittently act prior to receiving the Parliament's formal opinion.

Building on the Isoglucose ruling, the Parliament used its Rules of Procedure "to create" a consistent mechanism for indefinitely postponing the delivery of its formal opinion within the consultation procedure, an action that amounted to something of an informal rule legitimized by the ECJ's ruling. On this basis, the Parliament developed a practice of voting to send

[32] EU official, interview by the author, Council of Ministers, Brussels, May 5, 2003.

[33] The ECJ declared the Parliament's consultation power "an essential factor in the institutional balance intended by the Treaty. Although limited, it reflects at Community level the fundamental principle that the peoples should take part in the exercise of power through the intermediary of a representative assembly." See Cases 138/79 and 139/79.

206

a proposal back to committee if it found the Commission's response to its amendments unsatisfactory. In so doing, not only did the Parliament basically grant itself a *de facto* power of delay, which was not provided for in the Treaty, but it further discovered in its Rules of Procedure a tool it could use to make institutional adjustments and bring pressure to bear on the other organizational actors. In the run up to the SEA, the Parliament began to venture beyond the remit of the Treaty by its creative use of its legal right to draft its own internal rules—rules it would then attempt to foist on its stronger organizational counterparts.

Almost every one of the aforementioned informal accords in this section constitute *procedural accords*, the accord type comprising new institutional rules that alter the status quo, albeit not to the degree of *substantive accords*. As indicated in Chapter 1, the latter involve a reallocation of policy-making power while the former do not transfer power as much as they transfer authority—weaker organizational actors become better equipped to hold their stronger counterparts accountable and take them to task in organized settings. Because of the iterative nature of interorganizational interaction in the course of legislating policy, procedural type accords amount to something of substance; as such, over multiple iterations it becomes more difficult for pressured actors not to capitulate, at least partially, to pressuring actors. Across time and across issue areas in the EU, there is ample evidence that political outcomes have changed as a direct consequence of procedural accords in the informal sphere—to the advantage largely of the Parliament.[34] In most instances the changes have involved modest capitulations by the Council or Commission to the Parliament, albeit capitulations almost invariably of less consequence than what the Parliament was seeking.

In terms of theory confirmation, for most of these accords it was impossible to acquire evidence about my bargaining model's second-order constraints, as evidence about the dynamics surrounding the specific negotiations of these accords is buried along with the officials at the time their creation. Most of this batch of accords involved taking the Parliament more seriously and providing it with better information. In terms of the model's predicted first-order constraint changes and their effects on outcomes in the informal sphere, constraints on the Parliament had for the most part not shifted until after 1979; moreover, the Parliament lacked

---

[34] EU official, interview by the author, European Commission, Brussels, January 23, 2002; EU official, conference remarks, "The European Parliament at 50" conference, Aberystwyth, Wales, July 13, 2002.

much in the way of formal powers to use as bases for additional influence attempts. Nor had the Council Presidencies yet become focused on comparing themselves with their predecessors. These accords stem mostly from the lone remaining predicted constraint, namely an increase in pressure on the Council to democratize the EU. However, without the other constraint shifts yet in operation and due to the meager degree to which the Council was being pressured to transfer power to a consultative assembly, the causal effects are minimal. Thus, these outcomes are in fact consistent with the model in the following manner: in the absence of first-order constraint shifts, few informal accords were negotiated and the newly created rules were hardly integrative.

Other dynamics in the EU's informal sphere related to legislative procedures involve the Petitions Procedure. According to Rule 156 of the Parliament's Rules of Procedure, any citizen of the EU has "the right to address . . . a petition to the European Parliament on a matter which comes within the European Union's fields of activity and which affects him, her or it directly."[35] This right was originally introduced by the Parliament in 1963. Member State citizens made scarce use of it until the numbers began rising in the 1970s. Since direct elections the yearly average of petitions received by the Parliament has risen substantially and has for a considerable period remained at a level above 1,000. Originally they were dealt with by the Parliament's Legal Affairs Committee, but since 1987 the specially created Petitions Committee has been charged with processing them. It is empowered by the Parliament to draw up reports, organize hearings, conduct investigations, and request information and action from the other organizational actors. The Petitions Committee prepares an annual report which is debated in plenary and six months later issues a general statement in plenary. Yet, until 1989 the Council and Commission officially did not recognize this sphere of EU activity.

For years one of the Parliament's chief problems was approaching Member States for information and assistance. But in April of 1989 the Presidents of the Parliament, Council, and Commission signed a solemn declaration, which took on the configuration of an informal accord in the *Official Journal* in May of that year.[36] The accord consists of three short paragraphs, the first of which notes the Council's full support of the Parliament's "efforts to encourage and assist, in an appropriate manner, the custom of petitioning" and expresses their mutual pleasure that the procedure based

---

[35] Rule 156, June 1994, Rules of Procedure, the European Parliament.
[36] OJ No. C 120/90, 1989.

on this informal precept had become increasingly widespread. In paragraph two they agree that the Parliament should continue to rely on the Commission for assistance or ask the Commission to forward requests for assistance to the Member States concerned. And in the final paragraph they collectively express their desire for full cooperation from the Member States and underlined the principle enshrined in Article 10 of the Treaty, which requires the Member States to fully cooperate in applying the Treaty.

Member State governments have subsequently formalized the right of petition in the Maastricht Treaty. The text of Article 194 is identical to the text of the Parliament's Rule 156, demonstrating that the Parliament can of its own accord create a new sphere of EU activity (by including certain provisions in its Rules of Procedure and beginning to act on that basis), codify it in an informal accord, and then win its sweeping up in an amending treaty by demonstrating its usefulness to the other organizational actors (the very same has happened with committees of inquiry), even with the precise wording it would have chosen on its own. Although no powers of any kind were created or transferred as a result of this particular accord, the Parliament's freedom to carve out new spheres of EU activity—on the basis of a unilaterally declared informal institution—was confirmed.

The Arrangements for the Proceedings of the Conciliation Committee Under Article 189B is an informal accord, although it is commonly referred to as "the interinstitutional agreement on codecision."[37] Because it comprises a series of specific commitments made by both actors, it is a salient example of an informal accord that might at some stage be deemed legally binding by the Court.[38] The first paragraph states that the existing practice of holding discussions prior to the Council's adoption of a common position under the cooperation procedure can also be applied under the Article 251 procedure, commonly known as codecision.

The accord provides for a series of "arrangements"—or rules—related to conciliation elements of the codecision procedure. Arrangements 1 and 2 (the convening of the Conciliation Committee and the conciliatory role of the Commission, respectively) are both lifted verbatim from Article 251. Arrangement 3 calls for the Presidents of the Council and the Parliament to chair the Committee, cementing operation of the ad hoc procedure at the highest level. Most of the rest of the arrangement rules are concerned with placing the Parliament and the Council on equal terms with respect to availability of documents, finalization of joint texts, meeting place, etc.

---

[37] OJ No. C 329/141, 1993.
[38] Monar (1994: 713).

Arrangement 8 is of particular significance in that it provides for transparency in the operation of the Committee. Outcomes of votes and explanations of votes within each of the organizational delegations must be forwarded to the Committee.

The accord stresses the view that in order to make the codecision procedure operable in the day-to-day policy process, its provisions needed to be more sufficiently fleshed out. "A very similar process of 'filling out' the provisions of the treaties through constitutional convention and interinstitutional agreement occurred after the 1970 and 1975 Budgets Treaties and [occurred again] with the implementation of the Maastricht Treaty."[39] As the accord is largely concerned with establishing how the conciliation aspect of the formal codecision procedure will operate—along with stipulating several trilogue meetings—one can conclude that at a minimum it involves further institutionalization of one of the major formal changes brought about by Maastricht.

Finally, it is important to take stock of the two most freshly consecrated informal accords, the two that "couldn't wait for the Constitutional Treaty to get ratified"—the 2006 Comitology accord (see the following text) along with the 2007 Codecision IIA.[40] Although the Parliament was slated to receive some additional powers in this amending treaty, MEPs moved rapidly to press their position in the informal sphere despite its demise.[41] This came to pass in the form of the Lisbon Treaty, grafted onto the EU's cumulative Treaty, sweeping up a series of informal institutions into the formal sphere. As has become evident in previous chapters, however, informal accords can create the same rules that EU laws can, which in practical terms make no difference to everyday policy-making.

What is especially unique about this accord is how the Commission is actually the take away winner, for which there is no precedent in the EU's informal sphere. Because the impetus for informal interorganizational dynamics normally comes from the Parliament, it is hardly surprising that the Commission over the years has lost ground to its counterparts while the

[39] Westlake (1994*b*: 143).

[40] EU official, interview by the author, European Commission, Brussels, July 4, 2007.

[41] The Constitutional amending treaty was agreed by EU Member States in 2004; however, a year later the ratification votes in France and the Netherlands seemed to sink the agreement that would have defined the EU Treaty as a constitution for the first time. Nonetheless in June of 2007, largely at the behest of Chancellor Angela Merkel the treaty was salvaged and rebranded the Reform Treaty—this amending treaty, shorn of its ambitious preamble and the like, was subject to ratification in all 27 Member States and voted down in the Irish referendum seemingly killing the Treaty. Rebranded again the Lisbon Treaty, the treaty overcame considerable odds and subsequent to a positive re-vote in Ireland was finally ratified in autumn 2009.

Parliament has gained considerable ground. The only other influence attempt the Commission has made in the informal sphere resulted in the 2003 Better Lawmaking IIA (see Chapter 5), but it did not achieve nearly as much as it hoped to at the outset of negotiations over that accord. The 2007 Codecision IIA is different.

Although the Parliament portrays itself as the catalyst behind this accord, in fact the codecision department of the Commission in particular and the overall Commission in general constituted the prime mover for this the EU's final informal accord prior to Lisbon's ratification. The Parliament actually had to be persuaded to move beyond its initial reluctance, and the Council grudgingly came along: "The Council is still very hostile [to informal accords], so it's always a rearguard action."[42]

Discussions among the Three over the possibility of a new accord regarding codecision kicked off under the Austrian Presidency, after a few exploratory "probes" took place under the UK Presidency; however, these discussions amounted to little at the time as the Austrians on behalf of the Council were much more focused on the comitology accord analyzed above. Because the Council had more to gain from that accord, these informal discussions sort of lapsed until they were picked up by the Council again under the subsequent Finnish Presidency. Without exception, each Council President-in-Office over the course of the 2000s has demonstrated evidence of the first-order constraint shift regarding the desire of each one to achieve "success," as predicted; and the Scandinavians have been particularly prone to seek cooperative relations with the Parliament.[43]

At certain times in certain places this ultimate causal factor is complemented by a related trigger, if not issue linkage or time horizons then the second-order constraints shifter of intense preferences. In the case of this accord as with the 2006 Comitology accord, this and the time horizon trigger were catalytic. Both the Austrians and the Finns were generally predisposed to achieving successful presidencies; however, lacking enough other areas in their brief six-month tenures to point to as successes, each came to eye an informal accord with the Parliament and Commission as a prize worth possessing.[44] The temporary dynamic worked to the Parliament's particular benefit for the comitology accord and the Commission's particular benefit for the codecision accord. The Finns overcame a general reticence in the Council, for Finland wanted good relations with the

---

[42] EU official, interview by the author, European Commission, Brussels, July 4, 2007.

[43] EU official, interview by the author, Council of Ministers, Brussels, July 6, 2007.

[44] EU official, interview by the author, Council of Ministers, Brussels, July 6, 2007.

211

Parliament and found few of Parliament's suggested rules objectionable: "thus, they got it done in short order."[45]

Negotiations nearly broke down in early April 2006 at a trilogue meeting where the Council expressed a combination of misunderstanding and opposition from the ministerial level of Coreper, aimed more at the Parliament than the Commission. However, acting as an ally the Commission drafted a new text and sent it to the Parliament, who amended it as desired before taking it back to the Council. However, this move was resisted staunchly by the Commission, which then went to the Council and said the altered text was not agreeable to it. There were then two more trilogue meetings brokered by the Finns in which all three had to give up some of their preferences to get a final deal.

Thus, a final deal was done in mid-spring 2007 after a flurry of meetings at two different levels: at the technical level of civil servants from the secretariats of the Three and at the political level involving politicians from the Three (MEPs, Council ministers, and Commissioners). A few years earlier the Parliament amended its Rules of Procedure to incorporate an examination of all draft informal accords by its Constitutional Affairs committee, whose sign-off is required in order for the Parliament to finalize its commitment to a given accord in its plenary legislative session; as for the comitology accord, this was achieved at its May session. Interestingly, the Parliament considers these actions to be formal adoptions of what technically are informal accords—yet another indication of the overall trend toward informal accords that are sufficiently substantive in content and official in process and written down in the *Official Journal* that they seem more and more akin to treaty provisions.

This accord sweeps up a series of previously agreed informal institutions that have sprung up on their own since the previous 1999 Codecision accord, including the procedure of confirmatory letter from the Council at first or second reading stage of the policy-making process, as well as the same type of letter from the Parliament after the Parliament's first reading but before the Council adopts its so-called common position. The crux of the accord places major emphasis on the series of trilogue meetings it stipulates between the Three at several points in the process. This does help the Parliament, but it particularly brings the Commission back in after informally being cut out of a series of bilateral deals between the Council and Parliament on various pieces of draft legislation. The Commission now

---

[45] EU official, interview by the author, European Commission, Brussels, July 4, 2007.

once again has its voice in any negotiation to dispense with the rest of the codecision process if the Council and Parliament can come to an early agreement. The Commission thus benefits from "the emphasis on clear channels of communication and the reinforcement of the trilogue system for negotiations at all stages of the procedure" and the "codification of best practices at the 1st and 2nd reading stages of the procedure," not to mention the link established between the codecision process and the Better Lawmaking accord.[46]

For the Council the most important part of the accord is its preference achievement for new procedures for the finalization of legislation texts, in particular the legal-linguistic verification mechanism of the accord (the Parliament had been using disaccord in this area to hold up various pieces of legislation). However, this is small potatoes compared to what the Parliament and especially the Commission achieved, as it merely gets the Council back to the previous status quo. As for the Parliament, it gained somewhat more: a new commitment from the Council for Presidency officials attending Parliamentary committee meetings, a Council commitment on the Parliament's requests for information on the Council's position, a Council commitment for the Parliament's linguistic and legal services to be allowed equal footing with the Council's counterpart services, codification of the procedure of finalizing legislative deals reached via an exchange of letters, a Council commitment to begin signing draft legislation texts at press conferences alongside the Parliament and issuing joint press releases ahead of time. Overall the Parliament and Commission concur that the new accord makes EU policy-making more transparent, coordinated, efficient, and democratic.[47]

Improving the comitology procedure

As aforementioned, one of the more contentious elements of democratic control in the EU concerns the implementation and management of secondary legislation. The Treaty of Rome cast the Commission in the executive role, responsible for implementing, promulgating, and overseeing EU policies inscribed in law. In some areas the Treaty grants specific executive powers to the Commission, such as competition policy, limits on state aid

---

[46] EU official, correspondence with the author, European Commission, August 12, 2007.
[47] EU official, interview by the author, European Commission, Brussels, July 4, 2007; EU official, interview by the author, European Parliament, Brussels, July 3, 2007.

to industry, and coal and steel production. However, in the 1960s, the Council invoked its own executive authority and gradually began exercising day-to-day control over the Commission's implementing actions through a steadily growing network of supervisory committees of Member State civil servants. As previously discussed, over the years this practice came to be known as comitology.

In response to burgeoning criticism from the Parliament and the Commission for allegedly usurping the latter's traditional role as the EU's executive authority—and for using EU funds in the process—in the SEA Member State governments amended the Treaty explicitly to allow the Council to confer implementing powers on the Commission, while reserving the right to impose certain restrictions and in "specific cases" to exercise these powers itself.[48] Owing to incessant criticism from the other organizational actors, particularly for not specifying these cases "in advance" as called for by the Treaty, the Council issued a formal Decision in July 1987 based on a Commission proposal laying down the procedures for the exercise of the implementing powers conferred on the Commission.[49]

To reiterate, the Decision instituted a series of procedures for three types of oversight committees: advisory, management, and regulatory committees. Advisory committees can do nothing beyond offer advice to the Commission. Management committees can block a Commission decision with a qualified majority. And regulatory committees can effectively block Commission decisions without doing anything, for Commission action must be approved by qualified majority. The Parliament's strong aversion to management and regulatory committees stems from its inability to directly control their decision-making; it has only indirect control over advisory committees. In the view of the Parliament these committees are unaccountable to elected officials.

In response to the 1987 Decision, the most the Parliament has been able to do is systematically attempt to alter the Council's preferred choice of oversight committees in the course of second readings. In its efforts to procure the ability to scrutinize and monitor comitology decisions, the Parliament and the Commission established an informal accord in which the latter endeavors to keep the Parliament fully informed of the proposals the Commission submits to the oversight committees. This informal accord was codified in a 1988 exchange of letters between the Presidents of the Commission and the Parliament and has thus become known as the

---

[48] Treaty establishing the European Community, consolidated version, Article 202.
[49] OJ No. L 197, 1987.

Plumb–Delors procedure. The terms of the accord stipulate that, except for routine management documents or those related to matters of urgency or confidentiality, the Commission shall forward to the relevant Parliamentary committees all draft implementing measures in the same working languages and at the same time as they are forwarded to the oversight committees. This accord-based procedure has been in place since May 1989.

With the deluge of single market-based legislation in the wake of the SEA and with the widening of the scope of the cooperation and codecision procedures after Maastricht, the workload for the oversight committees increased dramatically. In the form of the 1993 De Giovanni Report, the Parliament adopted its strategy to close this gap. Since then it has adhered to its December 15, 1993 Resolution calling on the Council to agree to a new joint mechanism for Council–Parliamentary political supervision of implementing acts to be cast in the form of an informal accord. In the view of the Parliament, all legislative acts under Article 251 are by definition acts of codecision between it and the Council; therefore, the Parliament should be co-legislator in every respect, including policy implementation. The terms "codecision" and "co-legislator" are not present in the Treaty, yet the Parliament has in effect won an important rhetorical battle by succeeding in making these terms subject to common usage throughout the EU.

On this basis it refused to support the introduction of management and regulatory committees in draft legislation subsequent to entry into force of Maastricht on November 1, 1993. At that time there were a host of legislative proposals classified under Article 251 at various stages in the legislative pipeline.[50] The Parliament began intimating that it might reject some of them unless the Council acquiesced in some form to its desire for increased oversight powers in comitology. When the Council refused, the Parliament raised its rhetoric to the point of making direct threats to derail the various proposals one by one until the Council acceded to its demands.

The Council began to take the threat seriously, and in June 1994 it agreed to enter into negotiations with the Parliament to broker an informal accord to resolve the conflict. However, this process could not begin in earnest until the new Parliament took office in July. Negotiations began but little progress was made initially. The Council was apparently attempting to stall the proceedings. The first legislative proposal to come up for final

---

[50] Any legislation that had been under the cooperation procedure had to go back to a first reading if its legal base had been switched to Article 251 under Maastricht.

agreement was the directive on voice telephony. The Council had accepted a number of Parliament's amendments, but in the conciliation committee it refused to give in to the Parliament's demands regarding comitology. In light of the stalled negotiations of the comitology informal accord, in July the Parliament rejected the joint text in plenary—the piece of legislation was wholly stymied in a highly salient unprecedented fashion.

This action was critical for interorganizational relations. On one level the Council viewed the Parliament's actions over a piece of legislation with wide implications for industry as thoroughly irresponsible; on a separate level it was forced to take note of the seriousness of Parliament's influence attempt. By this time Germany had taken over the Council Presidency, and the Parliament was intent on taking advantage of the traditional support from Bonn (the German government was already on record as advocating increased powers for the Parliament in the context of the 1996 IGC). By November little progress had been made in the negotiations. There were four Article 251 classified proposals in conciliation at that time (the Directive on waste packaging, the Socrates Program, the Directive on petrol emissions, and the Directive on Youth for Europe), and with France due to take over the Council Presidency in January, the Parliament was intent on concluding an accord before the year's end.

In the negotiations the Parliament linked the comitology negotiations and its actions over the four pending proposals by refusing to take action on them until the Council agreed to an informal accord. At one point the Parliament refused to call for a meeting of one of the conciliation committees. The Council found it had no choice but to conclude the informal accord, which it did relatively swiftly on December 20. Officially known as the *Modus Vivendi between the European Parliament, the Council and the Commission concerning the implementing measures for acts adopted in accordance with the procedure laid down in Article 189b of the EC Treaty*, its name reflects the Council's extreme reluctance to give the accord the status of an IIA—again, EU parlance for an informal accord of the substantive type. In practical terms that is precisely what it is, considering it was negotiated in a trilogue meeting, signed by the Three, and published in the *Official Journal*.[51]

Although the Parliament did not achieve all that it had hoped to, it made significant gains in the accord. First, all comitology proposals from the Commission must be sent to the Parliament under the same conditions as

---

[51] OJ No. C 102, 4.4.1996. The accord was agreed in 1994 but for some reason was not published in the OJ until two years later.

those from the national civil servants on the committees. Second, the Parliament was granted the newfound power of consultation, including the right to be informed if final adoptions of proposals are not in accordance with the Parliament's opinion. Finally, the Parliament secured a commitment that the issue "will be examined in the course of the revision of the Treaties ... as the request of the European Parliament, the Commission, and several Member States."[52]

While the Parliament made some gains, they were far from its *ex ante* aims. The Council was vulnerable due to issue linkage, but the Parliament proved perhaps more vulnerable with an ironic reversal in this instance: on this occasion its preference intensities were stronger, and time horizons shorter, than the Council's. In more immediate terms, the Parliament's capitulation concerning its objective of obtaining voting rights on the oversight committees was due to the Council's successful delaying tactic and its playing on the Parliament's fears of a less favorable Presidency under the French. Nonetheless, the accord was a highly significant development, for the Parliament gained a toehold in the area of comitology for the first time—and on the basis of some hard bargaining in the informal sphere.

The 2006 Comitology IIA has already gone down as one of the two most significant informal accords in EU history, next to the 1995 Commission Investiture accord.[53] As discussed previously in Chapter 5, for years comitology issues have been among the most contested by the Three due largely to the Parliament's view that it should possess equal policy implementation powers to the Council's for any primary legislation created by the codecision procedure—which involves the broad range of legislation in the 2000s, though the Lisbon Treaty would later sweep up the 1994 Comitology. While the Constitutional Treaty would have swept up the 1994 Comitology IIA and created additional rules akin to Parliament's preferences for EU policy implementation, the Parliament launched an informal influence attempt aimed at winning some of the same powers from the Council in the informal sphere.

The Council acceded to the Parliament's wishes for negotiations on the matter in early 2006 under the Austrian Presidency, though final agreement on a new informal accord did not come until July under the Finns. For several years after the Lamfalussy accord negotiations, the Council pressured the Parliament to cooperate by fully delegating implementing powers to the Commission, but the Parliament began introducing the so-called sunset clauses into legislation that would lead to the expiration of such

---

[52] European Parliament, Minutes of the plenary session, January 18, 1995, PE 186.410.
[53] EU official, interview by the author, European Parliament, Brussels, July 5, 2007.

implementing powers. This was a major irritant to both the Council and the Commission and therefore a classic instance of the Parliament attempting to gets its counterparts over the barrel and temporarily augment its bargaining power; it was successful, for the major reason the Council eventually agreed to share veto powers with the Parliament in a new informal accord was to put an end to the use of sunset clauses.[54] Moreover, the Commission was so out of sorts about the "ghastly" issue that it went to the Council and said "this must be done."[55] Herein lies evidence of a shift in the second-order constraint involving preference intensity in the Council and the additional constraint shift of issue linkage by the Parliament.

These constraint shifts triggered a mandate given by the Council for negotiations on the matter under the 2005 British Presidency, though negotiations officially were organized under the Austrians. These negotiations lasted for nearly six months, leading to finalization of the accord with an appearance both in the *Official Journal* and a Council Decision.[56] The Council has sought to maintain the appearance of controlling the comitology sphere, hence its decision to also issue a Council Decision even though the IIA was printed in the *Official Journal* of the EU: "The Council decides this alone; there is no participation of the Parliament on these modalities."[57] Yet, reality would seem to belie such spin attempts. Throughout the negotiations the Council and Commission insisted that the Parliament relinquish sunset clauses permanently, though in the end the Parliament resisted successfully enough—direct evidence of Council and Commission preference intensity— that the wiggle words of the accord do not actually amount to a permanent capitulation by the Parliament. Indeed, MEP ire at the suggestion of anything contrary cropped up immediately: concerning legislation in the policy-making pipeline at that juncture coming under the Parliament's Economic and Monetary Affairs Committee, MEPs immediately began pushing anew for sunset clause passage.[58]

Yet it was the determination of both the Commission and the Council to end them once and for all that led to its internal decision to launch its most cooperative effort to date vis-à-vis the Parliament in the informal sphere. "We wanted to be sure the new procedure would be acceptable to the Parliament...the aim of the new procedure is to make the Parliament happy regarding its normal complaints."[59] Evidence of this could be seen

---

[54] EU official, interview by the author, Council of Ministers, Brussels, July 6, 2007.

[55] EU official, interview by the author, European Commission, Brussels, July 4, 2007.

[56] OJ C 200/11, 22.7.2006; Council Decision 2006/512/EC of 17 July 2006.

[57] EU official, interview by the author, Council of Ministers, Brussels, July 6, 2007.

[58] EU official, interview by the author, European Parliament, Brussels, July 5, 2007.

[59] EU official, interview by the author, Council of Ministers, Brussels, July 6, 2007.

in the setting up of two parallel sets of informal negotiations with the Parliament alone and also involving the Commission. The Commission was long opposed to callback, but it decided that if it were to grant this to the Parliament, the latter would grant it greater flexibility in turn (i.e., fewer sunset clauses). The original draft informal accord advance by the Commission did not contain a veto for the Parliament; this was acceded to later in the negotiations by the Council. Interview evidence testifies to evolution of a view in the Council that the Parliament did in fact deserve to be brought in from the comitology cold because of its coequal position with the Council regarding codecision.

The 2006 Comitology accord introduces a new informal institution referred to as the "regulatory procedure with scrutiny." While it only covers legislation created by the codecision procedure, it is a marquee example of the Council transferring a significant power to the Parliament in a manner neither foreseen nor called for by the Treaty, all in the informal sphere. This power amounts to a co-veto power alongside the Council of Commission draft measures, that is, Commission proposals for a particular policy implementation provision. Now, if either the Council or the Parliament rejects such measures—which in the Parliament requires an absolute majority vote within three months—the Commission must drop them.

This is a major advance for the Parliament, for in the policy implementation sphere it now possesses a full-fledged veto power over the vast majority of EU legislation and all on the basis of an informal accord; Lisbon formalize this power.[60] While the Parliament will continues to be consulted on Commission draft measures that emanate from policy-making procedures other than codecision, because many old pieces of legislation did not have the new regulatory procedure with scrutiny applied to them at the time, the Commission had to go back and reintroduce more than 200 pieces of already passed legislation for the Parliament's approval. "It is a very significant improvement, more or less what we wanted."[61] No doubt the Parliament will pursue veto power across the board in future influence attempts.

Other informal accords

With the conclusion of Maastricht, for the first time in EU history an amending treaty called directly for the negotiation of informal accords—

---

[60] EU official, interview by the author, Council of Ministers, Brussels, July 6, 2007.
[61] EU official, interview by the author, European Parliament, Brussels, July 5, 2007.

several in fact. That it did so provided a profound indication that the previous informal accords were not only accepted by the Council but also valued enough to be opted for on future occasions when they might prove mutually useful. This afforded informal accords legitimacy and cemented their presence on the EU landscape. Though they were still, strictly speaking, informal, that the accords eventually negotiated were called for by formal treaty provisions testified to the trend of certain accords taking on a more formal configuration. The Council also called for informal accords just after the conclusion of the Maastricht negotiations at the December 1992 Edinburgh Council. In the Edinburgh communiqué, the Council called specifically for a renewing accord for the next budgetary framework, as well as an accord on the implementation of the subsidiarity principle.

The Parliament managed to tie together the Council's call for an accord on subsidiarity, its own wish to conclude an accord fleshing out the codecision procedure, and those called for by the treaty into one omnibus negotiation package (the Council insisted only on keeping negotiations for the budgetary accord on a completely separate track). For the most part these flowed directly from the negotiation of Maastricht and its implementation, just as the first Code of Conduct flowed fairly directly from the SEA, as well as the 1975 and 1982 Joint Declaration accords from the Luxembourg and Brussels Treaties. According to Westlake, "all three institutions have increasingly come to recognize that the treaty amendments, and particularly the new procedures created by them, can only be successfully implemented if fleshed out with agreements as to how they are to be put into practice."[62]

Negotiations between the Three began under the auspices of the EU's first ever Interinstitutional Conference on November 10, 1992 (six months after Maastricht was signed).[63] The Belgian Presidency in the second half of 1993 expended considerable effort to achieve a compromise, which was finally accomplished in September. Multiple informal accords were the result (each will be described in succession).

The Interinstitutional Declaration on Democracy, Transparency, and Subsidiarity is part informal accord and part prelude to the four accords.[64] It

---

[62] Westlake (1994*b*: 217).

[63] This reference to the interorganizational negotiations was originally used only by the Parliament, which unilaterally began referring to the Maastricht-prescribed negotiations in this manner. The Council resisted but by late 1994 acquiesced as the Parliament again succeeded in framing the rhetoric in its favor.

[64] OJ No. C 329/133, 1993.

essentially provides for a limited series of practical measures to enhance democracy and transparency. It specifically stipulates that as soon as the Parliament adopts its resolution on the Commission's annual Work Program, the Council shall state its position on the program and undertake to implement the provisions it prioritizes as soon as possible. This institutional rule obliges the Council to respond directly to the Parliament's views and opens the way for a bona fide political dialogue on the legislative program, provided the Council adopts a clear and detailed position.[65] It is actually the only aspect of the accord that supposedly relates to democracy.

The bulk of the accord involves commitments of the Council and the Commission to adopting a lengthy list of measures to increase transparency. Among other things, the Council undertakes to open some of its debates to the public, publish records and explanations of its voting, publish its common positions and the accompanying explanatory statements, and provide access to its archives. In the same paragraph the Commission undertakes to conclude or initiate a series of measures, including wider consultations before presenting its proposals, including the publication of Green or White Papers on 1993 legislative program items; introduction of a "notification procedure" involving the publication of a brief summary of all planned proposals in the *Official Journal*; and a variety of other minor measures to augment the general public's understanding of and increase its contact with the Commission.

Regarding the effectiveness of these measures on transparency, much depends on whether and how some of the vague rules are implemented and/or adhered to. As it carries the label of "declaration," the tenor of the accord is one of declaratory intent as opposed to binding intent. It bears almost no relation to the Treaty, and thus far in practice, at least as far as the Council is concerned, the majority of the rule-based measures have either been only partially implemented or not at all. For example, in the immediate aftermath of the conclusion of the Interinstitutional Conference, the Council held several allegedly public debates, but they proved to be exercises in public relations rather than substantive discussions. As Monar concludes, on an imaginary continuum of informal accords "it would range quite close to the threshold connecting these with mere political declarations"—in other words, that of a standard accord by the taxonomy set out in Chapter 4.[66]

---

[65] Monar (1994: 710).
[66] Monar (1994: 710).

The Interinstitutional Agreement on Procedures for Implementing the Principle of Subsidiarity specifically states that its contents shall in no way alter the provisions of the Treaty, the *acquis*, or the interorganizational balance.[67] As its title indicates, this accord concerns only the implementation of the subsidiarity principle of governing as closely to the citizens as possible; it seeks neither to interpret nor actually apply it. This accord is more official both in structure and in language than the above accord. Its structure consists of a preamble, general provisions, two main sections, and final provisions, while each provision includes the word "shall." The preamble explicitly refers to Article 5 of the cumulative Treaty and Article 2 of the Maastricht Treaty, and paragraph IV.2 stipulates that the accord became operable from the date Maastricht legally came into force.

Concerning the content of informal institutions, the document calls on the Three to dutifully take full account of the subsidiarity principle in their policy deliberations, including their internal procedures, and to demonstrate that they have done so in the content of Commission proposals and Commission and Parliamentary amendments. The Commission is further obliged to produce an annual report on the EU's compliance with subsidiarity, which is the subject of a debate in the Parliament. One of its key provisions, III.1, stipulates that compliance with the principle must be reviewed "under the normal Community process, in accordance with the rules laid down by the Treaties." This is significant, for the Council had originally intended the document to call for preliminary consideration of prospective legislative proposals exclusively in light of the subsidiarity principle. This institutional rule precludes such from occurring.

No transfers or creation of new policy-making powers for any of the organizational actors are found in the accord. Ironically, in this case it was the Council, not the Parliament, that pressed most vigorously for an agreement. But, in a twist, its shorter time horizons and more intense preferences did not prove to its disadvantage in the negotiation. In fact, the Parliament actually did all it could to prevent the conclusion of a densely detailed document, for it had determined that the more precise an accord of this nature turned out to be, the more it would stand to lose in future deliberations. In essence, an accord based primarily or wholly on principle—as opposed to the standard emphasis on creating and altering policy-making rules—turned the standard informal dynamics on their head.

---

[67] OJ No. C 329/135, 1993.

The Commission originally produced a complicated and weighty discussion document outlining its views on how to apply practically the subsidiarity principle, but as discussion wore on it eventually came over to the Parliament's view on the issue, which in practical terms was that it was nearly impossible to apply an objective set of criteria that could adequately foresee and manage all scenarios. For its part the Council had been aiming for a more binding accord, but under pressure from the other two—who were willing to drag out the negotiation proceedings considerably—it was eventually forced to relent. Hence, the final form of the accord represents a bit of a climbdown from the conclusions of the Edinburgh Summit. In practice, the political effects of this standard type accord have been negligible.

The 1993 *Decision of the European Parliament on the Regulations and General Conditions Governing the Ombudsman's Duties* is commonly considered and referred to as an informal accord, but officially it is precisely what its title declares—a decision of the Parliament.[68] It stems directly from the Treaty, which stipulates that the Parliament shall "after seeking an opinion [nonbinding] from the Commission and with the approval of the Council acting by a qualified majority, lay down the regulations and general conditions governing the performance of the Ombudsman's duties."[69] Thus, in accordance with Articles 195 of the cumulative Treaty, 20D of the European Coal and Steel Community Treaty, and 107D of the Euratom Treaty, the accord qualifies as a "decision" arrived at in the manner described above. With the general procedural roles reversed—the Council acting on a common position from the Parliament—it is a unique procedure, applicable only to this circumstance. It is certainly the most peculiar informal accord in terms of both political and legal status.

With regard to its content, the accord performs several functions: defining who can bring a complaint to the Ombudsman, against whom, how it can be done, and by when the complainant must register his complaint (the two-year statute of limitation was a matter of much dispute during the negotiations); setting out the powers and tasks of the position of Ombudsman (including the highly contentious restriction of access to EU documents "on duly substantiated grounds of secrecy"); restricting the Ombudsman's freedom to disseminate information; governing the Ombudsman's interaction with Member State officials; laying down an election procedure for the position; and sorting out a host of mundane but necessary administrative

---

[68] OJ, No. C 329/136, 1993.

[69] Treaty Establishing the European Community, Article 195.

details. Independent in the performance of his duties, the Ombudsman is nevertheless linked to the Parliament in numerous ways.

As this accord concerns the creation of a new element of the political system independent of the Three, none of them gain much to speak of by the Ombudsman's creation. The Parliament gains in the sense that it has long advocated the creation of such a post; however, this accord must be viewed more as a policy victory for the Parliament, rather than a qualitative gain in its influence over the conduct of the other organizational actors.

Another example of the Parliament using its Rules of Procedure to create a new legal instrument of the EU, entirely on its own behalf, can be seen in the informal accord on committees of inquiry, one of the Parliament's principal means of exercising its supervisory role. Committees of inquiry have enabled the Parliament to conduct in-depth investigations of issues and problems in the wider EU. They have further acted as a means of shedding light on particular issues and placing them on the political agenda. The Parliament first began making use of them after direct elections. The first to be created was a 1979 committee of inquiry into the situation of women in Europe. The Parliament has created ten other committees of inquiry since.

Committees of inquiry were incorporated in Maastricht in an unorthodox way. Because Member States in the treaty negotiations could not agree on what precisely to do with "the detailed provisions governing the exercise of the right of inquiry," having defined the parameters of their duties and powers the Member States felt it would be innocuous enough to let the Parliament in on deciding the specifics. Prior to Maastricht, committees of inquiry had to rely on the cooperation of the other organizational actors and national authorities, for it had no legal recourse. Despite receiving a fair amount of cooperation from the other organizational actors, committees of inquiry have been incessantly viewed as feeble mechanisms.[70]

Under Maastricht's provisions the Parliament can set up a temporary committee of inquiry with a favorable vote of at least a quarter of the MEPs in order "to investigate, without prejudice to the powers conferred by this Treaty on other institutions and bodies, alleged contraventions or maladministration in the implementation of Community law."[71] Highly significant, the Maastricht provision adopted practically the precise wording of Rule 136 of the Parliament's Rules of Procedure.

---

[70] Westlake (1994*b*: 179).
[71] Treaty Establishing the European Community, Article 193.

The 1994 *Decision of the European Parliament, the Council and the Commission on the detailed provisions governing the exercise of the European Parliament's right of inquiry* is technically a decision but qualifies as an informal accord because it was negotiated between the organizational actors.[72] Unlike most other informal accords, it has a treaty base. The Parliament continues to operate the committees under the conditions laid out in the agreement: secrecy must be preserved; hearings and testimony shall take place in public; matters before a national court cannot be investigated, etc.

Given the Parliament's objective for committees of inquiry to have complete access to officials and documents from the Member States and the Council and Commission, several provisions proved contentious in the negotiations. The accord calls on them to authorize the appearance of their officials on reasonable requests, except on the grounds of secrecy and national security. It calls on them to turn over requested documents under the same conditions. No documents can be obtained without the consent of proper national and EU authorities. Committees are concluded with the issuing of a final report, which may make recommendations to the Member States or the other EU organizational actors.

This agreement holds particular significance in that it stemmed originally from an informal precept created by the Parliament that rose in stature enough to attain a treaty base giving the Parliament the power to launch its own legal inquiries. However, the provisions do not pertain to the EU's legislative process and therefore contribute nothing to changes in policy-making. Furthermore, the Council prevailed in the negotiations, as the Parliament was forced to compromise on all of its important objectives.

The 1994 *Interinstitutional agreement on an accelerated working method for official codification of legislative texts* has little political significance.[73] It simply involves the creation of an accelerated procedure for replacing existing legal acts with new legal acts without the requirement of going through the normal legal proceedings as stipulated by the Treaty. Its stated objective is "simple codification of existing texts" and is intended for use in renewing existing pieces of legislation while stipulating that no substantive changes can be made. Long pursued by the three legal services of the organizational actors, it has no implications for their relations in the normal course of policy-making.

---

[72] European Parliament, Minutes of the plenary session, January 18, 1995, PE 186.410.
[73] European Parliament, Minutes of the plenary session, January 18, 1995, PE 186.410.

Conclusion

The majority of changes brought about by the complete range of nonbudgetary informal accords in the EU have provided the Parliament with a collection of favorable outcomes from its perspective: general influence-related, policy-related, and power-related. In terms of the first of these, the Parliament has gained improved access to better quality and larger amounts of information, a greater number of instances in which the Parliament must be either consulted or informed by the Council and Commission, multiple opportunities to take part in legislative discussions with the other organizational actors, increased contact with officials from them, and even a greater level of respect from its organizational counterparts. Yet, if these were the only advantages gained by the Parliament from informal interorganizational dynamics, then clearly their effect would not extend beyond the institutionalization of previous procedural norms. However, the Parliament made an array of more significant gains in the process.

Also stemming from the full collection of bi- and trilateral informal accords in the EU—particularly those of the *procedural* and *substantive* types—the Parliament has benefited in other ways. On the one hand, the Parliament made a number of policy advances—although most of these, for example the standout greater ability to classify expenditure as noncompulsory (it has no powers over compulsory expenditure), stem from budgetary accords. On the other hand, the Parliament has made numerous advances in legislative power. *Inter alia*, it was able to create additional procedures relating to the appointment of the Commission, gaining increased supervisory authority in the process. It garnered indirect approval from the Council and the Commission to use its Rules of Procedure to create new policy areas. It acquired new powers of consultation in relation to implementing acts for comitology oversight committees. It obtained a new power to bring to a complete halt proposals it rejects under the codecision procedure. And it won the creation of innumerable meetings and negotiating sessions not prescribed by the Treaty.

Therefore, across the board the Parliament has gained additional authority in the EU policy-making process that it did not possess prior to becoming a party to the accords analyzed in this chapter. As a consequence, both institutionalization and integration are in evidence. When informal accords in the budgetary sphere are added to the mix, the Parliament's overall gains from the EU's informal interorganizational dynamics are considerable. Beyond any doubt, exclusive focus on the EU's formal institutions—

created by intergovernmental treaty-making negotiations—would overlook a significant source of integration at the supranational level of Europe.

Not only do innumerable treaty-based institutions have informal institutions as their original source, but a diverse array of informal accords contains informal institutions that, although not swept up into the EU's formal sphere, serve to reallocate influence and power among the Three and *ipso facto* policy outcomes. Therefore, in order fully to account for variance in European integration, informal interorganizational dynamics must be incorporated in the explanation.

8

Conclusion

Although not called for in the Treaty of Rome, five decades later informal accords have established themselves as a permanent fixture on the European Union's institutional landscape. Informal accords clearly have "come of age."[1] As recently as the early 1990s there was ample reason to view them in ephemeral terms, but, notwithstanding their different aims, the Parliament, Commission, and Council have come to recognize the utility of further fleshing out treaty-based interorganizational relations.[2] More significantly, in adding informal accords to its strategic repertoire, the Parliament has become increasingly deft at deploying them as instruments for wresting influence and power as well from its organizational counterparts, thereby directly contributing to the deepening of the EU alongside its even consistent widening to a total now of twenty-seven Member States.

The evidence of the preceding four chapters has shed considerable light on the phenomenon of institutional change, highlighting the crucially important role of informal institutions and the dynamics of incessant strategic interaction that create them. Thus, the foresight of NIE scholars like Douglass North and political scientists like Jack Knight is demonstrable. As such, evidence for the explanatory power of the theory presented in Chapter 2 is rife in the empirical sections of this book. This evidence declares open season on scholarly canards: Moravcsik-like arguments are herin felled, unable to take flight again.

My RCI-based bargaining model sufficiently predicts dynamics in the informal sphere of the EU, both when new informal institutions get created and when they do not, as well as how integrative they are. Changes in its first-order constraints are necessary for institutional change, but insufficient

---

[1] EU official, interview by the author, European Commission, Brussels, July 4, 2007.
[2] EU official, interview by the author, Council of Ministers, Brussels, July 6, 2007.

without changes in second-order constraints—the proximate catalysts for variation in the outcome of occasionally fierce competition among the EU's three primary policy-making actors. Moreover, as a result of institutional creation in the EU's informal sphere, the Member States of this proto European policy are *ipso facto* more integrated.

The catalytic amending treaty that shed light on dynamics in the EU's informal sphere was the Maastricht Treaty, which in particular demonstrated a key shift in a constraint on the Parliament. It facilitated informal interorganizational dynamics in three ways: first, it was a catalyst for several specific informal accords between the organizational actors; second, it demonstrated that the "life cycle" of informal accords often culminates in their being swept up into the cumulative Treaty; and third, for the first time an amending treaty actually called on the organizational actors to draw up specific informal accords, therein providing one of the most cogent testaments to date of not only their attractiveness as legitimate political devices but also their effectiveness. That the Treaty is now directly mandating them has the effect of legitimating all existing informal accords, as well as the myriad less formal ones.

In fact, the Nice amending treaty provides an even more cogent testament in the form of a specific provision found in one of the treaty's formal Declarations. Declaration 3 on Article 10 of the Treaty of Nice states:

> The Conference recalls that the duty of sincere cooperation which derives from Article 10 of the Treaty establishing the European Community and governs relations between the Member States and the Community institutions also governs relations between the Community institutions themselves. In relations between those institutions, when it proves necessary, in the context of that duty of sincere cooperation, to facilitate the application of the provisions of the Treaty establishing the European Community, the European Parliament, the Council and the Commission may conclude interinstitutional agreements [IIAs]. Such agreements may not amend or supplement the provisions of the Treaty and may be concluded only with the agreement of these three institutions.[3]

Herein lies the most solid evidence to date that the Member States in the Council not only recognize the importance of informal accords but also take them seriously—enough to state as much formally in the most recent amending treaty. Twice placing informal accords under an aegis of a "duty of sincere cooperation" and with specific reference to "facilitat[ing] the

---

[3] Treaty of Nice, *Official Journal* of the European Communities (October 3, 2001): C 80/01.

application of" treaty provisions, this Declaration serves to infuse informal accords and the dynamics surrounding them with a level of legitimacy beyond corollary language in the Maastricht Treaty. It must, moreover, be recognized that the pro forma admonition that informal accords "may not amend or supplement" treaty provisions is something of a higher fiction.

Contrary to what meets the eye, this rider is not expected by any EU official to change the long-standing reality that informal accords in numerous cases do in fact supplement formal provisions—and in a few instances actually amend and even in several instances replace them.[4] Instead, the spirit of this Declaration is widely interpreted practically as a legitimation of the EU's informal sphere, with the clear implication that informal accords are not only valid devices but also devices containing rules that must be adhered to.

The evidence in the preceding chapters indicates that the Three are increasingly reliant on more impactful varieties of informal accords—procedural and substantive accords—as devices for resolving policy problems and political conflicts that arise in-between the grand formal bargains that comprise amending treaties. Indeed, the number of informal accords has shot upward over the course of the late 1980s and 1990s, a trend that has continued in the 2000s. Moreover, the evidence testifies to a steadily increasing level of quasi-formality of informal accords: they have become more integrative over time. Furthermore, informal accords are increasingly sophisticated, as evidenced by the seriousness of the negotiations, the attention of the press, and the concerns being raised in Member State parliaments (especially the United Kingdom and Denmark).

Somewhat less clear, however, is what sort of aggregate effect informal accords—and Category III in particular—are having. The evidence indicates that the impact of informal interorganizational dynamics, when viewed as a whole, is modest but significant. The central question of this book asked whether informal accords contribute to mere institutionalization or actual integration of the EU's Member States—or both. These three potential outcomes were delineated for the purpose of providing a test for the primary hypothesis of this inquiry, that is, an appropriate yardstick by which to measure the findings of the study. They constitute the parameters within which the overall outcome is likely to lie. Extensive institutionalization or extensive integration? While instances of each type of outcome are readily

---

[4] EU official, e-mail exchange with the author, European Commission, April 23, 2003.

230

demonstrable, the cumulative empirical evidence points to the conclusion that the effect of informal accords actually lies somewhere in-between.

Having confirmed that informal interorganizational dynamics engender both institutionalization *and* integration, the phenomenon of national-to-supranational sovereignty transfers over time can no longer be fully explained by examining the conventional unit of analysis—the interstate Treaty. Analysis of the formal treaty agreements that comprise the overall Treaty must be supplemented by analysis of the informal accords that at times serve to supplement them, and at others to supplant them. Moreover, numerous rules contained in formal treaties are nothing more than the incorporation of previous informal accords, transforming specific bundles of informal rules into formal laws via their being swept up under treaty auspices, usually with minimal alteration of content. Thus observers of the EU cannot afford to ignore the informal sphere; and even if they were prohibitively to do so, paying exclusive attention to the formal sphere one is forced to acknowledge a multiplicity of rules whose origins are directly traceable to the informal sphere.[5]

The EU's principal organizational actors have become accustomed to carrying out their relations both formally in terms of the Treaty's provisions for policy-making and informally in terms of a vast array of informal rules that largely serve to fill in treaty gaps and complement the formal rules. Early accords in the budgetary and foreign relations spheres endured, as the Three discovered they could rely on their counterparts to uphold the commitments underlying them. Notwithstanding the absence of hierarchy, iterative interaction and a low discount rate—supplemented by self-enforcement among the Three based on occasional political sanctioning—have cemented compliance with the informal institutions contained in the accords, despite the lack of a third-party enforcer.[6]

In addition, in accordance with its organizational ethos, the Parliament is naturally disinclined to deal with its counterparts wholly on the basis of either *basic* or *standard accords*. As a directly elected legislative body, it has a natural proclivity for openness, clarity, and acting on vote-based mandates, rather than negotiating "behind closed doors" in accordance with the formation of these types of oral or tacit accords. Instead, the Parliament prefers to organize relations with the Commission and the Council on the basis of *procedural accords* and particularly their *substantive* counterparts,

[5] EU official, interview by the author, European Parliament, Brussels, January 22, 2002.

[6] EU official, interview by the author, European Commission, Brussels, July 20, 1994; EU official, interview by the author, European Parliament, Brussels, May 5, 2003.

accords that have a quasi-formal status. Hence, the Parliament's push for Category II and III accords is not only driven by its power preferences but also because of its organizational culture.[7] The Commission has gotten into the act less often, but it was somewhat successful in using its White Paper on governance to stimulate an eventual informal accord that left it better off.

On one hand the creation of an increased number of formal procedures under treaty auspices has necessitated the creation of an increased number of informal bargains for new rules to flesh out the formal rules and render them more practicable. On the other hand, with each new formal bargain particularly the Parliament has become better positioned to pursue its strategy of persuading, cajoling, and even on occasion forcing the other organizational actors to accede to its own broad interpretation of its newly received powers. Since the SEA, Maastricht, Amsterdam, Nice, and Lisbon Treaties, the Parliament has had many more formal powers in recent years to try to expand on informally. In attempting to parlay activity in the EU's informal sphere into an outcome consistent with its preferences, the Parliament is better placed to succeed if the starting point for the next round of the power game represents a more powerful position than in previous rounds.

Thus, in the process of "clarifying" the gray areas in amending treaties—thereby necessitating at least a modicum of informal interorganizational dynamics—not only do the Three iron out problems in policy-making processes based on strict interpretations of the Treaty, but the Parliament and Commission also use the process of informal rule creation in an incessant attempt to augment its position vis-à-vis each other but especially the Council. Always attempting to garner more power at the expense of its counterparts, the Parliament has learned that if it continues to "shoot for the moon"—occasionally undershooting for strategic purposes—it is bound to end up with at least partially achieving its aims, a time-tested and fairly reliable strategy by all accounts. In part by overcoming its long-standing political fecklessness, the Parliament has proved increasingly deft at playing the power game with its partners/rivals in the EU's informal sphere. In this sense, of its own accord the Parliament has endogenously changed one of the chief constraints on its ability to realize its preferences, viz. the organizational ineptitude that plagued the Parliament in the first two decades of its existence (or at least it has responded effectively to the exogenously determined inception of direct elections in 1979).

[7] EU official, interview by the author, European Commission, Brussels, July 20, 1994.

More significant still, because constraints on the Council's ability to achieve its preferences have changed, it is increasingly difficult for the Council to stonewall; moreover, the Council's own interests are occasionally served by brokering informal accords. With regard to the Commission, little has changed concerning its influence in the EU policy-making process—overall it is worse off due to the Parliament's gains—for the constraints on the pursuit of its preferences have not changed in ways advantageous to it. Or, put in a different way, the Commission has in fact continued to achieve its primary aim, viz. maintaining its power as sole legislative initiator.

Informal interorganizational dynamics and the Council

The Parliament's success prompts several questions: Why has the Council acceded to the Parliament's wishes, if only on the odd occasion? Given its preference of maintaining the level of authority prescribed to it by the Treaty, what circumstances have caused the Council to relinquish some of its authority? What specific changes in constraints have effected an erosion of the Council's power vis-à-vis the other organizational actors?

Due to its more powerful position, the Council has always played a crucial role in the EU's informal interorganizational dynamics and *ipso facto* the Parliament's ability to improve its position in the organizational hierarchy outside the formal sphere. Quite simply, unless the Council decides to give way or is forced to do so, the Parliament's incessant pursuit of greater power is stymied. In fact, this is reflected in the long-standing typical result of interorganizational skirmishes: the Parliament demands changes in the rules governing its relations with the Council, and the Council roundly refuses (only during the 1990s did this begin to change).

Such an outcome is hardly surprising given the Council's preference for maintaining the interorganizational balance of power and keeping its allotment of policy-making powers intact. Accordingly, its official position has long been that the Treaty must be adhered to by the letter, without exception; hence, activity in the informal arena shall in no way be allowed to alter the *acquis*.[8] Yet, as made clear in the above evidence, the Council has failed to achieve its preferences consistently, as the Parliament has

---

[8] EU official, interview by the author, Council of Ministers, Brussels, July 26, 1994.

made inroads in defiance of the Council's traditional dictum. Its preferences have not changed: whereas the constraints on its behavior have.

In layman's terms the Council succumbs to the Parliament's wishes under one of two scenarios: either when the Council's interests dictate trade-offs that give the Parliament greater influence, or when the Parliament successfully pressures the Council into brokering an informal accord. Under the first scenario, in the interest of maintaining at least a semblance of amicable relations, the Council on occasion finds it necessary to make concessions to the Parliament. Prior to the advent of direct elections in 1979, the Council was under little pressure to transfer policy-making powers to the Parliament. In the 1980s, however, buttressed by its new-found democratic legitimacy, the Parliament became increasingly antagonistic in its demands of the other organizational actors. Only gradually did the Council begin to respond to these novel, constraint-changing dynamics.

In terms of modeling informal interorganizational dynamics, the two constraints that have evinced flux are in fact somewhat intertwined with each other: the Council's accountability constraint and the Parliament's deficient leadership/expertise constraint. Post-1980 the Council began to feel increased pressure to take steps to democratize the EU, particularly as Member States began to transfer greater segments of sovereignty to the supranational level. Whereas the Parliament, motivated by its desire for greater legislative muscle and viewing the "democratic deficit" as something of an Achilles heel for the Council, has over time sought to decrease its political ineptitude.

In terms of the latter, in resolutely refusing to yield early on, the Council acted contrary to the unspoken rule of upholding the EU's consensus-based ethos. Initially unconcerned about decorum, the Council soon discovered that, unless the Parliament's demands were at least partially—if infrequently—met, then the Parliament would prove to be highly obstructive, often going to considerable lengths to scuttle the Council's aims if only by substantially delaying various procedures and even rejecting the EU budget at one point in the 1980s.[9] Gradually, due to a substantially improved political ability of the Parliament, as well as the evolution of a specific political strategy among the Parliament's talented civil servant staff, this constraint became attenuated. The relaxation of this constraint transpired directly in sync with the Parliament's increased ability to cause

---

[9] Even under the consultation procedure in which the Parliament seemingly possessed no political power of substance, it did have the power to delay any given piece of policy legislation.

234

interorganizational havoc. On these occasions, the Council rightly accused the Parliament of putting politics above principle; nonetheless, with time the Parliament increasingly failed to relent.

The Parliament resisted the Council on many occasions, but the yearly budget negotiations were particularly beset by interorganizational strife. Although more often than not the Council achieved its aims, rarely was it able to do so without expending prodigious time and resources, not to mention the considerable inconvenience of Council officials having to travel from Brussels to Strasbourg and spend the whole of their only night there in the throes of contentious negotiations. Often exasperated, they felt it was "like going into the parlor of the EP spider to do the deal; we felt weak."[10] Moreover, with much more at stake at the supranational level after the amending treaties from the SEA through Lisbon—in terms of both transferred sovereign powers and policy competencies—the Council felt it could not afford ongoing interorganizational strife.

Because rampant discord proved costly to the Council—the Parliament was growing increasingly adept at delaying and blocking legislation—it began seeking ways to appease or "buy off" the Parliament without sacrificing its primary objectives. Informal accords provided a ready solution. As an indication of the Council's strenuous efforts to mitigate the budget-related dissension, it agreed at that time to what was the EU's most significant informal accord to date: the 1988 budgetary accord was a landmark, and the Council itself actually requested it of the Parliament.

The other significant constraint in question is that which impinged on the Council's ability to achieve its preferences due to the pressure on the EU to become more transparent and democratic. Perceptions of EU citizens that Brussels officials are "out of touch" as well as the bias of a mildly pro-Parliament international press corps have both contributed to this pressure. As a result, according to one senior Council official, when dealing with problems "the Council is driven by a 'be nice to Parliament' orthodoxy."[11] Because of its democratic legitimacy, "in an official or public position it is quite impossible to criticize the Parliament."[12] Officials in the Commission speak of an incipient post-Maastricht conventional wisdom that one "needs to have the Parliament with you."[13]

---

[10] EU official, interview by the author, Council of Ministers, Brussels, July 25, 1994.

[11] EU official, interview by the author, Council of Ministers, Brussels, January 21, 2002.

[12] EU official, interview by the author, Council of Ministers, Brussels, January 21, 2002.

[13] EU official, interview by the author, European Commission, Brussels, July 20, 1994.

In terms of ultimate causes, the final constraint change causally acting on the Council's change in behavior has been a steadily rising pressure on the Council's President-in-Office to achieve success during its six months occupying the Council Presidency. This shift was unforeseen by the Parliament and the Commission, but each has been happy to take advantage of it—occasionally viewing a particular Members State occupying the Presidency as an ephemeral ally. The desire to be "successful" has not only concerned newer, smaller Member States like Finland or Greece but also older, larger ones like the United Kingdom and France.

Thus, although the Council has rejected far more of the Parliament's demands than it has accommodated, over the past several decades the pace of its interorganizational deal making has increased markedly. Typically, the Council will negotiate informal accords with the Parliament when either its own interests necessitate striking a compromise (such as not being perceived as anti-democratic) or it concludes that continuing pressure from the Parliament is too costly, either of which augments the Parliament's influence. The changing nature of these constraints have largely accounted for the greater divergence of the Council's interests from its unchanged preferences, viz. the need to mitigate interorganizational conflict and the pressure on the EU to become more transparent and democratic. The Parliament has proved capable of enticing, and on occasion forcing, the Council to enter into informal negotiations with it.

As these constraints have changed, outcomes of informal interorganizational dynamics have *ipso facto* changed. In sync with the gradual shifts in these key constraints, the organizational actors—as indicated quite starkly in Figure 4.1—have not only generated an increased number of informal accords but also an increased number of accords of a more formal nature, especially substantive accords. Stemming directly from changes in three important constraints regarding the Parliament and the Council, the former has achieved a relative increase in the realization of its power preferences while the latter has experienced a relative decrease in the realization of its power preferences. As no important constraints pertaining to the Commission have changed, except the change involving the Parliament's increased expertise, it has not made any power inroads via informal interorganizational dynamics. If anything, it has become increasingly weakened as a result of a string of bilateral accords with the Parliament.

Neither institutionalization nor integration?

The effects of informal accords do involve a substantial degree of institutionalization—the entrenchment of existing procedural norms. Yet, clearly something more significant is also taking place: interorganizational power relations have shifted discernibly. The Parliament is stronger, the Commission is relatively weaker, and the Council is clearly weaker.[14] Nonetheless, despite the increased activity in the informal sphere in evidence, the cluster of informal accords reached do not amount to a massive degree of hard and fast integration—a wholesale redistribution of legislative power among the organizational actors. In fact, while the amount of direct policy-making power transferred from one organizational actor to another is far from negligible, it is more accurate to argue that integration has indeed occurred though largely in terms of a modest amount.[15]

It is difficult to ascertain the precise number of formal treaty rules that started out as informal rules, for the historical record involving an array of basic and standard type informal accords is either incomplete or absent. However, officials among the Three concur on my own measurement of between one-sixth and one-fifth formal treaty provisions being reincarnations of rules first created in the EU's informal sphere, all either verbatim or with slightly altered wording but no discernible alteration of the substance.[16] This is a significant percentage, demonstrating the important link between the formal and informal spheres. Nonetheless, because this book has demonstrated the intrinsic and direct importance of the every day role played by the contents of informal accords, the EU's policy-making process in which legislation is regularly produced simply could not function in their absence (nor could a vast array of Parliament's fully realized policy aims been possible to achieve). Thus, the appropriate perspective to take as an outsider looking in is quite literally to consider the EU's informal institutions as part of the policy-making process itself, with the informal sphere comprising a sort of shadow treaty. All told there are some 600 informal rules that operate all the time in relations among the Three, and EU officials are so accustomed to this that they simply make no day-to-day distinction between formal and informal rules—in a classic European sense, they just get on with it and muddle through.

[14] EU official, interview by the author, Council of Ministers, Brussels, May 6, 2003.

[15] EU official, interview by the author, European Parliament, Brussels, May 5, 2003.

[16] EU official, interview by the author, European Parliament, Brussels, May 5, 2003; EU official, interview by the author, Council of Ministers, Brussels, May 6, 2003.

It is more appropriate to speak of informal interorganizational dynamics having engendered a slow, steady shift in the organizational balance of the EU, a shift which involves more than a mere entrenchment of the status quo but less than a dramatic transfer of powers. Thus, interspersed between the more notable large-scale institutional transformations engendered by formal treaty bargains, relations between the organizational actors are also changing as a result of informal bargains brokered separately from and temporally "in-between" amending treaties.

This change is neither overt nor even deliberate at times; rather, it takes place gradually—sometimes over rather protracted periods—as new accords require time to congeal into quasi-fixed behavioral patterns. This phenomenon can be appropriately characterized as "institutional displacement," for the informal accords serve gradually to displace previous policy-making frameworks with slightly altered frameworks. The relational change between the Three occurs in haphazard series of small steps, as opposed to large leaps. While EU officials sometimes lack perspective on how much ground has been gained over the years—unable to see the woods for the trees in the course of their every day legislative activities—when they step back and reflect on the cumulative effect of activity in the EU's informal sphere they often marvel.[17]

However gradual the displacement, informal accords taken together are clearly tantamount to an outcome of interregnum integration, one that has reengineered the EU in constitutional terms (in-between history-making events). The cumulative effect of informal interorganizational dynamics has been to make the Commission and the Council more accountable to the Parliament and to place the Parliament and the Council on more equal terms.[18] The Parliament has augmented its scrutiny of and control over the Commission primarily by using informal accords to build on its formal power of dismissal, as exemplified by inroads made in the process of appointing the Commission (the Commission has begun to worry that its "right of initiative will be delayed or blocked" in the near future, perhaps by

---

[17] EU official, interview by the author, Council of Ministers, Brussels, July 6, 2007; EU official, interview by the author, Council of Ministers, Brussels, July 6, 2007; EU official, interview by the author, European Parliament, Brussels, July 4, 2007; EU official, interview by the author, European Commission, Brussels, July 5, 2007.

[18] Westlake would appear to concur. See Westlake (1994a: 38). However, as indicated earlier, informal accords have not always served purely as vehicles for the power drives of the Parliament. Originally they were used strictly for the purpose of filling in gaps in the Treaty, i.e. acting as "constitutional glue." In the course of implementing the SEA the Parliament saw the potential for using informal accords as negotiating tools and subsequently seized on the opportunity without looking back.

informal means).[19] However, the Parliament's primary game is being played with the Council, as most of its influence attempts target that organizational actor.

In the early days of the EU, the Parliament and the Council rarely came into contact with each other; in fact, the 1957 Treaty of Rome did not even grant the Parliament the power of asking the Council written questions. Now contact is frequent, routine, and on multiple levels, all of which has been directly enhanced by the informal accords that are brokered both as a result of formal treaty implementations and as an alternative to them.

The more two different individual actors or competing groups come in contact with one another, the less likely it is that the more powerful individual or group will completely ignore the less powerful individual or group. "Whatever their 'bottom line' in terms of formal powers, MEPs also exert influence by their very presence in the discussions...The fact that their formal rights in the legislative procedure have increased can only reinforce their informal role."[20] Hence, the Parliament is better positioned as a result of informal accords to make use of its formal powers, which have also been increasing substantially during the 1980s, 1990s, and 2000s.

The Parliament has shown itself rather adept at exploiting the opportunities it receives to engage both the Council and the Commission. Generally speaking, in its negotiations with the other organizational actors the Parliament has had a fair degree of success in managing to secure at least a handful of concessions by pressuring its counterparts to grant it a lot more authority than it is likely to receive. This is the Parliament's "shoot for the moon" strategy detailed earlier: by bombarding its organizational counterparts with requests and demands, and with an increasingly greater degree of relative authority, the Parliament tends to attain some if not all of its objectives. In this scenario the other two organizational actors find themselves hard-pressed not to give in to the Parliament in *some* way, if for no other reason than simply to appease it.[21] The necessary caveat here is that from the mid-1990s forward the Parliament has grown shrewder still, increasingly adept at holding back in an attempt to gain more by demanding less. In so doing it has garnered increased respect from its EU counterparts, particularly in the Commission but also in the Council.[22]

---

[19] EU official, interview by the author, European Commission, Brussels, July 4, 2007.
[20] Corbett et al. (2000b: 203).
[21] EU official, interview by the author, Council of Ministers, Brussels, July 25, 1994.
[22] EU official, interview by the author, Council of Ministers, Brussels, May 6, 2003.

Quite crucial is how the ratchet effect ensures that once something is agreed, it essentially will not be reversed in the future. Reversions are prevented because the binding nature of informal accords (backed up by political goodwill and the specter of political sanctions) prevents any significant changes in the arrangements made unless mutually agreed to by the organizational actors.[23] As the ratchet effect prevents any backsliding or unraveling of informal commitments made, there is a one-way direction to informal interorganizational dynamics. This is not a teleological claim. My argument is not that there is an inexorable element to informal interorganizational dynamics; rather, while they may or may occasion further integration, the expectation of any backsliding in the informal sphere is virtually nil due to the high costs involved for the Three. In fact, the ratchet effect not only "locks in" agreements but also increases the likelihood that future accords will be brokered. Occurring is a particular sort of path dependence cum institutional change, as accounted for by my RCI bargaining theory.

With more formal powers the Parliament is able to bring more pressure to bear on the Council and Commission some of which began as informal rules. Moreover, as the Parliament has lived up to its end of the bargain regarding informal accords, its legitimacy in the eyes of the other organizational actors has grown considerably.[24] No longer, it would seem, can the Parliament be maligned as the Don Quixote of European integration. While the Commission too has been involved in and at times pressed its agenda via informal means, based on the model's predictions it is the Parliament that has been the greater beneficiary. As has been demonstrated, the actor constraints that have changed significantly in the model pertain much more directly to the Council and Parliament, except insofar as the Parliament's ability to exercise greater influence over the Commission has increased.[25] Thus, in terms of how the alteration of constraints has altered outcomes, the Parliament has been the principal beneficiary of this type of influence attempt.

For example, the 1975 Joint Declaration accord in the budgetary sphere and its successors have achieved this by obliging the Council and Parliament to sit down with each other in a conciliation committee specifically designed to facilitate direct negotiation over their budgetary differences.

[23] EU official, interview by the author, European Commission, Brussels, January 22, 2002.

[24] EU official, interview by the author, Council of Ministers, Brussels, May 6, 2003.

[25] The Commission has begun to fear being cajoled into informal accords with the Parliament, but especially bilateral accords between the Parliament and Council that partially negate the Commission's policy initiation role in the codecision procedure (EU official, interview by the author, European Commission, Brussels, July 4, 2007).

Although the Council is still not under a formal obligation to agree to the Parliament's terms, the two sides have proved generally more able to reach consensus in this forum. "The Parliament constantly is playing the game and increasing its powers, and the Council is constantly stepping back."[26] Another salient example involves the 1994 Comitology accord under the provisions of which the Parliament garnered a legitimate legislative power, viz. consultation, which it lacked prior to the agreement. Whereas the 2006 Comitology accord amounts to one of the two most significant in EU history, in which the Council went well beyond the Treaty to grant the Parliament a long-sought power to veto a whole range of policy implementation decisions by the Commission—a power the Council zealously preferred to retain but eventually was forced to surrender.

A Council official describes the incessant struggle with the Parliament in the following manner: "It's always the same practice: you don't refuse to play the game, so we try to limit it. Then, at the end we always try to present a compromise text where we try as much as possible to stick to treaty-based practices, and in the end the Parliament is always 'Well OK, but X is a new practice that is needed.' [i.e., a new informal rule arrogating itself increased influence] So every day is a process of constantly defending, keeping up a role as arch defender of the institution. Welle is the new Ayatollah of the Parliament; Romer was the old one."[27]

Indeed, informal accords have impacted EU policy-making via a modest reallocation of the organizational actors' legislative powers, largely on the basis of informal accords falling into Categories II and III, the least informal types of accord. Although the impact of Category I accords has been minimal, overall this phenomenon is noteworthy. The Parliament has utilized these agreements to reframe the context in which specific policy outcomes are pursued. Although this means of augmenting its authority is more indirect—and more esoteric—than receiving new powers via formal amending treaties, it is no less important.

From the Parliament's perspective, winning the policy game is what its attempt to shift the organizational power balance is ultimately about. It has found that one of the best ways to play the game is to utilize informal accords to frame an issue or a scenario to its advantage: "We always want to progress institutionally, whether there is formal progress or not."[28] In part

[26] EU official, interview by the author, Council of Ministers, Brussels, May 7, 2003.

[27] EU official, interview by the author, Council of Ministers, Brussels, July 6, 2007. Here the official refers by name to two former prominent Secretary Generals of the Parliament.

[28] EU official, interview by the author, European Parliament, Brussels, July 5, 2007.

it has managed to succeed by pressuring the Member States to act to decrease the democratic deficit: "More and more there is a visible gap of democracy, and that's why the Parliament has got cards. It holds the cards in playing games with the Council."[29] This is what the Parliament has achieved in recasting the EU's budgetary framework and other legislative initiatives. Indeed, officials in the Council concur that instances of the Parliament persuading the Council to do something it otherwise would not have done are becoming more common.[30]

The Parliament has also honed its strategy over time. In the 1990s, strategists in the Parliament began to eye the informal sphere as a potential growth area. "Previously, we were not very good at horizontal efforts [strategy aimed at the Council and Commission]; for example, our committees operated like independent planets. In order to be strategic as an actor, we instituted a more universal strategy." Later, the same strategists in the Parliament's Political Groups noticed a Council weakness. As a result, increasingly during the 2000s it has sought to take advantage of chinks in the Council's armor, viz. sympathetic Member States. In recent years the Parliament has found the Nordic Member States some of the more pliable and/or sympathetic to its preferences. "Each Presidency gets two or three 'free shots,' so we try to take advantage of this."[31] The Presidencies of Finland and Sweden have been particularly helpful to the Parliament, as have the Austrians. "There is a tendency of the [EU] Presidency to give a lot to the Parliament. COREPER is not the problem; the problem is the minister. Once the negotiation really gets going, the minister doesn't know the file. This is the reason we prefer first reading resolution: to avoid the minister problem. Each Presidency must have success and [we] can't risk this [because] the Presidency can't see the position of the institution over the long haul."[32]

During the 2000s the cabinet of the Parliament's president became the locus of political strategy formation. The strategy came to involve the following key elements: getting MEPs involved in the strategizing; maximizing the Parliament's impact on agenda-setting, for example, the Parliament now passes official reports in its plenary sessions on what policy outcomes it desires before the Commission formulates its legislative program; looking for opportunities of issue linkage wherever they can be

---

[29] EU official, interview by the author, Council of Ministers, Brussels, May 7, 2003.
[30] EU official, interview by the author, Council of Ministers, Brussels, May 6, 2003.
[31] EU official, interview by the author, European Parliament, Brussels, July 5, 2007.
[32] EU official, interview by the author, Council of Ministers, Brussels, July 6, 2007.

found, for example, linking policy debates and budget debates; and maximizing its influence in terms of its coequal status with the Council on all budgetary matters, for example, although it has no formal foreign policy powers it does have veto rights over the funding of the EU's external ventures.[33] Council frustration has mounted as the Parliament has sharpened its strategizing: "The Parliament always tries to engage in conquest and shift the [interorganizational] balance. Because we will be in a corner if we appear obliging, we have to be hard; but often we end up soft."[34]

As a result, because it is achieving more of its policy and power objectives compared to earlier periods, the Parliament occupies a better position vis-à-vis the Council in an altered framework than it did in any previous framework. In other words, relative to where it was in the 1970s, notwithstanding its newer formal powers the balance between the two organizational actors has shifted less in the Council's favor. Hence, although the Parliament has not gained a full laundry list of desired advantages from informal accords—some of them include the ability to force the Commission to withdraw proposals it rejects under codecision, to offer its opinion for all comitology committees under Article 189b, to compel the Council to engage in budgetary conciliations, to convene budgetary trilogues, and to veto Commission policy implementation decisions—at a minimum the Parliament has modestly but significantly expanded its influence in the EU policy-making process.

In parallel, numerous informal rules have been swept up by the Member States into treaties, thereby formalizing them. It is a clear recognition of the overall importance of the rules contained in informal accords. The Council has come not only to live with but also occasionally to value their impact insofar as how much improved the policy-making procedures are with the parallel informal rules, not only filling formal gaps but also keeping the Parliament content and less combative. While Member States have not swept up all informal rules—for example, many key rules of the budgetary procedure remain informal—they have frequently codified their existence by sweeping them up during IGCs. "Very often things are codified after [an informal accord comes into existence]; there is evidence that they work and are often thereafter codified."[35]

Influence is by nature a difficult phenomenon to measure, partly because its increase or decrease is normally fairly gradual, and partly because it can

---

[33] EU official, interview by the author, European Parliament, Brussels, July 5, 2007.
[34] EU official, interview by the author, Council of Ministers, Brussels, July 6, 2007.
[35] EU official, interview by the author, European Parliament, Brussels, July 5, 2007.

take any number of forms. Influence can be exercised as a direct consequence of a particular structure of formal power; a political actor can strategically force or compel another political actor to do something it otherwise would not; and a political actor can set the agenda and reframe the policy process in such a way that its own preferences can be achieved without explicit coercion over others taking part in the process. Each of these is an example of the operation of influence.

Informal interorganizational dynamics in the EU exemplify all of these scenarios, most notably the third one. By causing shifts in the distribution of power among the EU's primary organizational actors, I have demonstrated that the new informal institutions have transformed the overall framework in which policies are made, enabling the traditionally weak Parliament to exercise greater ability to affect policy-making outcomes—and under certain conditions dictate them. By acting outside the scope of the Treaty and thus the law, the European Parliament has rendered EU Member States less sovereign.

Theoretical implications

In conclusion I maintain that the new institutional rules encapsulated in informal accords do indeed amount to integration (in addition to a degree of institutionalization and negligible disintegration), their having altered the formal status quo and, *ipso facto*, engendered integration beyond what is prescribed by the cumulative, Member State-brokered Treaty. The implications of my RCI-based theory, therefore, are multiple. First, as accounted for by it, interorganizational dynamics contribute to the accuracy of our understanding of how the EU actually works in practice: integration occurs not simply every five years or so but in-between amending treaties— that is, in the interregnum. The EU is nothing if not a mélange of incessant bargaining on multiple policy *and* power levels.

Second, although Member State-dominated IGCs account for a sizable variance portion of the integration outcome, a modest portion is accounted for by the bargaining theory underpinning informal interorganizational dynamics. Moreover, there is more to an IGC than meets the eye, for numerous formal treaty provisions seemingly introduced in the Member State forum are in fact reincarnations of previously extant informal rules that first resided in informal accords. Third, the results indicate that pure P/A theoretical accounts of European integration could do well to be expanded to incorporate not only shirking but occasional defiance. Instead, the bargaining theory proffered here is rooted in a branch of rational choice institutionalism that places strategic interaction and distributional concerns front and center among postulated causes. Fourth, in more general terms the theory underpinning this project is nothing if not a theory of institutional change and would thus appear to apply to a wider array of comparative and world politics phenomena.

For example, beginning in the early 2000s the Basel, Switzerland-based Bank of International Settlements (BIS), to which virtually all central banks around the world belong, has been effecting considerable worldwide banking system change entirely via informality. The BIS possesses no formal authority over individual banks around the world and cannot force them to do anything; however, over time it has amassed a high degree of informal authority and become an effective regulator of individual bank behavior with regard to their attempts to hedge against risk. Indeed, it has promulgated substantial change as to how much capital banks need to have on hand to deal with risks to their well being and significantly impacted how they assess and manage these risks. Other international organizations like the International Association of Insurance Supervisors (IAIS) and the International Organization of Security Commissions (IOSCO) are increasingly operating in a similar manner, not to mention a variety of international standards setting organizations like the International Organization for Standardization (ISO) and the International Electrotechnical Commission (IEC).

Likewise, international war tribunal-type organizations face a similar challenge to organizational actors in the EU, viz. how to operate with effectiveness and legitimacy when there is not a great deal of precedent to look to (what I referred to earlier in the EU case as circumstances involving the lack of a constitutional settlement). The highly significant International Criminal Tribunal of the former Yugoslavia (ICTY) has prosecuted thousands of individuals for various war crimes in the region, and the bulk of the institutional rules it has abided by stem not from the series of formal United Nations Security Council resolutions that created the ICTY, but from informal precedents set by its administrators and judges. Similarly, the recently created International Criminal Court (ICC), which is designed to expand on ICTY's success and handle war crimes around the world, is proceeding in accordance with the formal treaty prescriptions from the Rome Treaty; however, it too is creating a bevy of informal institutions to govern its first set of cases stemming from alleged war crimes in the Sudan.

Back in the EU, if evidence can be found not only that informal interorganizational dynamics is extant but also that they contribute to an integration outcome—that is, explain a portion of the outcome's variance—then a distinction between types of integration would be necessary. As such, based on the evidence gathered in this project and recent contributions concerning the EU's legal sphere, it is advisable to recall the distinction between history-making integration and interregnum integration. *History-making integration* amounts to national-to-supranational sovereignty transfer on the basis of formal treaty bargains; this is to say that the decisions not only to give up sovereignty but also to design the forms that transferred sovereignty will take at the supranational level, are encapsulated in the provisions and rules of primary law-based, inter-Member State treaties.[36] As formal bargains, treaties tend to have a "big bang" sort of an effect on European integration; for this reason, they tend to attract a considerable degree of attention in the press.

However, *interregnum integration* amounts to national-to-supranational sovereignty transfers either on the basis of the ECJ's jurisprudence or on the basis of informal accords, which is to say that the decisions to transfer sovereignty on the supranational level either flow through court rulings from the ECJ or are encapsulated in bargains that lack both a legal basis and a third-party external enforcer (which is in fact the ECJ in the EU context). Informal accords are negotiated not between Member State governments, but between the supranational organizational actor which collectively represents them—the Council and its counterparts among the Three. The accords comprise far fewer rules than the bargains that are formal treaties; for this reason they attract less attention from the press and the public. Nonetheless, empirical evidence demonstrates not only that the integration process is furthered in-between formal amending treaties but also and more importantly that the primary source of interregnum integration is not the Member States, but the Council's supranational competitors instead. Moreover, the evidence further testifies to the fact that formal treaty provisions often trace their origins directly to the informal institutions found in informal accords.

Short of a wholesale transfer of power from the Council to the Parliament or the Commission, informal accords give rise to institutional

---

[36] Peterson and Bomberg offer a similar definition of "history-making decisions"—those that function by "altering its procedures…or adjusting the Union's remit"—which is consistent with my operationalization, though broader in scope and not consistently delineated. Moreover, their misjudgment that informal processes do not constitute institutions is perhaps why they give little credence to the EU's informal sphere, from which interregnum integration is possible. In spirit, however, our renditions of history-making interorganizational bargains are much the same. See Peterson and Bomberg (1999: 1–2, 10–11, 21).

displacement, a subtler but nonetheless significant outcome involving shifts in relations between the organizational actors more by altering the policy framework and improving the status of the weaker organizational actors than by strictly redistributing legislative powers—despite their being multiple documented instances of the latter. Beyond doubt, therefore, informal interorganizational dynamics serve to tilt the EU interorganizational balance of power more in the Parliament's favor and modestly augment the integration of its Member States. Informal accords thus contribute to an ongoing reengineering of the EU "constitution"—that is, the *acquis communautaire*—by formal *and* informal means.

Bibliography

Abbott, Kenneth W. and Duncan Snidal. "Hard and Soft Law in International Governance." *International Organization* 54, 3 (2000): 421–56.

Anderson, Jeffrey J. "The State of the (European) Union: From the Single Market to Maastricht, from Singular Events to General Theories." *World Politics* 47 (1995): 441–65.

Arthur, Brian. *Increasing Returns and Path Dependence in the Economy.* Ann Arbor, MI: University of Michigan Press, 1994.

Aspinwall, Mark and Gerald Schneider. "Same Menu, Separate Tables: The Institutionalist Turn in Political Science and the Study of European Integration." *European Journal of Political Research* 38, 1 (2000): 1–36.

—————— Eds. *The Rules of Integration: Institutionalist Approaches to the Study of Europe.* Manchester: Manchester University Press, 2001.

Axelrod, Robert. *The Evolution of Cooperation.* New York: Basic Books, 1984.

Ballman, Alexander, David Epstein, and Sharon O'Halloran. "Delegation, Comitology, and the Separation of Powers in the European Union." *International Organization* 56 (2002): 551–74.

Bates, Robert H. and William T. Bianco. "Cooperation by Design: Leadership, Structure, and Collective Dilemmas." *American Political Science Review* 84 (March 1990*a*).

—————— "The New Organizational Theory." Eds. Karen Schweers Cook and Margaret Levi. *The Limits of Rationality.* Chicago: University of Chicago Press, 1990*b*.

Bieber, Roland. "The Settlement of Institutional Conflicts on the Basis of Article 4 of the EEC Treaty." *Common Market Law Review* 21 (1984): 505–23.

Bryder, Tom. "Party Groups in the European Parliament and the Changing Recruitment Patterns of MEPs." Eds. David S. Bell and Christopher Lord. *Transnational Parties in the European Union.* Aldershot: Ashgate, 1998.

Bulmer, Simon. "The Governance of the European Union: A New Institutionalist Approach." *Journal of Public Policy* 13 (1994): 351–80.

Burley, Anne-Marie and Walter Mattli. "Europe Before the Court: A Political Theory of Legal Integration." *International Organization* 47, 1 (1993): 41–76.

Büthe, Tim. "Taking Temporality Seriously: Modeling History and the Use of Narratives as Evidence." *American Political Science Review* 96 (2002): 481–93.

Calvert, Randall. "Rational Actors, Equilibrium, and Social Institutions." Eds. Jack Knight and Itai Sened. *Explaining Social Institutions*. Ann Arbor, MI: University of Michigan Press, 1995.

Cameron, David. "The 1992 Initiative: Causes and Consequences." Ed. Alberta Sbragia. *Euro-Politics: Institutions and Policymaking in the "New" European Community*. Washington, D.C.: The Brookings Institutions, 1992.

Caporaso, James. "The European Union and Forms of State: Westphalian, Regulatory, or Post-Modern?" *Journal of Common Market Studies* 34, 1 (1996): 29–52.

Carey, John M. "Parchment, Equilibria, and Institutions." *Comparative Political Studies* 33 (2000): 735–61.

Checkel, Jeffrey. "Norms, Institutions, and National Identity in Contemporary Europe." *International Studies Quarterly* 43 (1999): 83–114.

—— "Constructing European institutions." Eds. Gerald Schneider and Mark Aspinwall. *The Rules of Integration: Institutionalist Approaches to the Study of Europe*. Manchester: Manchester University Press, 2001.

Christiansen, Thomas, Knud Erik Jorgensen, and Antje Wiener. *The Social Construction of Europe*. London: Sage, 2001.

—— Gerda Falkner, and Knud Erik Jørgensen. "Theorizing EU Treaty Reform: Beyond Diplomacy and Bargaining." *Journal of European Public Policy* 9, 1 (2002): 12–32.

Ciavarini Azzi, Giuseppe. "The Slow March of European Legislation: The Implementation of Directives." Eds. Karlheinz Neunreither and Antje Wiener. *European Integration After Amsterdam: Institutional Dynamics and Prospects for Democracy*. Oxford: Oxford University Press, 2000.

Commission of the European Communities. (2001) *European Governance: A White Paper*. COM (2002) 428 (final), Brussels, July, 25.

Corbett, Richard. *The European Parliament's Role in Closer EU Integration*. Basingstoke: Macmillan, 1998.

—— "Academic Modeling of the Codecision Procedure: A Practitioner's Puzzled Reaction." *European Union Politics* 1, 1 (2000*a*): 373–81.

—— Francis Jacobs, and Michael Shackleton. *The European Parliament*. 4th ed. London: John Harper, 2000*b*.

—— "Response to Garrett and Tsebelis." *European Union Politics* 2 (2001): 362–366.

Cortes, Cesar. *Co-decision: The Recent Developments*. Brussels: General Secretariat of the European Council, 2000.

Crombez, Cristopher. "The Co-Decision Procedure in the European Union." *Legislative Studies Quarterly* 22 (1997): 97–119.

David, Paul. "Clio and the Economics of QWERTY." *American Economic Review* 75 (1985): 332–7.

Deutsch, Karl. *Political Community and the North Atlantic Area*. Princeton, NJ: Princeton University Press, 1957.

Diermeier, Daniel and Keith Krehbiel. "Institutionalism as Methodology." *Journal of Theoretical Politics* 15 (2003): 123–44.

Diez, Thomas. "Speaking 'Europe': The Politics of Integration Discourse." *Journal of European Public Policy* 4 (1999): 652–68.

Diez Medrano, Juan. *Framing Europe: Attitudes to European Integration in Germany, Spain, and the United Kingdom*. Princeton, NJ: Princeton University Press, 2006.

DiMaggio, Paul J. and Walter W. Powell. "The Iron Cage Revisited: Institutional Isomorphism and Collective Rationality in Organizational Fields." Eds. Walter W. Powell and Paul J. DiMaggio. *The New Institutionalism in Organizational Analysis*. Chicago: University of Chicago Press, 1991.

Dogan, Rhys. "Comitology: Little Procedures with Big Implications." *West European Politics* 20 (1997): 31–60.

Dowding, Keith. "Institutionalist Research on the European Union: A Critical Review." *European Union Politics* 1 (2000): 125–44.

Driessen, Bart. *Interinstitutional Conventions in EU Law*. London: Cameron, May, 2007.

—— "Interinstitutional Conventions and Institutional Balance." *European Law Review* 33 (2008): 550–62.

Duff, Andrew. *The Treaty of Amsterdam: Text and Commentary*. London: Sweet & Maxwell, 1997.

Endo, Ken. *The Presidency of the European Commission Under Jacques Delors: The Politics of Shared Leadership*. New York: St. Martin's, 1999.

Eggertsson, Thrainn. "A Note on the Economics of Institutions." Eds. Lee J. Alston, Thrainn Eggertsson, and Douglass C. North. *Empirical Studies in Institutional Change*. Cambridge: Cambridge University Press, 1996.

Eichenberg, Richard C. and Russell J. Dalton. "Europeans and the European Community: The Dynamics of Public Support for European Integration." *International Organization* 47 (1993): 507–34.

Eiselt, Isabella, Johannes Pollak, and Peter Slominski. "Codifying Temporay Stability? The Role of Interinstitutional Agreements in Budgetary Politics." *European Law Journal* 13 (2007): 75–91.

Eisenstadt, Stuart N. *Essays on Comparative Institutions*. New York: Wiley and Sons, 1965.

Elster, Jon. Ed. *Rational Choice*. New York: New York University Press, 1986.

—— *Nuts and Bolts for the Social Sciences*. Cambridge: Cambridge University Press, 1989.

Falkner, Gerda. "Introduction: EU Treaty Reform as a Three-level Process," *Journal of European Public Policy* 9 (2002*a*): 1–11.

—— "How Intergovernmental are Intergovernmental Conferences? An Example from the Maastricht Treaty Reform." *Journal of European Public Policy* 9 (2002*b*): 98–119.

Farrell, Henry and Adrienne Héritier. "Formal and Informal Institutions Under Codecision: Continuous Constitution-Building in Europe." *Governance* 16 (2003): 577–600.

—— "Interorganizational Cooperation and Intraorganizational Power: Early Agreements under Codecision and their Impact on the Parliament and the Council." *Comparative Political Studies* 37, 10 (2004): 1184–212.

Fligstein, Neil and Alec Stone Sweet. "Constructing Polities and Markets: An Institutionalist Account of European Integration." *American Journal of Sociology* 107 (2002): 1206–43.

Finnemore, Martha and Kathryn Sikkink. "International Norm Dynamics and Political Change." *International Organization* 52 (1998): 887–917.

Franchino, Fabio. "Efficiency or Credibility? Testing the Two Logics of Delegation to the European Commission." *Journal of European Public Policy* 9 (2002): 677–94.

—— "Delegating Powers in the European Community." *British Journal of Political Science* 34 (2004): 449–76.

—— *The Powers of Union: Delegation in the EU*. Cambridge: Cambridge University Press, 2007.

Franklin, Mark N. and Susan E. Scarrow. "Making Europeans? The Socializing Power of the European Parliament." Eds. Richard S. Katz and Bernard Wessels. *The European Parliament, National Parliaments, and European Integration*. Oxford: Oxford University Press, 1999.

Gabel, Matthew J. *Interests and Integration: Market Liberalization, Public Opinion, and European Union*. Ann Arbor, MI: University of Michigan Press, 1998.

Garrett, Geoffrey. "Internal Cooperation and Institutional Choice: The European Community's Internal Market." *International Organization* 46 (1992): 533–60.

—— "The Politics of Legal Integration in the European Union." *International Organization* 49 (1995): 171–81.

Gelleny, Ronald D. and Christopher J. Anderson. "The Economy, Accountability, and Public Support for the President of the European Commission." *European Union Politics* 1 (2000): 173–200.

Genschel, Philipp. "The Dynamics of Inertia: Institutional Persistence and Change in Telecommunications and Health Care." *Governance* 10, 1 (1997): 43–66.

George, Stephen. *Politics and Policy in the European Community*. 2nd ed. Oxford: Oxford University Press, 1991.

Gourevitch, Peter A. "The Governance Problem in Strategic Interaction." Eds. David A. Lake and Robert Powell. *Strategic Choice and International Relations*. Princeton, NJ: Princeton University Press, 1999.

Grabitz, E. "The Sources of Community Law: Acts of the Community Institutions." *Thirty Years of Community Law, European Perspectives*. Luxembourg: Official Publications of the European Communities, 1983.

Greif, Avner. *Historical Institutionalist Analysis*. Unpublished manuscript, Stanford, CA, 2001.

Haas, Ernst B. *The Uniting of Europe*. Stanford: Stanford University Press, 1958.

—— "The Study of Regional Integration: Reflections on the Joys and Anguish of Pretheorizing." Eds. Leon N. Lindberg and Stuart A. Scheingold. *Regional Integration: Theory and Research*. Cambridge: Harvard University Press, 1971.

Hailbach, George. "The History of Comitology." Eds. Mads Andenas and Alexander Turk. *Delegated Legislation and the Role of Committees in the EC*. Boston: Kluwer Law International, 2000.

Hall, Peter A. *Governing the Economy: The Politics of State Intervention in Britain and France.* Oxford: Polity, 1986.

—— and Rosemary Taylor. "Political Science and the Three New Institutionalisms." *Political Studies* 44, 5 (1996): 936–57.

Hasenclever, Andreas Peter Meyer, and Volker Rittberger. *Theories of International Regimes.* Cambridge: Cambridge University Press, 1997.

Helmke, Gretchen and Steven Levitsky. "Informal Institutions and Comparative Politics: A Research Agenda." *Perspectives on Politics* 2 (2004): 725–40.

Héritier, Adrienne. *Policy-Making and Diversity in Europe: Escaping Deadlock.* New York: Cambridge University Press, 1999.

—— *The White Paper on European Governance: A Response to Shifting Weights in Inster-institutional Decision-Making.* Jean Monnet Working Paper No. 6/01. October, 2001.

Hix, Simon. "The Study of the European Community: The Challenge to Comparative Politics." *West European Politics* 17 (1994): 1–30.

—— "The Study of the European Union II: The 'New Governance' Agenda and Its Rival." *Journal of European Public Policy* 1 (1998): 38–65.

—— *The Political System of the European Union.* New York: St. Martin's Press, 1999.

—— "Parliamentary Oversight of Executive Power: What Role for the European Parliament in Comitology?" Eds. Thomas Christiansen and Emil Kirchner. *Europe in Change—Committee Governance in the European Union.* Manchester: Manchester University Press, 2000.

—— "Constitutional Agenda-Setting Through Discretion in Rule Interpretation: Why the European Parliament Won At Amsterdam." *British Journal of Political Science* 32, 2 (2002): 259–80.

—— Abdul G. Noury, and Gerard Roland. *Democratic Politics in the European Parliament.* Cambridge: Cambridge University Press, 2007.

Hoffmann, Stanley. "Reflections on the Nation-State in Western Europe Today." *Journal of Common Market Studies* 21 (1982): 21–37.

Hooghe, Liesbet. Ed. *Cohesion Policy and European Integration: Building Multi-Level Governance.* Oxford: Oxford University Press, 1996.

—— and Gary Marks. *Multi-Level Governance and European Integration.* Boulder, CO: Rowman & Littlefield, 2001.

Hug, Simon. "Endogenous Preferences and Delegation in the European Union." *Comparative Political Studies* 36 (2003): 41–74.

Hummer, Waldemar. "From 'Interinstitutional Agreements' to 'Interinstitutional Agencies/Offices'?" *European Law Journal* 13 (2007): 47–74.

Jabko, Nicolas. *Playing the Market: A Political Strategy for Uniting Europe, 1985–2005.* Ithaca, NY: Cornell University Press, 2006.

Jachtenfuchs, Marcus. "The Governance Approach to European Integration." *Journal of Common Market Studies* 39 (2002): 245–64.

—— Thomas Diez, and S. Jung. "Which Europe? Conflicting Models of a Legitimate European Political Order." *European Journal of International Relations* 4 (1998): 409–45.

Joerges, Chrisian and Jurgen Neyer. "Transforming Strategic Interaction into Deliberative Problem-Solving: European Comitology in the Foodstuffs Sector." *Journal of European Public Policy* 4 (1997): 609–25.

Judge, David, David Earnshaw, and Ngaire Cowan. "Ripples or Waves: The European Parliament in the European Community Policy Process." *Journal of European Public Policy* 1 (1994): 27–52.

Jun, Hae-Won. "Catching the Runaway Bureaucracy in Brussels." *European Union Politics* 4 (2003): 421–45.

Jupille, Joseph. *Procedural Politics: Issue, Influence, and Institutional Choice in the European Union.* Cambridge: Cambridge University Press, 2004.

—— and James Caporaso. "Institutionalism and the European Union: Beyond Comparative Politics and International Relations." *International Review of Political Science* 2 (1999): 429–44.

—— —— and Jeffrey Checkel. "Integrating Instituitons: Rationalism, Constructivism, and the Study of the European Union." *Comparative Political Studies* 36 (2003): 7–40.

Katzenstein, Peter, Robert O. Keohane, and Stephen J. Krasner. "International Organization and the Study of World Politics." *International Organization* 52 (1998): 645–85.

Keck, Margaret and Kathryn Sikkink. *Activists Beyond Borders: Advocacy Networks in International Politics.* Ithaca, NY: Cornell University Press, 1998.

Keitz, Daniela and Andreas Maurer. "The European Parliament in Treaty Reform: Predefining IGCs Through Interinstitutional Agreements." *European Law Journal* 13 (2007): 20–46.

Kelemen, Daniel. "The Politics of 'Eurocratic' Structure and the New European Agencies." *West European Politics* 25 (2002): 93–118.

Keohane, Robert O and Stanley Hoffman. "Institutional Change in Europe in the 1980's." Eds. Robert O. Keohane and Stanley Hoffman. *The New European Community.* Boulder, CO: Westview Press, 1991.

Kiewiet, D. Roderick and Matthew D. McCubbins. *The Logic of Delegation: Congressional Parties and the Appropriation Process.* Chicago: University of Chicago Press, 1991.

Kirschner, Emil. *Decision Making in the European Community: The Council Presidency and European Integration.* Manchester: Manchester University Press, 1992.

Knight, Jack. *Institutions and Social Conflict.* Cambridge: Cambridge University Press, 1992.

—— "Models, Interpretations, and Theories: Constructing Explanations of Institutional Emergence and Change." Eds. Jack Knight and Itai Sened. *Explaining Social Institutions.* Ann Arbor, MI: University of Michigan Press, 1995.

Kohler-Koch, Beate and Berthold Rittberger. "The 'Governance Turn' in EU Studies." *Journal of Common Market Studies* 44 (2006): 27–49.

Kollman, Kenneth. "The Rotating Presidency of the European Council as a Search for Good Policies." *European Union Politics* 4 (2003): 51–64.

Krasner, Stephen J. "Approaches to the State: Alternative Conceptions and Historical Dynamics." *Comparative Politics* 16 (1984): 223–46.

Kreppel, Amie. *The European Parliament and the Supranational Party System*. New York: Cambridge University Press, 2002.

Ladrech, Robert. "Europeanization of Domestic Politics and Institutions: The Case of France." *Journal of Common Market Studies* 32, 1 (1994): 69–88.

Laffan, Brigid. *Integration and Cooperation in Europe*. London: Routledge, 1992.

Lake, David A. and Robert Powell. *Strategic Choice and International Relations*. Princeton, NJ: Princeton University Press, 1999.

Levi, Margaret. "A Logic of Institutional Change." Eds. Karen Schweers Cook and Margaret Levi. *The Limits of Rationality*. Chicago: University of Chicago Press, 1990.

Lieberman, Robert. "Ideas, Institutions, and Political Order: Explaining Political Change." *American Political Science Review* 96, 4 (2002): 697–712.

Lindberg, Leon N. *The Political Dynamics of European Economic Integration*. Stanford, CA: Stanford University Press, 1963.

—— "Political Integration as a Multidimensional Phenomenon Requiring Multivariate Measurement." *Journal of Common Market Studies* 24 (1970): 649–50.

Lindner, Johannes and Berthold Rittberger. "The Creation, Interpretation, and Contestation of Institutions—Revisiting Historical Institutionalism." *Journal of Common Market Studies* 41 (2003): 445–74.

Lipson, Charles. "Why Are Some International Agreements Informal?" *International Organization* 45 (1991): 495–538.

Majone, Giandomenico. *Regulating Europe*. London: Routledge, 1996.

Mancini, G. Federico. "The Making of a Constitution for Europe." Eds. Robert O. Keohane and Stanley Hoffman. *The New European Community*. Boulder, CO: Westview Press, 1991.

March, James G. and Johan P. Olsen. "The New Institutionalism: Organizational Factors in Political Life." *American Political Science Review* 78 (1984): 749–84.

—— —— *Rediscovering Institutions: The Organizational Basis of Politics*. New York: Macmillan, 1989.

—— —— "The Institutional Dynamics of International Political Orders." *International Organization* 52 (1998): 943–59.

Marks, Gary, Liesbet Hooghe, and Kermit Blank. "European Integration Since the 1980s: State Centric Versus Multi-Level Governance." *Journal of Common Market Studies* 34 (1996): 341–78.

Marshall, Geoffrey. *Constitutional Conventions: The Rules and Forms of Political Accountability*. Oxford: Oxford University Press, 1984.

Mattli, Walter. *The Logic of Regional Integration: Europe and Beyond*. Cambridge: Cambridge University Press, 1999.

—— and Anne-Marie Burley. "Europe Before the Court: A Political Theory of Legal Integration." *International Organization* 47 (1993): 41–76.

—— and Anne-Marie Slaughter. "Law and Politics in the European Union: A Reply to Garrett." *International Organization* 49 (1995): 183–90.

—— —— "Revisiting the European Court of Justice." *International Organization* 52 (1998): 177–209.

McCubbins, Mathew and Thomas Schwartz. "Congressional Oversight Overlooked: Police Patrols versus Fire Alarms." *American Journal of Political Science* 28 (1984): 165–79.

McKelvey, Richard D. "Intransitivities in Multidimensional Voting Models and Some Implications for Agenda Control." *Journal of Economic Theory* 12 (1976): 472–82.

McLean, Iain. *Rational Choice and British Politics: An Analysis of Rhetoric and Manipulation from Peel to Blair.* Oxford: Oxford University Press, 2001.

McNamara, Kathleen R. *The Currency of Ideas: Monetary Politics in the European Union.* Ithaca, NY: Cornell University Press, 1998.

Meerts, Paul W. and Franz Cede. *Negotiating European Union.* London: Palgrave, 2004.

Meunier, Sophie: "What Single Voice? European Institutions and EU–US Trade Negotiations." *International Organization* 54 (2000): 103–35.

Middlemas, Keith. *Orchestrating Europe: The Informal Politics of the European Union, 1973–95.* London: Fontana Press, 1995.

Milner, Helen V. *Interests, Institutions, and Information.* Princeton, NJ: Princeton University Press, 1997.

—— "Rationalizing Politics: The Emerging Synthesis of International, American, and Comparative Politics." *International Organization* 52, 4 (1998): 759–86.

Moe, Terry M. "An Assessment of the Positive Theory of Congressional Dominance." *Legislative Studies Quarterly* 12 (1987): 475–520.

Monar, Jorg. "Institutional Agreements: The Phenomenon and Its New Dynamics After Maastricht." *Common Market Law Review* 31 (1994): 693–719.

Moravcsik, Andrew. "Negotiating the Single European Act: National Interests and Conventional Statecraft in the European Community." *International Organization* 45 (1991): 651–88.

—— "Preferences and Power in the European Community: A Liberal Intergovernmentalist Approach." *Journal of Common Market Studies* 31 (1993): 473–524.

—— *The Choice for Europe: Social Purpose and State Power from Messina to Maastricht.* Ithaca, NY: Cornell University Press, 1998.

—— and Kalypso Nicolaïdis. "Explaining the Treaty of Amsterdam: Interests, Influence, Institutions." *Journal of Common Market Studies* 37 (1999): 59–85.

Moser, Peter. "The European Parliament as a Conditional Agenda-Setter: What are the Conditions? A Critique of Tsebelis." *American Political Science Review* 90 (1996): 834–8.

Nelsen, Brent F. and James L. Guth. "Exploring the Gender Gap: Women, Men, and Public Attitudes Toward European Integration." *European Union Politics* 1 (2000): 267–91.

Niedermayer, Oskar and Richard Sinnott. "Democratic Legitimacy and the European Parliament." Eds. Oskar Niedermanyer and Richard Sinnott. *Public Opinion and Internationalized Governance.* Oxford: Oxford University Press, 1995.

North, Douglass C. *Institutions, Institutional Change, and Economic Performance.* Cambridge: Cambridge University Press, 1990.

—— "Epilogue: Economic Performance Through Time." Eds. Lee J. Alston, Thrainne Eggertsson, and Douglass C. North. *Empirical Studies in Institutional Change.* Cambridge: Cambridge University Press, 1996.

Nugent, Neill. *The Government and Politics of the European Union.* 5th ed. Durham: Duke University Press, 2003.

Nye, Joseph S. *The Paradox of American Power.* Oxford: Oxford University Press, 2002.

O'Nuallain, C. Ed. *The Presidency of the European Council of Ministers.* London: Croom Helm, 1985.

Ostrom, Elinor. *Governing the Commons: The Evolution of Institutions for Collective Action.* Cambridge: Cambridge University Press, 1990.

Parsons, Craig. *A Certain Idea of Europe.* Ithaca: Cornell University Press, 2003.

Pentland, Charles. *International Theory and European Integration.* London: Faber and Faber, 1973.

Peters, B. Guy. "Bureaucratic Politics and the Institutions of the European Community." Ed. Alberta Sbragia. *Euro-Politics: Institutions and Policymaking in the "New" European Community.* Washington, D.C.: The Brookings Institutions, 1992.

—— *Institutional Theory in Political Science: The "New Institutionalism."* London: Pinter, 1999.

Peterson, John. "Decision-Making in the European Union: Towards a Framework for Analysis." *Journal of European Public Policy* 2 (1995): 69–93.

—— and Elizabeth Bomberg. *Decision-Making in the European Union.* New York: Palgrave, 1999.

Phillips, O. Hood. *Constitutional and Administrative Law.* 6th ed. Oxford: Oxford University Press, 1978.

Pinder, John. "Positive Integration and Negative Integration: Some Problems of Economic Union in the EC." Ed. Michael Hodges. *European Integration.* Harmondsworth: Penguin, 1970.

Pierson, Paul. "The Path to European Integration: A Historical-Institutionalist Analysis." *Comparative Political Studies* 29 (1996): 123–63.

—— "Increasing Returns, Path Dependence, and the Study of Politics." *American Political Science Review* 94 (2000a): 251–67.

—— "The Limits of Design: Explaining Institutional Origins and Change." *Governance* 13 (2000b): 475–99.

—— and Theda Skocpol. *Historical Institutionalism in Contemporary Political Science.* Paper prepared for the meeting of the American Political Science Association. Washington, D.C. August, 30–September 2, 2000.

Pollack, Mark. "The New Institutionalism and EC Governance: The Promise and Limits of Institutional Analysis." *Governance* 9, 4 (1996): 429–58.

—— "Delegation, Agency, and Agenda-Setting in the European Community." *International Organization* 51 (1997): 99–135.

—— "The End of Creeping Competence? EU Policy-Making Since Maastricht." *Journal of Common Market Studies* 38, 3 (2000): 519–38.

—— *The Engines of European Integration: Delegation, Agency and Agenda Setting in the EU.* Oxford: Oxford University Press, 2003.

Polsby, Nelson W. "The Institutionalization of the U.S. House of Representatives." *American Political Science Review* 62 (1968): 144–68.

—— *Congress and the Presidency*, 4th ed. Englewood Cliffs, NJ: Prentice-Hall, 1986.

Powell, W. W. "The New Institutionalism." *The International Encyclopedia of Organization Studies.* Thousand Oaks: Sage Publishers, 2007.

Puchala, Donald. "Institutionalism, Intergovernmentalism, and European Integration: A Review Article," *Journal of Common Market Studies* 37, 2 (1999): 317–331.

Puntscher Riekmann, Sonja. "The Cocoon of Power: Democratic Implications of Interinstitutional Agreements." *European Law Journal* 13 (2007): 4–19.

Riker, William H. *The Theory of Political Coalitions.* New Haven, CT: Yale University Press, 1962.

—— "The Heresthetics of Constitution-Making: The Presidency in 1787, with Comments on Determinism and Rational Choice." *American Political Science Review* 78 (1984): 1–16.

—— *The Art of Political Manipulation.* New Haven, CT: Yale University Press, 1986.

Risse-Kappen, Thomas. "Exploring the Nature of the Beast: International Relations Theory and Comparative Policy Analysis Meet the European Union." *Journal of Common Market Studies* 34, 1 (1996): 53–80.

Risse, Thomas. "Social Constructivism and European Integration" Eds. Antje Wiener and Thomas Diez. *European Integration Theory.* Oxford: Oxford University Press, 2004.

Rittberger, Berthold. "Impatient Legislators and New Issue Dimensions: A Critique of Garrett and Tsebelis' 'Standard Version' of Legislative Policy." *Journal of European Public Policy* 7 (2000): 554–75.

—— *Building Europe's Parliament: Democratic Representation Beyond the Nation-State.* Oxford: Oxford University Press, 2005.

—— and Jeffrey Stacey. "Conclusion: Stepping Out of the Shadow of History-Making Integration." *Journal of European Public Policy* 10, 6 (2003): 1020–32.

Rohrschneider, Robert. "The Democracy Deficit and Mass Support for an EU-wide Government." *American Journal of Political Science* 46 (2002): 463–75.

Rosamond, Ben. *Theories of European Integration.* New York: St. Martin's Press, 2000.

—— "The Future of European Studies: Integration Theory, EU Studies, and Social Science." Ed. Mette Eilstrup-Sangiovanni. *Debates on European Integration: A Reader.* Basingstoke: Palgrave Macmillan, 2006.

Sandholtz, Wayne. "Choosing Union: Monetary Politics and Maastricht." *International Organization* 47 (1993): 1–39.

—— "Membership Matters: Limits of the Functional Approach to European Institutions." *Journal of Common Market Studies* 34, 3 (1996): 403–29.

Bibliography

Sandholtz, Wayne and Alec Stone Sweet. *European Integration and Supranational Governance.* Oxford: Oxford University Press, 1998.

Sartori, Giovanni. *Parties and Party Systems: A Framework for Analysis.* Cambridge: Cambridge University Press, 1976.

—— *Comparative Constitutional Engineering.* London: Macmillan, 1992.

Sbragia, Alberta M. "Thinking about the European Future: The Uses of Comparison." Ed. Alberta M. Sbragia. *Europolitics: Institutions and Policymaking in the "New" European Community.* Washington, D.C.: Brookings Institution, 1992.

—— "The European Community: A Balancing Act." *Publius* 23 (1993): 23–38.

Schalk, Jelmer, Rene Torenvlied, Jeroen Weesie, and Frans Stokman. "The Power of the Presidency in EU Decision-Making." *European Union Politics* 8 (2007): 229–50.

Scharpf, Fritz W. "The Joint Decision Trap: Lessons from German Federalism and European Integration." *Public Administration* 66 (1988): 239–78.

—— "Community and Autonomy: Multi-Level Policy-Making in the European Union." *Journal of European Public Policy* 1 (1994): 219–42.

—— "Negative and Positive Integration in the Political Economy of European Welfare States." Eds. Gary Marks, Fritz Scharpf, Philippe C. Schmitter, Wolfgang Streeck. *Governance in the Emerging Euro-Polity.* London: Sage, 1996.

Schneider, Gerald. "European Union Politics Editorial Statement." *European Union Studies* 1 (2000): 5–8.

Schusterschitz, Gregor and Sabine Kotz. "The Comitology Reform of 2006: Increasing the Powers of the European Parliament Without Changing the Treaties." *European Union Politics* 1 (2007): 318–39.

Scully, Roger. "The European Parliament and the Co-Decision Procedure: A Reassessment." *The Journal of Legislative Studies* 3 (1997): 58–73.

—— *Becoming Europeans? Attitudes, Behaviour, and Socialization in the European Parliament.* Oxford: Oxford University Press, 2005.

Shackleton, Michael. *Financing the European Community.* London: Pinter Publishers and Royal Institute of International Affairs, 1990.

—— "The Politics of Codecision." *Journal of Common Market Studies* 38, 2 (2000): 325–42.

—— Paper presented at the 7th Biennial Conference of the European Union Studies Association. "Codecision Since Amsterdam: A Laboratory for Institutional Innovation and Change." Madison, Wisconsin. May, 31–June, 2, 2001.

Shepsle, Kenneth A. "Institutional Arrangements and Equilibrium in Multidimensional Voting Models." *American Journal of Political Science* 23, 1 (1979): 27–59.

—— "Institutional Equilibrium and Equilibrium Institutions." Ed. Herbert Weisberg. *Political Science: The Science of Politics.* New York: Agathon Press, 1986.

—— "Studying Institutions: Some Lessons from the Rational Choice Approach." *Journal of Theoretical Politics* 1, 2 (1989): 131–47.

—— "Old Questions and New Answers About Institutions: The Riker Objection Revisited." Eds. Barry R. Weingast and Donald A. Wittman. *The Oxford Handbook of Political Economy.* Oxford: Oxford University Press, 2006.

Schotter, Andrew. *The Economic Theory of Social Institutions*. New York: Cambridge University Press, 1981.

Shugart, Matthew A. and J. M. Carey. *Presidents and Assemblies*. Cambridge: Cambridge University Press, 1992.

Sinclair, Barbara. *Unorthodox Policy-Making: New Legislative Processes in the U.S. Congress*. 2nd ed. Washington, D.C.: Congressional Quarterly Press, 2000.

Skyrms, Brian. *Evolution of the Social Contract*. Cambridge: Cambridge University Press, 1996.

Stacey, Jeffrey. Paper presented at the 7th Biennial Conference of the European Community Studies Association. "Constitutional Re-engineering in the European Union: The Impact of Informal Interinstitutional Dynamics." Madison, Wisconsin. May, 31–June 2, 2001.

—— "The Newest New Institutionalism in EU Studies." *European Union Studies Review* 15, 2 (2002): 15–17.

—— "Displacement of the Council via Informal Dynamics? Comparing the Commission and Parliament." *Journal of European Public Policy* 10, 6 (2003): 936–55.

—— and Berthold Rittberger. "Special Issue: Dynamics of Formal and Informal Institutional Change in the EU." *Journal of European Public Policy* 10, 6 (2003): 858–83.

Stein, Arthur A. "The Limits of Strategic Choice: Constrained Rationality and Incomplete Explanation." Eds. David A. Lake and Robert Powell. *Strategic Choice and International Relations*. Princeton, NJ: Princeton University Press, 1999.

Steinmo, Sven and Kathleen Thelen. "Historical Institutionalism in Comparative Politics." Eds. Sven Steinmo et al. *Structuring Politics: Historical Institutionalism in Comparative Analysis*. Cambridge: Cambridge University Press, 1992.

Stone Sweet, Alec. *Governing with Judges: Constitutional Politics in Europe*. Oxford: Oxford University Press, 1999.

—— "European Integration and the Legal System." Eds. Tanja Börzel and Rachel Cichowski. *The State of the European Union, Vol. 6—Law, Politics, and Society*. Oxford: Oxford University Press, 2003.

—— and Thomas Brunell. "Constructing a Supranational Constitution: Dispute Resolution and Governance in the European Community." *American Political Science Review* 92, 1 (1998): 63–81.

—— Neil Fligstein, and Wayne Sandholtz. "The Institutionalization of European Space." Eds. Alec Stone Sweet, Wayne Sandholtz, and Neil Fligstein. *The Institutionalization of Europe*. Oxford: Oxford University Press, 2001.

Strasser, Daniel. *The Finances of Europe*. 7th ed. Luxembourg: Official Publications of the European Communities, 1992.

Tallberg, Jonas. *Leadership and Negotiation in the European Union*. Cambridge: Cambridge University Press, 2006.

Thelen, Kathleen "Historical Institutionalism in Comparative Politics." *Annual Review of Political Science* 2 (1999): 369–404.

Thelen, Kathleen (n.d.). "How Institutions Evolve: Insights from Comparative-Historical Analysis." Manuscript.

Tsebelis, George. *Nested Games: Rational Choice in Comparative Politics*. Berkeley, CA: University of California Press, 1990.

—— "The Power of the European Parliament as a Conditional Agenda Setter." *American Political Science Review* 88 (1994): 128–42.

—— and Geoffrey Garrett. "Agenda Setting, Vetoes and the European Union's Co-decision Procedure." *Journal of Legislative Studies* 3 (1997): 74–92.

—— —— "Legislative Politics in the European Union." *European Union Politics* 1 (2000): 9–36.

—— —— "The Institutional Determinants of Intergovernmentalism and Supranationalism in the European Union." *International Organization* 55 (2001): 357–90.

Wallace, Helen. "European Governance in Turbulent Times." *Journal of Common Market Studies* 31 (1993): 293–303.

—— "The Institutions of the EU: Experience and Experiments." Eds. Helen Wallace and William Wallace. *Policy-Making in the European Union*. Oxford: Oxford University Press, 1996.

—— and Alasdair R. Young. "The Single Market: A New Approach to Policy." Eds. Helen Wallace and William Wallace. *Policy-Making in the European Union*. Oxford: Oxford University Press, 1996.

Wallace, William. "Less Than a Federation, More Than a Regime: The Community as a Political System." Eds. Helen Wallace, William Wallace, and Carole Webb. *Policy-Making in the European Community*. London: Wiley & Sons Ltd, 1983.

—— "Introduction: The Dynamics of European Integration." Ed. William Wallace. *The Dynamics of European Integration*. London: Pinter, 1990.

—— *Regional Integration: The West European Experience*. Washington, D.C.: The Brookings Institution, 1994.

Weber, Max. "Politics as a Vocation." Eds. H. H. Gerth and C. Wright Mills. *From Max Weber: Essays in Sociology*. Oxford: Oxford University Press, 1942.

—— *Economy and Society, Vol II*. Eds. Guenther Roth and Claus Wittich. Berkeley, CA: University of California Press, 1978.

Weiler, Joe H.H. "The Transformation of Europe." *Yale Law Review* 100 (1991): 2403–83.

—— "The Community System: The Dual Character of Supranationalism." *Yearbook of European Law, Vol. 1*. Oxford: Oxford University Press, 1992.

Weingast, Barry R. and Mark Moran. "Bureaucratic Discretion or Congressional Control? Regulatory Policy-Making by the Federal Trade Commission." *Journal of Political Economy* 91 (1983): 765–800.

Wellens, K. C. and G. M. Borchardt. "Soft Law in European Community Law." *European Law Review* 14 (1989): 267–321.

Westlake, Martin. *The Commission and the Parliament: Partners and Rivals in the European Policy-making Process*. London: Butterworths, 1994a.

—— *A Modern Guide to the European Parliament*. London: Pinter, 1994*b*.

Wheare, K. C. *Modern Constitutions*. Oxford: Oxford University Press, 1966.

Williamson, Oliver. *The Economic Institutions of Capitalism: Firms, Markets, Regional Contracting*. New York: Free Press, 1985.

Wincott, Daniel. "Looking Forward or Harking Back? The Commission and the Reform of Governance in the European Union." *Journal of Common Market Studies* 39 (2001): 897–911.

Wurzel, Rudiger K. W. "The Role of the EU Presidency in the Environmental Field: Does it Make a Difference Which Member State Runs the Presidency?" *Journal of European Public Policy* 5 (1998): 209–34.

Zysman, John and Wayne Sandholtz. "Recasting the European Bargain." *World Politics* 41, 1 (1989): 1–30.

Index

Index